ENLARGING THE CHANGE

ENLARGING THE CHANGE ❧ ❧ ❧
THE PRINCETON SEMINARS IN LITERARY CRITICISM 1949–1951

ROBERT FITZGERALD

NORTHEASTERN UNIVERSITY PRESS
BOSTON ❧

Northeastern University Press
Copyright © 1985 by Robert Fitzgerald

Publication of this volume was assisted in part by a grant
from the Publications Program of the National Endowment
for the Humanities

Library of Congress Cataloging in Publication Data
Fitzgerald, Robert, 1910–
    Enlarging the change.
    Includes bibliographical references.
    1. Literature — Congresses.   I. Title.
PN33.F57   1984   809   84-7993
ISBN 0-930350-62-6

Manufactured in the United States of America
89 88 87 86 85 84   5 4 3 2 1

To R. W. B. Lewis

CONTENTS 🐌

Contents

He observes how the north is always enlarging the change,
With its frigid brilliances, its blue-red sweeps
And gusts of great enkindlings. . . .

WALLACE STEVENS
"The Auroras of Autumn"

PREFACE ❧

THE READER should be briefly informed of how and why this work came into existence. Richard Blackmur conceived the idea of it in the spring of 1951, after I had spent an academic year at Princeton as his assistant in Creative Writing and as a seminar leader in the Princeton Seminars in Literary Criticism. The faculty committee directing the seminars commissioned me to write a chronicle and study of that program, and the Rockefeller Foundation, which had partially subsidized the program, supported this effort as well. Originally it was to cover the program's first three years, but the committee and the foundation settled for an account of the first two.

Submitted and duly noted, my report no doubt found a place in a file. As the years passed it seems to have mouldered away, figuratively speaking, for no top copy can now be found. A carbon copy, buried in a file of my own, lay forgotten for years until I was reminded of the post-war Princeton circle by a scholar and critic who had come on that scene just after I left it and now looked back on it with attachment. I dug my carbon out and showed it to him. The next thing I knew he had mentioned it in print as "eminently publishable," and the Northeastern University Press had asked to see it. In due course Princeton kindly yielded its rights to the work.

These, then, are the circumstances of publication. But what are the reasons? For one thing, the enterprise reviewed here was the genesis of the Gauss Seminars, as they have latterly been called, a singular institution still very much alive at Princeton. In that setting at any rate, the beginnings of "the Gausses" must seem worthy of record. I am persuaded, however, that they have in fact a broader interest. The story is that of a fresh humanistic adventure carried out in a remarkably liberal and warm center of intellectual life. Time, place, and persons coincided in promise, justifying the élan of large ambition. How this came to be tempered, though not quenched, by difficulties local and general is part of the story.

But are not those old occasions ghostly now? Have not those who took part in them faded into impalpability, as Stephen Dedalus puts it in *Ulysses,* "through death, through absence, through a change of manners"? Yes and no. Ghostliness and permanence both are of the nature of good literature, and persons devoted to it partake of both. We have indeed seen changes of manners. At the mid-point of the century in American society at large we looked for no sexual or electronic revolutions, no landings on the moon. Literary society barely registered the stir of Structuralism, not to speak of later twists and intensities in the ancient study of letters. I do not think that any of these changes, or all of them, render obsolete the course of discussion recorded in this book.

ENLARGING THE CHANGE

PROLOGUE ❧

THE WRITER would like this chronicle to be taken as endlessly corrigible by finer minds and better informed ones. To have as one's subject two years of discourse on great matters among persons of unusual ability . . . this is delightful, but it leaves the chronicler no choice but to declare his limitations and his hope to stay within them. He will try to be accurate, but he will make no misguided effort to be impersonal, much less magisterial. This had better be stated at once, so that the reader can begin to regard what he finds here as a partial—and miniature and faded—image of a certain life.

IN THE SCENE ITSELF, the setting, one has the illusion of greater fixity or slower change. Princeton remains across the meadow, at the end of the railroad spur, town and university, a pretty place. One boyish American generation discerned the Princeton quality as speed and lightness at football. The writer, at seventeen, felt a peculiar awe, in a Princeton undergraduate club, when his host appeared in riding boots, ready for polo. How cavalier—and how rich. In the years before the Second Great War the writer, as a New Yorker, made friends with Princetonians from whom he learned to think of Princeton, again, as a community in which handsome and simple things counted. Such things might be understood as dramatically ambiguous or amusing, but they counted all the same.

Of what is sometimes meant by intellectual life, the Bohemianism of the cities and the shiver of the advanced in art and thought—of this, Princeton seemed curious but not envious. The college town stood apart from the metropolis and content to keep its distance. If there was something smart and moneyed about the college, there was also something old-fashioned, Presbyterian American, almost pastoral. Professor George MacLean Harper, the distinguished and beloved, had brought himself, but only with pain and in the cause of scholarship, to reveal his discovery of Wordsworth's mistress. Professor Paul Elmer More had called hopefully on the converted Tommy Eliot in London, but had come away to report, with tactful regret, that Eliot would continue to write verse as he had written it before.

IN 1949 the writer spent a day in Princeton at the invitation of two men whom he had known more or less well for years. Richard Blackmur he had first met in Boston in 1932 carrying a large parcel of research on the *Cantos* of Ezra Pound; it was a cold night, and Blackmur sat huddled over his parcel, saying nothing, in the backseat of an unheated car. Francis Fergusson, in the writer's earliest memory of him, sat amid a budding grove of Bennington College girls in 1935, talking about Euripides. These men were six years older than the writer, and belonged to the generation of his instructors. Each, too, belonged to a milieu, a ramification of friendships, prized by the younger man.

In neither case had these shared interests or affections ever had anything to do with Princeton. The university that the writer had in common with Blackmur and Fergusson was Harvard, and the friends they had in common were of Harvard and New York. Neither of the two men had set out to

4

be a scholar or teacher; each had practiced an art, and conspicuously well: Blackmur the art of writing, Fergusson the art of the theater. They, like the writer, though earlier than he, and like other men of their calling, had taken to teaching presumably because it gave them a living. But what had brought them to Princeton?

Once, before the war, the writer had gone to a dinner party in Princeton at which the principal guest was H. T. Lowe-Porter, the translator of Thomas Mann. Her husband, a humanist and paleographer, had become a member of the Institute for Advanced Study. Until then the writer had thought of this foundation, established in Princeton by the Bamberger fortune of Newark, as a preserve of scientists and mathematicians of whom the most famous was Albert Einstein. He had not thought of it as attracting to Princeton people interested in the art of letters, or in any art: people with whom one might have dinner.

Such, however, was indeed the case. And the presence of the Institute, so one might think, worked a change in the atmosphere of Princeton. It was as if a garage staff devoted to the gasoline engine had received a cyclotron for Christmas. A community could scarcely be called provincial in whose midst there were the internationally great, the showy dazzlers of the world. Thomas Mann himself lived in Princeton for a time; the writer heard him lecture there on Goethe. The displacement of eminent persons from Germany began early, but it was to continue—and not only from Germany—during and after the war

There were other causes, but the Institute appeared to be one, for the fact that the university bestirred itself to seek a fresh, and broader, distinction. At any rate, Blackmur, who had never in his life been on a class list in a college, much less the recipient of a college degree (he had attended lectures at Harvard with the consent of the professors), and who therefore had no academic standing, as it is called, had been invited to teach creative writing at Princeton in 1940. More exactly, the university invited the poet Allen Tate, and when Tate invited Blackmur the university concurred.

Up to that point Blackmur, who was thirty-five, had not only never enrolled in a university class, he had never taught one either. He was a professional and absolutely independent writer. After helping to edit the *Hound and Horn,* a quarterly started in Cambridge, and a Harvard product if there ever was one, he had composed in the thirties a number of literary studies wonderful for their verbal and formal connoisseurship and strength of attention, among them the first really good critical essays on Pound, Cummings, and Stevens. Any highbrow writer would have said that Princeton was lucky to get him; and the Princeton community continued to keep him when the creative writing course at the university was suspended during the war. From 1943 to 1946 it was the Institute that offered Blackmur hospitality, along with such other guest intellects as Bertrand Russell and Niels Bohr.

Of these facts the writer learned vaguely during a couple of casual meetings with Blackmur in 1948, both at symposia of literary people. By this time Blackmur was an associate professor at Princeton. If, at their first meeting long before, he had been impressively silent, he was now impressively articulate, self-possessed and lucid in open forum. He had the air of one who had prevailed, and he had; in what sense, and to what end, will perhaps appear in the course of this chronicle. At the second of the symposia the writer also met Francis Fergusson again. He too was, or was about to be, at Princeton as a guest of the Institute, where he intended to finish a book on dramatic art that he had been meditating for twenty years.

This was the year of the Russian blockade of West Berlin and the Berlin airlift, interpreted by some beholders as theatricals cheaply produced by the Russians to divert attention in Europe and America from the Communist conquest of China. The writer, as it happened, looked in on the United

6

Nations meeting at the Palais de Chaillot in Paris and thought it served chiefly to make the diversion more successful. He had been in Spain and Italy, and returned to New York the next year. In late September 1949, Fergusson wrote to invite him down to Princeton for a talk about some seminars.

THE IMPRESSION of this visit was that the Princeton now given to the visitor for contemplation—for the first time, the university itself—had put on a new dress and faced the ominous world. In visible aspect the principal change was the lately opened library, a mass proportioned with discretion in the fine Goodhue tradition, like an architectural Carthage founded from the Tyre of West Point, but far glassier, more gracefully recessive, and faced with warmer stone. There, in a bright vacant office, listening to Blackmur and Fergusson, the writer felt that for the time being something like an open academic society existed at Princeton.

Common sense would tell him that this must be partly illusory; but his friends, at any rate, were living in a universe of possibility, and what they envisioned they were apparently in a position to bring about. The idea was to keep up, during the course of three academic years, a running discussion of literature among a small and intent group of people who were not only interested but competent, including others besides university people, and any of the highest competence who were available. T. S. Eliot, for example, had been a guest of the Institute the year before; he might return, and if he did he would take part.

The method was to organize an annual program of seminars, four series of six weekly sessions each, each series to be conducted by someone with something to say. Kenneth Burke had led a pilot series the preceding spring at the Institute, and Robert Oppenheimer, director of the Institute and an old friend of Fergusson's, was sympathetic to the program. So were the people on the Humanities side of the university, chiefly Donald Stauffer, Whitney Oates, and Ira Wade, heads respectively of the English, Classics, and Modern Languages departments. The Rockefeller Foundation had put up $10,000. Fergusson, as director of the seminars, had a university appointment as associate professor in modern languages.

The first series of seminars had already started, led by a German scholar named Erich Auerbach, one of the two or three greatest Europeans in Romance philology; and one of the others, the renowned Ernst Robert Curtius of Bonn, under whom Auerbach had studied, was also a guest of the Institute and had attended the first meeting. Jacques Maritain, then holding a professorship in philosophy at Princeton, would be a participant. Fergusson proposed that the writer, too, give a series of seminars.

Fergusson is a quiet man with an undeluded eye. Meeting it, the visitor realized in a moment that there had been no mistake, that neither Fergusson nor Blackmur took him for a scholar, and that they wanted not only men who had mastered the Muse, in Auerbach's way or another, but occasionally one still relatively callow in her company. They also wanted a seminar in some subject out of Greek literature. The academic year in question would be 1950-1951, and Blackmur proposed that the writer come to Princeton that year as assistant in the Creative Writing Program. This job had been held after the war by the poet John Berryman; a younger poet, William Meredith, had the position now, while Berryman lived in Princeton and worked on a biographical study of Stephen Crane.

BERRYMAN and Meredith, and the writer as well, were men for whom the making of verse was a vocation, so far as they could manage it; they were poets if they were anything, writers in general as a consequence of being poets in particular; and for any university this was rather a high concentration in that

category. Serious writers in the United States had most often
done their work alone; that is, at best, though alone, they
had done it. But: "The best things come, as a general thing,
from the talents that are members of a group," Henry James
had written in 1879, with regard to Hawthorne's loneliness.
How could a group be formed, or to what group could one
attach oneself? In 1940, the year Blackmur went to Princeton,
he had published "A Feather-Bed for Critics: Notes on the
Profession of Writing" in which the following sentences
appeared:

> Serious men require the institutions of society almost
> more than they require to change them to fit their will
> and imagination, require them sometimes in the offing
> and sometimes at hand. Serious writers are no different;
> for them it would seem today that the university is the
> only available institution, whether in the offing or at hand
> cannot certainly be said, except by the university itself.
> I think at hand.

Further:

> It is not that the university, even when properly em-
> ployed, furnishes the ideal guarantee of the writer's
> profession; not at all—too many mistaken choices, too
> much misled energy are certain to appear; but it is the
> thing at hand, and it is the business of the positive critic,
> when he can momentarily bring himself to exist as pos-
> itive, to lead writers where they necessarily are going.

Now, in reflecting on the Princeton tableau of 1949, the
writer had decidedly the sense that these programmatic sentences were being enacted before his eyes. It was clear that
the Princeton Creative Writing Program and the Princeton
Seminars in Literary Criticism would together, for their all-
inclusive effect in his own case, make him for a year and
possibly longer a part of the institution that was Princeton
University; and it was clear that nobody had done more than

Blackmur to bring this to pass. The writer had little of the passion of professionalism, so marked in his friend, nor had he felt that he precisely required, except in the sense of employment, the institutions of which he had up to then been a part. Blackmur on the other hand was engaged, as the phrase went in those days. Part of his strength lay in knowing the extent to which others including the writer were not, but might become so; and another part lay in the fact that he was engaged on the side of the university as well as on theirs.

If the university, a house of studies, were to become a patron of the art of letters, as Blackmur had foreseen, it would necessarily do so through cultivation of the study of literature. In the end, whatever residential appointments or equivalents of research fellowships might be imagined, this meant teaching, in some effective and acceptable sense, of literary matters. Here was the tide-rip between the life of the imagination and the life of scholarship. "These people think they can tell us how to teach literature; but we know how to teach literature," one of Princeton's elder professors had said; how to amend either half of the statement was a delicate question.

Among the younger teachers by trade at Princeton there were many of more generous mind; and there was, besides, behind Blackmur and his friends, the encouraging presence of the venerated Christian Gauss, for years professor of French and dean of the college, who had in fact been the prime mover in the Creative Arts Program, started in 1939 under a grant from the Carnegie Foundation. This grant, and the one lately made by the Rockefeller Foundation for the Princeton Seminars, appeared to indicate something else: the gentle pressure of assistance from thoughtful people near the central switchboard of society. How did these lofty agencies, with so much money to dispense, justify the dispensations in question? The answer would no doubt be elaborate. What the men of letters at Princeton had to offer, essentially, was a disinterested approach to mysteries, recognized as such. It may have seemed that these mysteries—having to do with the work of the human spirit in language and in imagination—were worth honoring, or at least acknowledging, in a time very low in fruitful mysteries but very high in barren ones: too close for comfort, in fact, to chaos and the void.

More general and more easily formulated was the sense that during the breaking of nations certain substructures of tradition had been laid bare for the United States to take account of. The twentieth-century fling at the purely experimental life had begun to look unnecessarily wasteful. Circumstances in the world at large appeared to demand a certain centering, grounding, and girding up—hence the new attention the universities were giving to humanistic studies on their own grounds, not as adjuncts of social or other sciences, and not as adornments of the politely educated. This, which might have been called the critical movement in the colleges, antedated the war, but the war had made it more earnest. At Princeton, undergraduates were invited to enroll in something known as the Special Program in the Humanities, an interdepartmental collaboration. One avowed and obvious purpose of the new seminars was to strengthen this program at the top.

However profoundly and almost unrealizably threatened abroad, the United States had enjoyed after the war a breathing space at home in which the citizenry might take thought, if they cared to and were capable of it, about the significance of the life of which they found themselves still in possession. They had the money and the leisure that are held propitious to the arts, and they had the incentives that have been mentioned to pull themselves together and make use of the sources of wisdom. Many others besides the writer had consciously tried to do so. So far as he was concerned, Princeton fitted in with this effort, and the seminars should instruct it . . . so, at least, ran his first speculations.

Chapter One

PARADOXES OF A DWINDLING FAITH ❧ ERICH AUERBACH ON PASCAL AND BAUDELAIRE

THE PRINCETON SEMINARS in Literary Criticism formally began on the evening of Thursday, October 6, 1949, with Erich Auerbach's series on Pascal, Baudelaire, and Flaubert—a triptych in itself worth meditation. Thinker, poet, and novelist, the three established a certain range for the seminars at the start; all French, they established what would in fact be a recurrent if not dominant cultural sounding board or backstop of literary reference; and it would have been difficult to choose three figures with more magnetism for the modern educated world of thought and letters. In the case of Pascal there was presumably an interest that the scientific personages at the Institute could share, and in all three there were varieties of interest for those to whom the difficulties of thought and art terminate in religious difficulty—a class of persons rather augmented, at Princeton as elsewhere, during the preceding decades. Auerbach's approach to all three was in terms of "stylistics," as became the critic trained in philology. Anyone could see how appropriate this was to Baudelaire and Flaubert, who represented sheer literary power at its apogee in styles that had carried over into the twentieth century and were as influential in the English-speaking world as in continental Europe.

Auerbach's method was to devote each evening to the discussion of a text, brief enough in each case to be mimeographed on a single sheet and thus put in the hands of everyone present. This procedure had obvious advantages in tethering the random horses of discussion to a single pin, a datum for minds to meet on. It was no doubt vain to hope, and it would have seemed impertinent to the director, Fergusson, to require that all subsequent seminar leaders adopt the same technique; but several in fact did so to good effect. With Auerbach it was standard operating procedure, a convention employed throughout the series of essays in his book *Mimesis,* a work of massive learning and considerable vivacity, published at Berne in 1946 and at once a *succès d'estime* among scholars, though at the time of the seminars not yet translated into English. Auerbach's seminar papers were further essays in the same mode, put into English by himself for the Princeton occasion.

THE EVENINGS on Pascal were not attended by the writer but, with the aid of Auerbach's paper (published in the spring 1951 issue of the *Hudson Review*), one or two verbal reports, and some notes to be described hereafter, he was able to form an idea of them. The text chosen for the first was *Pensée 298.* There were about thirty persons on hand. Auerbach first analyzed the logical and syntactical structure of the passage, remarked on the interpretation it invited from the modern reader on mere inspection, and then demonstrated at some length the different and graver interpretation called for if the passage were understood in the light of Pascal's thought as a whole. Thus Auerbach had to discuss the religious affair of Port-Royal and the political situation in France in the middle of the seventeenth century. This progressive enlargement of focus apparently corresponded to a practice Auerbach had adopted or would adopt in teaching.

The given passage of Pascal is a cold and acrid set of symmetrical antitheses between *la force* and *la justice,* ending with the conclusion that since it is impossible to make what is right powerful, it has proved necessary to make what is powerful right (that is, to regard it as right). Auerbach argued that this was more than an irony, that it had behind it more than the victory of absolutism in France after the failure of the Fronde, the rebellion of 1650, and that in fact Pascal saw politics as a matter of force and practically undifferentiated evil and held that it was right that this should be so. The duty of the Christian was to suffer the evil of the world, or to fight it without hope of winning, for injustice among men was the justice of God.

No later performance by Auerbach equalled in concentrated intellectual passion his treatment of this "political theory" of Pascal. A Jew, an *émigré* from Germany, for years homeless, putting his big book together in Istanbul without benefit of the great libraries he longed for, Auerbach had faced with his flesh and blood the reality of evil force; the extremity of Pascal's thought answered, for him, an extremity of experience. Pascal, too, had lived in a totalitarian state. In the little audience at Princeton there were not lacking minds to observe that Pascal had made an antithesis of ideas not logically antithetical; the opposite of force, as Gauss brought out in the discussion, is not justice but *impuissance*. But when Gauss wished to go on to say that Pascal was relating incommensurables, that justice was in another realm of discourse, Auerbach violently took the part of experience; he insisted upon what was indeed the case, that, at a certain level known to him and his audience, justice *was* the opposite of force despite the logical incongruity.

It was to be noted that the mathematician and physicist present, Klein, appeared to accept the antithesis that minds of philosophic and literary training—Gauss and Fergusson at least—tended to criticize. Klein's mind, however, was working along quite another line, fascinated by a resemblance he saw between the tension of opposites in Pascal and the thinking of Niels Bohr, the theoretical physicist, which he described as Pascalian—a way of thinking in which, he said, "certainty was corrected by uncertainty." He felt that there were always two souls speaking in Pascal. When Klein spoke it was as if a curtain rose and fell fitfully on the underworld of twentieth-century physical speculation, a place of radical alternatives and discontinuities beneath all thoughts of the real.

There was also a diverting glimpse of the Old World of tournament scholarship, or at least of the armory where hang the hearty bludgeons and neat stilettoes of Renaissance and later *philologismus*. As the discussion ranged, and Auerbach recalled Pascal's view of human affection as larceny from God, the redoubtable Curtius stirred testily and spoke in a manner that made his former pupil turn momentarily a little pale. Let Pascal's theology be dismissed with a smile, he said; it was heresy and poppycock. Let the company look again at the text, consider the usages *in Pascal's time* of the important participles. Stylistics, science of literature!

This call to order had in fact the useful consequence of bringing out, a little later, from Americo Castro, professor of Spanish, the best phrase of the evening for the stylistic quality of the passage from Pascal: "The mathematical and the extrarational in tragic anguished clash."

It was, of course, impossible to dismiss the theology, and on the second evening, a week later, Auerbach pressed on with it. He remarked that there had been much talk between him and Curtius (who was not present this evening), but that he could not wholly agree to leave questions of ideas to specialists, in this case to historians of theology; it was his purpose to make understandable the immediate human thing on the basis of information and help. To abandon all fact to specialists—that he would not do.

The text for the second evening was a letter of Pascal's written in 1661 to a friend in Clermont, reflecting on the attitude of some of his companions in the struggle with the

16

Jesuits and the Church. Auerbach said this letter in his opinion was among the great texts of Christian ethics. If the line of thought in the *Pensée* were to be followed it might seem that a Christian should never fight for justice and truth, but Pascal himself fought and in this letter described the state of mind required for the fight. It was to be remembered that the same God who inspired the struggle permitted the opposition; it was one and the same spirit who produced the good and permitted the evil. It was even much more certain that God permitted the evil, horrible as it might be, than that He had chosen us to effect the good. Our inner assurances were less valuable on this point than our external attitude. If we desired nothing but the will of God, we should have to be equally satisfied if the truth were doomed and remained hidden, or if it were victorious and became known: in the second case it was God's mercy that triumphed, in the first, His justice.

Auerbach returned now to the text of the *Pensée* and noted Pascal's mastery of expression, in which could be found several levels of understanding in depth. It was, he said, sharp as a sword and deep as the sea; the old tricks of rhetoric, in countless instances used as ornament, here became the weapons of a passionate mind, fighting against common sense for the tragic paradoxes of a dwindling faith. The thud of this last formulation was muffled by a brief coda referring to the traditional and Thomist philosophy of "natural law"—with which Pascal was said to have nothing in common—and the Machiavellian political theory, *raison d'état,* with which Pascal was in agreement but on far profounder premises, according to Auerbach.

The first important question raised in the discussion was naturally whether or not Pascal's premises were acceptable. Delmore Schwartz, a poet and critic down from New York for the evening, asked what would happen to Pascal's meaning if we refused to adopt his "attitude," and added that his arguments were not the central Christian ones. Were they acceptable to the skeptic? Auerbach, clearly replying for himself, said no. Now Alba Warren, a Catholic in the English department, holder of a faith that Auerbach had described as "dwindling" in the seventeenth century, objected to Auerbach's tendency to identify Augustine plus Pascal with Christianity. He cited Augustine's *extra ecclesiam nulla salus* (no salvation outside the Church)—a saying controverted by St. Thomas and condemned by the Church. Auerbach replied that Warren was certainly right, that Pascal had been on the verge of heresy in overstating the case for grace and trying to extinguish the *lumen naturale.* The point admitted, it disappeared easily from the discussion—too easily, one might well think.

Somewhat as Curtius had broken in on the first evening, Meredith now broke in to inquire, Where was literature? He evidently had little sympathy with Christian theology in general, and still less with Pascal's. In rather a long colloquy he kept after Auerbach to make a distinction between Pascal's ideas and his style. When Auerbach refused to do so, Meredith said then he would be unable to discuss a second-rate mind in a great poem, such as some by Tennyson and Hugo. Auerbach said he didn't care for Tennyson and Hugo. He consented, however, to distinguish between literary work in which ideas had stylistic importance and that in which they scarcely appeared at all, as in the poems of Mallarmé.

The members of the group who knew Pascal best—Elbert Borgerhoff and Fergusson, both of the Romance Languages department, and Russi, a visiting professor from Pisa—engaged now and then in brief efforts to qualify Auerbach's sharp presentation. Auerbach had remarked on Pascal's refusal to subject the realm of intellect, where *grandeur* was possible, to the evil world of power, the world of *misère;* one or two people thought more should be made of this, and Auerbach repeated that he thought it an inconsistency. Klein wished to treat this, again, on his modern physicist's analogy of opposite truths correcting one another; again he referred to Bohr, and this time even found a stylistic similarity in the

18

way both Pascal and Bohr forced new meanings, drawn directly from reality, upon a received vocabulary. Auerbach was pleased to agree and incautiously added that Pascal was one of the first writers to acknowledge several levels of statement, at one of which a proposition might be true and at another untrue. He ended by reverting to the subject of the reality seen by Pascal—his extreme Augustinism in theology—and Castro put in the last word: "There is an *acute* impression of good and evil in Pascal." That was link enough with the next topic: Baudelaire.

ON THE EVENING of October 20 new mimeographed sheets were passed around to a somewhat smaller audience, twenty-two persons this time. The sheets contained these poems of Baudelaire: *Spleen* (IV), *Je te donne ces vers afin que si mon nom, La Mort des Artistes,* and in between the two first-named the sestet from *Le Mauvais Moine.* Auerbach began by stating that his subject was the unique fusion, in certain poems of Baudelaire, of two categories of style previously separate and distinct in the European tradition: the Sublime and the Low. In treating this he proposed to use the terms "realism" and "symbolism," not because these words had, or could have, absolute content, but because with good will they could be serviceable. He read the poem, *Spleen,* rapidly and flatly—as a text, not a poem. Then he gave a syntactical analysis of the text: a singular movement in three temporal clauses, each introduced by *quand,* each a stanza in length; then a main clause in stanza four, ending the grammatical period; then a conclusion, stanza five. The unity of syntax and the Alexandrine meter, he said, assisted the general tone of sombre sublimity. In further and lengthy analysis he showed Baudelaire converting "realistic" details (that is, as the new realism of his time was understood, unbeautiful ones) into a symbolism of much greater power, an evocation of the hopelessly terrible. Auerbach remarked that this was one traditional form of the sublime. Certain expressions, however, were at odds with that tradition. The most dramatic of these was the sudden image in stanza four of bells bounding in steeples, raising a blubbering howl. Seventy years later such expressions would be thought merely surrealist, but in Baudelaire's time they carried the shock of originality. The last stanza, silent again while hearses in procession move through the soul, surpassed all that had preceded by its intensity in representing a complete moral collapse—a loss of dignity not before God, for God was nowhere in this poem, but before "Fear" (this appeared to be Auerbach's translation of *Angoisse*).

Auerbach recalled that most critics in Baudelaire's time attacked *Les Fleurs du Mal* for these violent breaks in the traditional high style. Baudelaire's admirers, however, and modern critics in general have declared, he said, that there are no sublime and low subjects, only good and bad verses. To say this was to miss the historical point: the old categories corresponded to general European feeling; and the fundamental change in the nineteenth century, continued and developed in the twentieth, was a revaluation of subject. It became possible to present things as great and tragic that were formerly considered necessarily low or comic. Baudelaire was the first to treat, as sublime, subjects that seemed incompatible with sublimity. The "spleen" in his poem meant hopeless despair and paralyzing fear. Auerbach could discover no religion or philosophy in the poem, not even courage; only the *triste misère* alluded to in *Le Mauvais Moine*. For Baudelaire's work this *misère* was at once the condition and subject: the utmost degradation, the most paralyzing depression, were the sources from which he drew poetry of the highest dignity.

Auerbach made no effort to connect this *misère* with that of Pascal. He took up its erotic aspects, noting, in *Je te donne ces vers,* the slow infusion of malice into a traditional theme that at first recalled Ronsard, and the apostrophe at the end to the angel of evil. So in other poems, instead of the old motifs of love, the details of sexual lust were emphasized relentlessly, with cold sensuality but also with hatred and scorn. In this, too, Baudelaire's new and tormented kind of sublimity had such an impact upon European literary tradition that the light and pleasant treatment of sexual love thereafter became trash or pornography or both. Auerbach acknowledged that among the poems to Mme. Sabatier there were some that seemed of a different order, in which the beauty of the flesh was positively spiritualized and worshiped. But Auerbach judged that the poet could not stand the disharmony between this attitude and his dominant one; evidence of this could be seen in such a poem as the famous *A celle qui est trop gaie* in which the poet, in hatred, threatens poisonous vengeance on natural joy.

To enforce the contrast between the old tradition and this sort of thing in Baudelaire—the morbid desire of tormenting others and himself—Auerbach read a lovesick sonnet of Petrarca, *Zefiro torna*. It was a curious choice, for it ended with these lines:

E' n belle donne oneste atti soavi
Sono un deserto, e fere aspre e selvagge.

Something not entirely remote, after all, from the Baudelairien. And in the discussion which now followed much more was said to question the sharp terms of Auerbach's argument than in the case of Pascal.

Auerbach must have foreseen this, for he remarked almost at once, in answer to some objection, that he could not do in a lecture what Baudelaire did in his poems—meaning he could not communicate the full complex of Baudelaire's qualities. Berryman recalled Hamlet "lugging the guts" of Polonius, and inferred that the fusion of high and low styles was new in Baudelaire only as a deliberate form of the lyric. Even so, there was such a poem as Donne's *Apparition* to show what there had been of that sort before.

Curtius now with benignity posed Auerbach three stupefying questions: first, did Baudelaire have any psychological importance; second, did it lead anywhere to define a style as a mixture of two styles; third, ought we not to avoid such vague notions as "realism." He added a fourth: was it quite right to use the term "viciousness" of Baudelaire? Auerbach replied that there was a lot of venom in Baudelaire, that in the matter of style he would agree as to the unity of inspiration, and would place the emphasis on *fusion;* as for "realism" he thought the word meant something in the historical context. . . . He did not get around to answering Curtius's first question, because Jacques Maritain answered it for him.

Poetic experience, said Maritain, was a form of knowledge deep in the consciousness; Baudelaire discovered his own knowledge deep in his own denuded human nature and expressed his poetic intuition of it in the most exact manner, not in his style but in a deeper way. He discovered something new, and once for all, in the very sources of poetry. Maritain's interjection seemed to provoke a little shy talk about Baudelaire's *words.* Curtius urged that the critic get everything out of the words that can be gotten, and when Russi asked if words were not related to psychology, Curtius replied flatly that words make shapes of beauty, not states of consciousness but artistic states. Maritain suggested a different way of putting it: that there was a melody of images circumscribing the inexpressible flash of intuition, not as concept, but as poetry, and that this was knowledge. Not, added Curtius in apparent agreement, attained by other methods.

Harold Cherniss, a Greek scholar from the Institute, asked Curtius if he could explain the beauty of the line *Vaisseau favorisé par un grand aquilon* —"vessel favored by a following gale" (the poet alluding to his own fame) and Curtius replied yes, perhaps, in time. Cherniss said it was beautiful but he didn't know an intelligible reason why. A little later, with quaint phrasing, Auerbach remarked that Beauty cannot be explained to whoso does not feel it, but to whoso does feel it much can be explained. Before the discussion broke up, Meredith put in a word of praise for Auerbach's lecture, adding that if there was a modern style in English it was what

Baudelaire had taught. All who know modern poetry, said Auerbach, find Baudelaire the initiator; he is the point where everything converges, then radiates again. "But I have a personal confession," he said. "I don't like him very much."

THE FIRST of the Princeton Seminars attended by the writer was Auerbach's second evening on the poetry of Baudelaire, October 27, 1949. The visitor did not reread *Les Fleurs du Mal* in advance of the meeting. His first reading was distinctly present to him, however, even to the sound the book made when he dropped it on the floor beside his bed, at three o'clock of a cold winter night nineteen years before. This was in Hollis Hall, in Cambridge; the spirit of Thoreau, who had once lived in the next room, interfered little with the influence of Baudelaire. Now in 1949, however, the writer was in a mood not to like Baudelaire very much himself. He had been irritated not long before by a poor translation of Baudelaire's journals by Christopher Isherwood. Literary talk about Baudelaire embarrassed him. He had, too, something else on his mind of a nature to keep him clear about the respective claims of life and literature. A friend of whom he was fond, wife of the Princeton friend of earlier years whom he has mentioned, was dying that fall and had been moved from New York, where they then lived, to Princeton to die. The October weather held warm and sunny, and on this trip the writer paid a last visit to her in a garden. The life of which leave was being taken had been, for him, the essence and fragrance of Princeton in another time, most pervasive against all that is idolatrous or alien to familial piety in the cults of art. Incongruity ruled more noticeably than usual by sending him in the evening to a session on Baudelaire.

The writer sat with Berryman. Behind them sat Blackmur with pad and pencil, carrying out a project he had set for himself of taking notes on the proceedings. There were about thirty people in four rows of folding chairs with tubular

23

metal frames. The speaker sat on the other side of a big table of glossy blond wood. A portable blackboard at his back bore two lines inscribed in chalk: *Sa chair spirituelle a le parfum des anges*—"Her spiritual flesh has the perfume of angels" and *Le destin charmé suit tes jupons comme un chien*—"Charmed destiny follows your skirts like a dog." Auerbach began without introduction, often dropping his typescript to talk without it. Here was the superlatively good European, practiced in the old languages, steeped in the old universities cosmopolitan as seaports, his dark eyes glowing with cultivated energy, amused, alive, disenchanted, ardent.

He made a résumé of what he had said the week before, referred to the lines on the board and read some others, including some of the sort condemned in 1857 by the same court that had acquitted Flaubert in the *Madame Bovary* case earlier that year. Then he came to the question raised by any intelligent reading of Baudelaire. He conceded that medieval Christian concepts of sex and sin had influenced the poet, as they did the romanticists, and that his "mental structure was that of a mystic" in that he sought the supernatural in the world of the senses. But as to the place of *Les Fleurs du Mal* in the Christian tradition, their character and tendency were, he said, entirely different from and incompatible with any of its forms. This for four reasons: Baudelaire sought neither grace nor eternal salvation but sensuous ecstasy or annihilation—*le néant;* Christ appeared in *Les Fleurs du Mal* only once, and then to be played off against God; the beauties of the flesh, far from being regarded as a snare, in the medieval way, were glorified in the poems; finally, degradation was treated not as an occasion for humility but as setting off the poet in his lonely pride.

In all this, Auerbach said, he was referring exclusively to *Les Fleurs du Mal:* he felt unable to deal with the problem of Baudelaire's soul and its later development. The interest of Catholic critics was understandable, but it was not his. He agreed with an essay by Jean-Paul Sartre to the effect that

Baudelaire consciously fought to dead ends without issue. It was essential to see that such a life and such a psychological structure could develop in the first half of the nineteenth century, revealing something hidden to earlier generations: thus the periods of history, Auerbach said, select and shape their representatives.

To later cogitation, at least on the writer's part, a crevice appeared here in which a wedge quietly tamped might split the underlying argument from stem to stern. If the poems alone were his subject, Auerbach would be on doubtful ground in characterizing Baudelaire's life and psychological structure; indeed he had professed himself incompetent on these subjects under the alternative heading of "Soul and Later Development." If he did not care to discuss Baudelaire's journals, in particular *Mon Coeur mis à nu*, the book on which Catholic critics like Du Bos relied in interpreting Baudelaire's experience as profoundly religious and progressively Christian, how could he bring in an essay of the existentialist, Sartre, written in fact as an introduction to a new edition of Baudelaire's *Écrits Intimes*? More dubious still was the idea of a period of history "selecting" anyone. When the writer came to think of it, this sounded like a glibness of an all too familiar sort.

At the time, however, Auerbach's *brusquerie* seemed refreshing. He now came back to the poems and treated his audience to an explication of *La Mort des Artistes*, the final poem in the 1857 edition of *Les Fleurs du Mal*. This poem illustrated the point that Baudelaire did not worship God but the idol of absolute poetical creation, absolute artificiality. According to the analysis there was a good deal of irony and contempt mixed in with the adoration—a suggestion, too, that the idol degraded its idolaters. As to this, Auerbach said that the poet wronged himself. The sincerity that made it impossible for him, in a time without gods, to worship the idols of his contemporaries—progress and wealth, liberty and equality—this was his greatness. His dandyism and his poses

25

were nothing but the distortions which such a struggle imposes on the desperate fighter. In the new style that he gave to poetry were to be found for the first time in literature certain surprising and incoherent combinations of ideas whose visionary power was a revelation to later poets; perhaps a revelation of present anarchy and dawning order. As much as Dostoievski's Ivan Karamazov, the human structure revealed in Baudelaire's poems was significant for the transformation—or perhaps the ruin—of the European tradition.

Auerbach's final point was that he, nevertheless, did not like the poetry of Baudelaire. This poetry is horrible, he said emphatically, and smiling. Some of the critics who denounced *Les Fleurs du Mal* comprehended it better than the average of its admirers. A book full of horror is better understood by those who are stricken with horror, even though it infuriates them, than by those who express nothing but delight with the author's art. Even Flaubert's admiration was too exclusively aesthetic. Later critics have insisted on the purely aesthetic approach; but to such a work it cannot be fully adequate. Baudelaire would probably not have agreed with this. But Baudelaire was contaminated by the idolatry of art, which still is keeping us under its spell.

As Auerbach waited pleasantly for someone to say something, the writer looked at *La Mort des Artistes*, which he had in his lap, and decided for the second time that it was not a successful poem. He put his head together with Berryman, who nodded emphatically: the second quatrain was strong, the rest labored. The writer felt that Baudelaire's art had not been particularly well represented; but the writer did not particularly care. Auerbach's paper had been incisive. What would the savants wish to make of it?

An Italian-English accent, a voice high and a little declamatory, drawling words in search for words, began to dispute from the back of the room Auerbach's assertion that the only mention of Christ in *Les Fleurs du Mal* came in the poem *La Reniement de Saint Pierre*—"Saint Peter's Denial"—

the point of which is that St. Peter did well in his denial. It was Russi. He had his book, and read the poem *L'Examen de Minuit* in which the poet bitterly acknowledges having blasphemed Jesus. Clearly Auerbach had overlooked something. With poise and quickness, shrugging, he admitted that there might be still other examples.

Would anyone care enough about the subject of Baudelaire's Christianity to widen the opening Russi had made? Auerbach had ended his own paper by saying that aesthetic appreciation was inadequate in the case of *Les Fleurs du Mal*. Now Fergusson, sitting at the extreme left in the front row, speaking by turns over his elbow to the group and then in Auerbach's direction, recalled Berryman's question as to whether Donne had not mixed the high and low styles long before Baudelaire. Had not Dante too, he asked, mixed Christianity and direct sensuality, as in the Paolo and Francesca episode of the *Inferno* and the "Pietra" canzone? Auerbach assented. Then Fergusson asked if Baudelaire did not present himself as damned in *La Mort des Artistes*. Auerbach at first thought not, then thought so.

The longest exegetical leap of the evening now took place. A stately silvery professor in the front row—Castro, the writer learned—linked *l'énorme bétise* of *L'Examen de Minuit* with the *grande Créature* of *La Mort des Artistes* and both with the Great Beast of Revelations—a conjunction in which he suggested there was Black Magic to be discovered. When Castro was through, a little silence fell, the company reflecting. Upon this Berryman broke in explosively to question the opposition Auerbach had made between aesthetic criticism and other criticism. Maupassant, at a dinner in his honor, had asked the diners to take off their shoes and stockings . . . a situation at once indelicate and ironical. "A good poet," said Berryman, "could take this and turn it into two Alexandrines. By thus removing the incident from life into poetry it is no longer shocking. I conceive it might be used as an exordium, as a middle, or as a conclusion."

"In your witty way," said Auerbach, "you make my polemics seem questionable, and so they would be if generally applied; but I applied them here exclusively to Baudelaire. His actual content and the weight of his outlook cannot be ignored."

A solid large man, bald, with a rather flat shy face, began speaking carefully from the back row, remarking on the shift of grammatical subject in the poem from *moi* to *nous* to *ils*: suggesting a series of frustrated seekers. It was Stauffer. Auerbach allowed that the poem was Mallarméan in this and other respects. There was a long and learned exchange from several quarters about the traditional figure of the archer's target. Then Castro brought up the Beast again, to which Auerbach replied by bringing up Platonism—the ambivalent struggle for the absolute in Baudelaire. Someone suggested that the poem in fact parodied the Platonic, the point being that the artist, despite his hellish desire for something better, always had formed *material* on his hands, was stuck with it.

"Stuck with it?" said Auerbach, all polite attention but puzzled at the idiom. Someone explained. Someone else adduced, in support of the point last made, the poem *La Géante*, in which love of women was developed into love of the material universe. Auerbach thought this might be indeed another incarnation of the *grande Créature*; but in *La Mort des Artistes* he thought there was high style and real despair, the poem was in dead earnest.

A small man, aged, attentive, with a touch of ruggedness, spoke up from the front row to suggest taking the poem with the other two poems in its series, *La Mort des Amants* and *La Mort des Pauvres*. This was Christian Gauss. He observed that these poems indicated the consolations of love and perhaps of Christianity—"You are more optimistic than Baudelaire," interposed Auerbach—but that the artists had only the insatiable struggle for beauty never found. But Castro had interrupted by proposing an analogy between Baudelaire's poem and *Aucassin et Nicolette*, both illustrating what he called "the

28

importance of hell in French literature." He went on by saying that the French were rationalistic and praised hell, and had done so since the eleventh century. Rationalist and demonic at once, they were, practicing reason and Black Magic. He continued to talk for a long time, rapidly, hands clasped as though in supplication—a historical analysis of the French soul as distinguished from the Spanish. When he finished, Gauss was patiently waiting with his point about the immediate context.

"Does not *La Mort des Artistes*," he said, "represent a new conception of the poet, a poet who uses no mimesis and no representation but who *creates* absolutely? Here is something not possible to the lovers or to the poor. . . . The artist is separated from the ordinary concerns of mankind. *La Mort des Artistes* follows after *La Mort des Amants* and *La Mort des Pauvres*, and so indicates a different destiny and a harder life."

Berryman, who had been growing red, began speaking now with overriding alarm and impatience. "Either I do not understand this poem or there has been a series of violent misconceptions. . . . Here is my interpretation for what it is worth, though I do not see how it can be wrong: In the first stanza the 'I' is all of the banal in which we live. In the second stanza, which is serious and terrifying and grave, the 'nous' are the serious artists, the real artists, the poets—not the painters and sculptors; and the death of these serious artists takes place in *userons*—that extraordinary word. Then 'Ils' take over, and we have a cold disdain for the false artists."

Castro, turning around, agreed. The sonnet, he began to say, broke in pieces. But a dissent, flat and urbane, came from across the room. Panofsky, an art historian from the Institute, stated that all the way through the poem the subject was the same kind of artist, the only exception being in the first line of the first tercet, which referred to vulgar people, the public, knowing nothing of art.

At this Russi lifted his voice again to complain that although the poem had been clear to him, it was becoming confused. He thought the *grande Créature* and the "target" in the poem were one and the same and were Beauty, a word he pronounced with great simplicity and respect. He read, insistently, other passages of Baudelaire in support of this. But the hour had come to an end, and Fergusson suggested, to everyone's amusement, that Auerbach should sum up.

"I should never have believed it possible," said Auerbach, "for Baudelaire to have produced such an un-Baudelairean hilarity."

IT WAS NOT Baudelaire who provoked the hilarity; in fact very little in the occasion was really provoked by Baudelaire. The man of that name may have affected each of these people in private. In company, Auerbach provoked them, or they provoked one another, or each provoked himself, or provocation was inveterate and needed only a passing twinge to burst into speech. One would not have supposed that a soul there was in touch with the hounded sick man who loved as if it were flesh the depth of summer twilight; who feared the rumble of firewood falling in courtyards, tocsin of the Paris winter; who hated his military foster father, hated *les cuistres* and *la femme Sand*. The author named in literary discussions is a peculiar being, with a peculiar relation to flesh and blood.

With *Les Fleurs du Mal* there was, on the other hand, all due familiarity. Russi went home and wrote a brief dissertation, complete with references to such sources as a Baudelaire item published in *Le Figaro* in 1931, proving that Beauty was what was meant in *La Mort des Artistes*. Blackmur wrote several pages of notes on the way the various readings of this poem, by their very conflicts and confusion, served to reduce each reader's private infatuation and to guide or enlarge each toward the true poem, which had been there all the time. Meredith tried to translate it. Vast labors and trouble had gone into the effort of the evening to agree on the meaning of fourteen lines of French. There was an irony, nearly indefinable, about it. A poet need not wish to efface himself in his work; he would be effaced, he needn't worry. And idolatry, if idolatry there was: who was the greater idolater, one might wonder, the man who made the verses and corrected the proofs and suffered trial, or the men who made literature an institution, who gave their days and nights to the mere expense of reading, to the *study* of poetry.

Such were the writer's reflections; yet he could not think that they were entirely perverse. Would they not conduce to a proper sense of difficulty and humility? The social task, the effort made in common, the method of the seminars—these were surely necessary; more necessary perhaps than ever before. The void regions between artist and university and society-at-large needed to be filled, for sanity's sake; and there was nothing to do but to set about filling them. It was a part of Auerbach's passion: "to make understandable the immediate human thing." And Auerbach was valuable, both for the immense range of what he knew, and for his drive to keep it centered on a simplicity. In his case the simplicity was History, and this itself seemed an idol of a sort. In some matters he knew perhaps less than was desirable, for instance in his remarks about the "mental structure of a mystic" in Baudelaire. But he could not be called evasive. He was attacking, broadside on, great literary and poetic powers. His next was Flaubert.

Chapter Two

A WHOLE TRAGIC EXISTENCE ❧ ERICH AUERBACH ON FLAUBERT'S *MADAME BOVARY*

ERICH AUERBACH's powerful work, *Mimesis,* was not published in the United States until May 1953, when it appeared from the Princeton University Press in a very good translation by Willard Trask. By that time at least two excerpts from it had been published: a long chapter on Stendhal, Balzac and Flaubert in the *Partisan Review,* and another long chapter on Dante in an issue of the *Kenyon Review.* These essays won Auerbach a much wider reputation in the United States than he had had before. In linguistic and historical range, at any rate, he pretty clearly surpassed any literary critic writing in English with comparable scholarship. This distinction, which *Mimesis* more than confirmed, had become evident in the fall of 1949 at least to the writer and, he supposed, to most other participants in the seminars at Princeton. Only a few, however, including Fergusson, had already read *Mimesis* in German and were acquainted not only with the full range of Auerbach's work but with its guiding interest or intention. Auerbach's method of exposition—the text with commentary—tended somewhat to obscure this intention, but with the two final evenings it emerged in reasonable clarity. The study of Flaubert might well be thought crucial not only to his seminars but to his whole work. For Auerbach's effort during those years in Istanbul when he wrote *Mimesis* had been to show, by stylistic study, the forms of

literary realism shifting from Homer and Petronius through
the ages to Zola—shifting toward, then away from, and then
again toward the serious, the "existential," treatment of
everyday life.

In the century between 1848 and 1949 there were, in this
line, probably but two artistic efforts of comparable temper
and density, Flaubert's *Madame Bovary* (1857) and the work
of James Joyce. The writer, like many of his contemporaries,
had first opened his eyes in literature upon a world created
by both. Existence itself, taken in by the sense of identity as
well as by the direct drinking of the senses until the mind
had all it could hold—this seemed to him at twenty, facing
Ulysses (1922), the primary donnée of the artist, to be retained, however transformed, in art. When he was twenty-
one he sat until he was stiff over the pages of a cheap copy
of *Madame Bovary* in a yellow paper cover, Bibliothèque
Charpentier, at a long window opening on the rainy odor of
the rue Molière. The book was printed from broken type in
gray ink rather than black, a torment to the retina. It was the
only French novel the writer would ever ponder sentence by
sentence, from beginning to end. His head ached from the
type and the cheap wine he drank with his lunch. He was
trying to learn something he might inadequately have called
the art of prose. Whether he learned it or not, he felt from
that April onward more respect for Flaubert's novel than he
could often feel for the verse of Baudelaire. The writer held
with those professionals, his predecessors, Ford and Pound,
who believed that poetry should be as well written as prose,
that is, as Flaubert's or Joyce's; by "well written" they would
understand "ordered, concrete, intense, and economical." He
had therefore an interest of long standing in what Auerbach
would perform on his chosen text in this instance.

THE CHOICE was modest: a paragraph near the end of Part
I, at the climax, one might almost say at the peripety, of

Emma's life in Tostes—the paragraph beginning: "Mais c'était surtout aux heures des repas qu'elle n'en pouvait plus." With his usual sharp delicacy in such matters, Auerbach pointed out that the scene is presented through Emma, yet what her consciousness contains is not rendered in her terms but in Flaubert's, of which she would be incapable. If she herself could have formed the sentence, "toute l'amertume de l'existence lui semblait servie sur son assiette," she would have outgrown herself and thereby saved herself. On the shape and texture of these sentences Auerbach was excellent, up to a point. He declared that Emma's disgust with the food was in the rhythm and was thus a part of the content of the sentence, likewise that the second sentence, "Charles était long à manger . . ." introduced a new rhythm; but he did not say anything in description of these rhythms. What he wanted to make clear, in the given passage and in a later sentence quoted from Chapter 12 of Part II, was the imposition by the artist of his own hand in the choice and ordering of detail, a trait that set the work apart from anything "naturalistic."

Taking the text as typical of Flaubert in particular and nineteenth-century realism in general, Auerbach then raised the question as to how it differed from the realism of earlier periods. The material and the scene, a man and wife at table, were usual in art. In the seventeenth century the scene might have been an idyll of family life, and in an older, more grotesque art, there might have been an amusing quarrel. But the story of Emma Bovary was neither sentimental nor satirical, nor was it a love story, *au fond;* it was "a serious representation of a whole tragic existence." Yet, said Auerbach, the tragic mode of past periods would scarcely have admitted as a minor climax a scene during a regular meal at home. The scene disclosed a wrecked marriage—not, said he, the marriage of the eighteenth century wrecked by mischief after mischief with a final solution, but the wrecked marriage that is a permanent condition. There is no quarrel, because there is no contact, and on Charles's part not even an awareness of this. Each of the two lives in a windowless world of his own, with no one to help, no one for company, and no genuine reality; moreover, this is true of everyone in the novel. People meet for business or by instinct, never for community, and they are hampered everywhere by their lying, silly hatreds. Their isolating *bêtise* prevents a common life. Their public officials are all like the priest who fails to see that anything is wrong with Emma. When an illusion breaks, it breaks not on truth but on another illusion—and the word *Bovarysme* has entered the French language to designate this kind of life in an unreal world.

"But what the world would really be, the world of the 'intelligent,' Flaubert never tells us," said Auerbach. "In his book the world consists of pure stupidity, which completely misses true reality, so that the latter should properly not be discoverable in it at all; yet it is there; it is in the writer's language, which unmasks the stupidity by pure statement." In this way he approached the matter of Flaubert's famous religion of art—his faith, as Auerbach put it, that every event, if one is able to express it purely and completely, interprets itself and the persons involved in it far better than any overt judgment could do. Auerbach noted that faith in the truth of language responsibly employed was a classic French tradition; Vauvenargues had said, "Il n'y aurait point d'erreurs qui ne périssent d'elles-mêmes, exprimées clairement"—"There are no errors that do not perish of themselves when clearly expressed." But Flaubert went further: he believed that the truth of the phenomenal world could also be revealed in linguistic expression. A true expression was a real happening, placed with its value clear, just as God would judge it. This "mystical-realistic" insight, as Auerbach put it, associated Flaubert with Baudelaire as a stylist, for it entailed a certain view of the mixture of styles. Since the universe was a work of art produced without any taking of sides, the realistic artist must imitate the procedures of creation, and every subject in its essence contains, in God's eyes, both the serious and the comic, both dignity and vulgarity; if rightly and surely reproduced, the level of style proper to it would be rightly and surely found.

Auerbach ended by discussing the question as to whether Emma could be considered a tragic heroine. He thought not. Neither author nor reader could ever feel sympathetic or at one with her, he said, because the style itself judged her silly as well as wretched. Balzac invested Père Goriot with tragic dignity, as Stendhal made Julian Sorel a tragic hero. Flaubert's attitude and tone were quite different and should be called, Auerbach said, quite simply "objective seriousness."

In the general talk that followed, various people seemed uneasy as they tried to match Auerbach's ever-incisive formulae with the novel as they knew it. Fergusson wanted to know if there was not something tragic in Flaubert's style itself. Curtius objected to the whole category of "realism" as applied to Flaubert, observing that Flaubert himself explicitly disavowed the intention of realism. He went on to say, even more cantankerously, that the critical study of the history of literature uses terms that won't bear examination; we should dispense with these venerable terms.

Auerbach (stung): Why question the characteristic things called realism in the textbooks?

Curtius (Olympian): Because the textbooks are all wrong.

Auerbach (fighting back): Isolated, the term has no meaning, but it is sufficiently understandable in the context—French nineteenth-century realism. No matter if Flaubert did not want to be called realist; he worked the same way whether he liked it or not.

But the mention of Flaubert's other work, especially *Salammbô* (1862), made Auerbach concede that only part of Flaubert was realist. "But," said he, no doubt putting his finger on what was, in a sense, the heart of the matter, "I was writing a book on the treatment of everyday life!"

The next relevant remarks were made by Ira Wade, and they were closely relevant. Flaubert, he recalled, once said that he wanted to fuse the tragic and the lyric—an intention that Auerbach had not mentioned, though it was clearly related to his discussion of the style of Baudelaire. Wade wanted to know how you could get along without using such terms to bring out Flaubert's transformation of reality to lyrical writing. In the passage Auerbach had discussed, he called attention to the alliteration on "s." The writer thought this a useful remark, and made use of it himself later to discover that in fact the alliteration in the passage was progressive, beginning with the explosive "p's" of impatience and ending with the "f" of disgust.

As to the matter of tragic tone, Gauss severely interposed that Emma was not tragic because the tragic are those who deserve to live, and deserve to live Emma did not. Curtius returned to the attack on the category of "realist," remarking that it was very interesting (that is, nonsense) that Stendhal, Balzac, and Flaubert should all be lumped in one category; did not Balzac and Stendhal enjoy life while on the contrary Flaubert was a prey to despair? What was important was not what novelists have in common but their differences. Auerbach mildly replied that you couldn't get at the individual in Flaubert without historical common denominators. Fergusson and Curtius tried again to slit the straightjacket in which they evidently felt that Auerbach had encased a living work of art. Borgerhoff, having thought the matter over, disputed one of Auerbach's principal points; the judgment in Flaubert's presentation of Emma and Charles at table, he said, was *sympathetic* to Emma; the reader shared Emma's feeling. Moreover—and this was Borgerhoff's liberating stroke—there was other evidence of the novelist's sympathy for Emma:

"Remember how Flaubert shows her at the time of extreme unction. . . . That is sad. To me, there is a quality like the ballads: something is celebrated, and properly."

BLACKMUR'S meditation on this session, written down afterwards, read in part as follows:

"No matter who hammers against him, Auerbach must insist on his 'realism,' his 'sublime and common' and his 'dead earnest' or 'seriousness,' these, I take it, representing mode, medium, and point of view. When he applies his method to three authors with whom he is out of sympathy, as he has here to Pascal, Baudelaire, and Flaubert, he comes out somehow narrow but penetrating. What is narrowed away is the humanity of his authors; what is penetrated is their defect: the point where their work did not reach the level of performance, for him, but turned to some form or formula or rationalization or mere method: the antithesis in Pascal, the fusion of sublime and common in Baudelaire, the contempt and seriousness in Flaubert. I think myself he gives too much credit to these formulas on the work of the authors, where they were only aids, and too little credit to the actual material that got into the work with their aid. . . . He forgets that every writer who survives is constantly wrestling with a burden of actual experience by no means amenable to anything but disposition (disponibleness) by the method. Thus he not only missed but denied the wrestling, swindling authority of life itself, apart from all categories, in the series of images that lead to the whiff of all human ill in Emma's soul—a whiff looking out its home in the smoking stove, creaking door, sweating walls, damp floor, and above all in the odor of the food; and missed, too, our chance at that whiff while Emma pecks at the hazel nuts or marks on the oil cloth—those creases that come and go—with her knife. No; for him it is *bêtise* judging *bêtise à la bête,* with a further cruel judgment in Flaubert's *style.* That was Auerbach's predilection; and it is true that he has made it present; it must be taken account of.

"The pity is that this goes along with the prejudice in favor of tragic figures—those who deserved to live; and with the worse, because human rather than artistic prejudice, that Emma could have fixed everything up if only she had been more intelligent: the prejudice, in short, that emotion is capable of maturity. There is mature thought or attitude or understanding about emotion, but maturity is not a concept which applies to emotion; a lesson one would have thought universally taught in art, and one of the signs of greatness. Maturity is the solution, not the experience of the tragedy of individuals, and the solution is commonly death.—At any rate that is the predilection I gain from my reading.

"Turning from Auerbach to Curtius, one sees the great protection from follies afforded him by his doctrine of *loci,* the common *places* of mankind's efforts to express itself, its conditions and aspirations, in the arts. Curtius is, relative to Auerbach, a deep anarch of the actual. Every blow he struck at Auerbach was meant to break down the formulas whereby we see how unlike things are like. . . . He understands why it is that the textbooks *must be wrong:* because they are designed to take care of the reading we do not do: a legitimate enterprise when provisional, fatal when permanent. . . . It seemed to me, then, that Curtius was potentially always on the verge of breaking through into Emma's life itself, or into the moving subject or locus of literature. Or—to put it the other way round, to put it critically . . . Curtius was struggling toward the development of a neutral vocabulary, good for any insights. . . . I do not say Auerbach does not see all this; that he would not concede it in any instance, as we might all of us do; but that he has not the magnitude of mind or sensibility . . . to emulate it in original practice. . . .

"Borgerhoff seemed to me to make the remarks of richest possibility, and especially when he compared the fusion of the lyric and the tragic in Emma Bovary to the kind of thing a ballad does: a celebration of the beautiful and the strange and the true, where the meaning is in the celebration, and the celebration is a mystery, with many voices. . . . Note well that, for the moment, in Borgerhoff's use of it, the word 'ballad' is neutral: and, so to speak, here engineers a whole human vocabulary—though one that conspicuously would not last. . . .

"[One might put] the question whether the members of the seminar find it part of the common enterprise of culture. If they do, it is at a lower level both of collaboration and of individualism than the level anyone would name as optimum. The enterprise is there, is common, and the commonalty is of individuals; but the members tend mostly to run off into the artificializing formulas which make problems easy to discuss and easier to escape in discussion. It seems to me . . . that there are two ways in which we can promote both greater collaboration and greater individualism. One: when 'history' is at issue, in any sense of the term, it is certain that literature provides us with . . . documents in the *experience* of ideas or thought or the mind; literature is the history of the experience of the mind. It is also the history of the experience with which the mind has been coping or—more important—what it must now cope with—and—most important—the experience with which the mind has never yet been able to cope. The other line is this: that it is a probable rule in literature, that whatever can be wholly subsumed under categories or formulas of any kind represents the work that the writer either could not do or was not interested in doing or refused to do. . . . Applied to criticism it means that categories, sets, formulas, slogans, and so on have constantly to be refreshed by the direct look: by the individual look in company with the collaborative look. These two lines, boiled down and made almost habitual, should provide the right questions and the living questions. They provide means for the reaccession to the experience *in* literature—of which the experience *of* literature is only a part."

AS THESE characteristic notes suggest, the Princeton colloquies had now moved into a region—that of narrative fiction—considerably broader and more various than that of either Pascal or Baudelaire. In attending to the thinker and the poet it had been possible to neglect, or take for granted, what Blackmur called "humanity"; but this was not possible with *Madame Bovary*. In retrospect, the writer found this the most interesting of Auerbach's sessions, the most one-sided, the least conclusive, and the most fertile. As humanity entered into the subject, the savants and craftsmen may have felt certain pressures from the world of flesh and blood where the novel *Madame Bovary* may be found in drugstore editions and in the hands of high school girls; it did not belong to critics, scholars and writers only but to the unknown people. A sense of the mystery involved in this—a large one—no doubt lurked in the minds of those who, like Curtius on the one hand and Borgerhoff on the other, fought shy of Auerbach's treatment. The week before, Berryman had attacked Auerbach and everyone else except Curtius for getting a work of art and the response proper to it mixed up with a human attitude and the response proper to *it*. This fascinating question might have been raised again, but was not, in relation to the work of Flaubert.

Either the term "realism" was indispensable, the writer thought, or the kind of study that Auerbach had been conducting was useless. Yet the quarrel over the term was not a waste of time, or rather it would not have been a waste of time if Auerbach had been able not only to defend it—as he did humbly and adequately—but to unfold fully the *differentia* within it. The great differentiating notion of "existential seriousness" for Flaubert seemed largely lost on the company. To the writer's mind this expression should have satisfied Blackmur's wish for a neutral vocabulary and, properly understood, would have obviated much of his and the other criticism. It would have done so, that is, if it had been understood to apply to the whole conception of the novel. Here Auerbach's method of concentrating on a slice of text betrayed more clearly than before its peculiar disadvantage.

As in the case of Baudelaire, the passage selected was a serviceable one for the analysis of style *in parvo* but not a great one that would represent the scope of Flaubert's art.

Suppose, the writer thought, Auerbach had put his mind on that later page in which Emma mounts to the attic window with Rodolphe's letter in her hand. One could scarcely imagine his being able to argue from the classically controlled and dramatic impact of that scene to the formula of Flaubert's style merely "judging" *bêtise*. Or suppose he had tried to deal with the sequence of Emma's death. Anyone not moved to pity and terror by that sequence must be insensitive indeed. By merely recalling it, Borgerhoff had in all mildness indicated what was lacking in Auerbach's paper: a sense of style *as the organization of the whole*. Not that Auerbach failed intellectually to grasp the fact that the novel was "the serious representation of a whole tragic existence," for he said so, at one point, in so many words. That recognized, Emma was either a "tragic heroine" or the equivalent; the quarrel over whether she was or not became almost entirely verbal. All Auerbach had to do was to take the next step and see Flaubert's art as constructive in the large sense, resembling in this, too, the traditional art of the tragedian.

If the restriction of "stylistics" to sentence structure obscured this for him on the one hand, on the other it would have been difficult for him to give it full value in the face of his powerful interest in Flaubert's realism as a criticism of bourgeois society. This interest he developed in his sixth and final evening with further and extensive reference to the life and work of Stendhal as a social realist who brought into fiction an acute sense of period, of the moving background of history. In Auerbach's essay, as later published, the order of treatment, beginning with Stendhal and Balzac and ending with Flaubert, was far more satisfactory and clearer than in the reversed order he followed at Princeton. All the requisite evidence of Flaubert's attitude toward his period—he hated it as Baudelaire did—was of course fully supplied. No doubt could be entertained of Auerbach's sensitivity as an intellectual historian. Not only did he know, and suggest with precision, the social and political facts in themselves and as the novelists responded to them; he also defined the subject of modern fiction as the relationship between society and personal life. Later seminars at Princeton were to explore it precisely as such.

What Auerbach scanted, however, was the relationship between fiction, fiction in general or this fiction in particular, and its subject. It was no doubt a tribute to Flaubert's art that his critic failed to distinguish between representation of the actual and presentation of the conceived, the created form. But it was a tribute too commonly paid, and criticism had too often achieved facility by omitting one or more of the essential conditions of work in the arts. Auerbach could certainly have discussed this very topic; he was of course acquainted with Flaubert's "sources" in his own life and the lives, such as Mme. Pradier's, that he deliberately studied, and Flaubert's own description of his transforming art as *une chimie merveilleuse* was even cited in the course of the paper. The simple fact was that the reality of Emma Bovary was an illusion created by art; she lived wholly in Flaubert's imagination and his imagination shaped her wholly in the work. The illusion exemplified laws of constructive art, as well as depths of emotion and intention in the artist, that Auerbach did not touch.

It interested the writer, moreover, that in this, one more critical effort on *Madame Bovary,* the defense of the novel by Maître Senard in 1857 was not so much as mentioned. But Maître Senard spoke for a large and by no means extinct class of readers, including in his own way Henry James, who have discovered in *Madame Bovary* what Flaubert himself called the *autorité imprevue* of profound moral understanding. Maître Senard was only a great lawyer, not a literary man, but Flaubert would no doubt have been pleased to liken him to the great doctor, Larivière, who appears in all his energy, compassion and sanity toward the close of *Madame Bovary.* The writer had the impression that Maître Senard was the last critic, as he was the first, to observe that the death of Charles Bovary is as beautiful and touching as the death of Emma is terrible. Emma had lived for her own gratification, and died mocked by her own image; Charles lived for others and loved another, and died with his love intact, however heartbroken, mocked by its object.

THE WRITER'S interests and business lying elsewhere, he was absent from Princeton during the rest of the academic year, and attended no further seminars except one of those given by his friend Fergusson on Dante. Of Auerbach's further activities at Princeton he saw nothing and heard little except that the hospitality of the Institute was enabling him to make further accumulations of research in the university library, where he busied himself as much in making lists of books as in reading them. By later correspondence the writer learned that Auerbach valued the seminars highly as an introduction to the vocabulary of American critics, with which, and no wonder, he confessed himself slow to become adept. His learning, clarity, and vitality as a teacher were so obvious that the writer assumed he would be offered a professorship at Princeton. As it turned out, the Yale Graduate School moved first and acquired him, so that he was no longer on the scene when the writer arrived in Princeton the following year. His only tangible deposit there was his big manuscript, which the University Press was pleased to undertake. In Blackmur's mind especially, however, there remained a deposit of protest against Auerbach's dismissal of Emma Bovary as "silly." It was partly this *scrupulum* that incited him a year or so later to develop an essay on Emma Bovary, entitled "Beauty Out of Place" and published in the *Kenyon Review* for summer 1951, in which sympathy for Emma positively ran riot. The more useful achievement of Blackmur's essay was to extract, with the critic's usual and unrivalled penetration, some of the symbolic and structural features of Flaubert's novel, hinting at the pain and subtlety and inventive power of his imagination.

Chapter Three

TOWARD A HISTRIONIC SENSIBILITY ข FRANCIS FERGUSSON ON DANTE'S *PURGATORIO*

THE WRITER'S NOTION of events at Princeton in the remainder of the academic year 1949-1950 was gathered afterward from various sources. No notes were taken on the ensuing seminars—Fergusson's on Dante's *Purgatorio*, Delmore Schwartz's on T. S. Eliot, and Mark Schorer's on "The Novel as Genre." Blackmur's copious record ended with Auerbach's evenings, for the reason that his notes on each evening took a couple of days' work to digest and transcribe. Blackmur, although spared a certain part of his "teaching load" for seminar purposes, could not manage that much time. The manuscripts from which Fergusson and Schorer delivered their talks were consulted for this chronicle, though neither man regarded his manuscript as completed work. In the case of Delmore Schwartz no such manuscript existed. Schwartz had been working for at least four years on a book-length study of Eliot and had already published, in the *Partisan Review* for spring 1945 and February 1949, two chapters entitled "T. S. Eliot as the International Hero" and "The Literary Dictatorship of T. S. Eliot." The material of these chapters as well as others unpublished was incorporated in his seminar talks, but he worked from notes according to an order different from that in his text; and he did not consider his notes intelligible in themselves. In surveying that year, therefore, the writer had to narrow his lens for a more distant and wider view. Some general matters seemed worth lingering over.

In the first place there was the question of the relationship between the seminar program and the Institute for Advanced Study. Ten years had passed since the Institute, under Frank Aydelotte who became director in 1939, had set up a School of Humanities for the broad purpose of welcoming as guests and occasionally embracing as members distinguished scholars or writers from other than scientific fields. The director at his discretion had invited a number of such persons for one-year renewable appointments, of which Blackmur, as has been already noted, had held three. In 1947 on Aydelotte's retirement the new director, J. Robert Oppenheimer, a well-educated physicist, seemed disposed to continue and even to expand this policy. Oppenheimer had known Fergusson since the twenties when they were both at Harvard. He invited Fergusson to the Institute for the year 1948–1949. He invited T. S. Eliot for the same year, and these men continued at the Institute important work that they had begun elsewhere: Fergusson his book, *The Idea of a Theatre*, and Eliot his play, *The Cocktail Party* (1950). It has already been mentioned that when Fergusson and Blackmur conceived the seminars they thought of them almost as a joint enterprise of university and Institute; they thought, at any rate, that one or more annual appointees at the Institute would be on hand not only to give a set of seminars but to take part in the others in the course of each year. It seemed likely at the time that Eliot would do this. Anyone might have supposed that the School of Humanities at the Institute would flourish under a director as sympathetic and knowing as Oppenheimer.

As 1949 passed into 1950 and 1950 wore on, these assumptions gradually underwent a certain change. The governing members of the Institute voted to dispense with the School of Humanities. They merged it in something henceforth known as the School of History and Politics. It was of

46

course nothing but an administrative reorganization, and interpretation had to await developments. Among these, there were no trenchant public statements from anyone. Precisely why the change was made, or rather what arguments could be made for it, remained as obscure to some of those closely concerned as it did to the writer. It slowly became clear at least that something had gone wrong with the prospect of Eliot's second visit, not to mention the possibility of his appointment to the Institute. He never came. It was difficult to credit, but the fact little by little apprehended seemed to be that some eminent members had rather ignored him while he was at the Institute and had rather retarded the processes of renewing hospitality. There was no doubt that Oppenheimer would have wished it otherwise. If the administrative change accorded with a change of attitude, it did not accord with his. One consequence seemed to be that he had to continue to act alone in such matters. The Institute as such, for example, did not give Auerbach his year in Princeton; the director did so on his own initiative in spite of some curious manifestations of disapproval.

A severe and partisan examination of these events might have concluded that the scientists and historians at the Institute were subject, in their Olympian way, to sentiments found among place-keepers and time-servers everywhere else. If they were willing to exclude Eliot and Auerbach, the fiery inference would be that they were capable of anything. Ernst Robert Curtius was probably the finest scholar-critic of literature who had written in German in the twentieth century. His studies of Joyce and Proust, his translation of *Ulysses*, his works on the civilization of France and the literature of the Middle Ages were of conspicuous authority throughout Europe. The writer did not know these works, for he knew no German, but he knew the essay of Charles Du Bos in which their quality had been most sensitively estimated from the French point of view. Yet it seemed that the Institute contrived to let Curtius go after no extravagant period of entertainment, nor did he return. Certainly neither in his case nor in Eliot's was there any question of discourtesy; both men had deep interests and commitments abroad, and a positive effort would have been needed to bring them to Princeton for any extended period. The point was that the opportunity for this was allowed to pass.

As to Oppenheimer's responsibility in these cloudy affairs, it had to be remarked that the Institute was after all a democratically governed body. In other words, it was a club in which few men but resolute could determine the exclusions. The director no doubt had his perplexities. It was even doubtful whether intransigence on his part could have preserved to the humanities a more handsome share in the perquisites of the Institute. One might hear both pro and con on this proposition. Larger events in any case soon settled it. By June 1950, the United States was at war in Korea, by October the war threatened to become serious, and Oppenheimer's brains were again, as they had been during the Second World War, at the service of the country. That ended any chance of his being able to contend steadily at the Institute for the honor of creative literary labor. The kind of advanced study that issues in literature would continue to take place elsewhere. "A man making a study of Dante could be appointed," as one member put it to the writer, "but Dante could not."

This slow crystallization at the Institute was an internal injury to the promise of the Princeton Seminars, an injury more or less grave according to how one viewed the promise. The possibility may have been remote, but there was a possibility of a rapprochement, through the medium of the seminars, not only between university and Institute, but between humanistic studies and scientific studies. It was a commonplace among thoughtful men at this stage of the century that pure science in its progress had gone over the hill from humankind. Scientists themselves—among them Oppenheimer—had recoiled from the powers their own researches had

48

put in the hands of men. The best among them were willing to look for a wisdom that would embrace both nature as newly conceived and human action. The humanists on their side and for the same reason were eager to vindicate such wisdom as they had or to improve on it until it should meet the demands of the scientists and the situation. This urgent and grand object could not be approached merely in a few seminars on literature, but if the seminars were supported in part by the Institute that had cradled them they would supply at least one common occasion for meditation.

Now, however, the Institute appeared to harbor somewhat less interest in this than had been supposed. The thinkers who represented the sciences and therefore stood in the position of highest intellectual prestige in modern society had shown themselves cool toward sharing that position with men of letters no matter how distinguished. Nowhere else, it might well be said, had the choice been put to men of science so squarely and under conditions so favorable to men of letters. It seemed a rebuff on the highest level, to borrow a phrase from diplomacy. Would it be just, then, to conclude that the men of science refused to entertain even the possibility of collaboration with literary men?

That was a natural conclusion, but the writer, after some reflection, thought it premature. The word "collaboration" raised a doubt in his mind, and he felt the doubt to be salutary; for it was not clear that collaboration was what the literary men were after. They were interested in the critical examination and improvement of their own kind of job and in reestablishing its credit in face of the sciences, and they took it for granted that the men of science would be interested witnesses. Well, that was true to some extent; a physicist from the Institute had for example attended the Auerbach seminars on Pascal, and Oppenheimer maintained his interest; occasionally he came. But were the literary men prepared to reciprocate? Would they care, concretely, to make the effort of learning and logic required to follow the public lectures given by members of the Institute whenever one of them felt that he had something important to say? If they would, they gave little evidence of it as far as the writer could see. And he imagined that the quiet withdrawal of the Institute might have seemed, to those responsible for it, nothing more than a recognition of the *status quo*. Sometime later, before the hospitable fire of one Institute member, the writer beheld a meeting of minds on the thesis that culpability in the matter lay far back and even among the terms with which it was approached. He heard it suggested, indeed, that the category of the "Humanities" would be a curse so long as it excluded the work of men's minds in mathematics and natural sciences, fields not perhaps as barren of values as the current humanists sometimes presumed.

This, besides, was taking the problem in its extreme alternatives. What about History and Politics? Here one would have supposed the humanistic interest intrinsically great. To the writer's ear there had come at least one echo—or so he suspected—of interchange at the Institute between literary study and the study of politics. George Kennan, a resident at the Institute in Fergusson's year, on leave from the State Department, had put into his little book on foreign policy certain conceptions of history, notably a realization of Consequences as Limits, that seemed derived not only from experience but from the reinspection of classic literature. An echo of this kind might reverberate in the great world. On the other side, for at least ten years Blackmur had been working off and on—and intensively while he was at the Institute—on a study of Henry Adams in which presumably the literary and the sociological interests were exercised together. It appeared that the Institute had nothing against such work as this.

In the given instance, however, beneath appearances that always remained cordial, a massive shoulder was turning and turning a little cold. And the effect on the seminars was an impoverishment, not only metaphorical but to some extent literal. Four sets of seminars in each year had to be provided for. The director had a fund of $4,000 for the purpose and his committee had established $1,500 as the normal stipend for each seminar leader brought to Princeton for residence. Traveling expenses were also to be paid for invited visitors to each session. This meant that two seminar leaders in every four had to be otherwise provided for—by residence and adequate compensation either at the university or at the Institute. The Institute, as slowly became clear, would assist on an occasional basis and chiefly by kindness of the director. No sooner were the seminars off the ground, so to speak, than one of the outboard engines began to fail. The director nursed it along and stayed on course, but it must have seemed to him at times a labored flight.

A CERTAIN confirmatory interplay, as ironic as one pleased, could be seen between the circumstances now outlined and the view of life implied by the brilliant extended essay on dramatic art that Fergusson published late in 1949, *The Idea of a Theatre*. This book, finished at the Institute and published by the Princeton University Press, came out of the author's twenty years of work as a director and teacher at the Laboratory Theatre in New York and the Theater Studio at Bennington. Experienced and qualified readers recognized it at once as one of those critical works whose value lies in the annexation of new ground. Fergusson brought to dramatic literature an executant's interest in writing and a sense of style cultivated by the symbolist poets, the novels of Henry James, and the work of T. S. Eliot; but his best personal insights were gained in the theater, in the exercise of what he called the histrionic imagination and in the study of that form of imagination as expressive of human understanding and culture.

The general conception of the "dramatic" as a mode of understanding had been imported long since into literary criticism and had proved fertile especially in the critical theory of Kenneth Burke; but Burke was an elaborator of "grammars." Fergusson pinned himself down to particular plays and to the actor's sense of psychic change underlying the verbal medium. He diverged thus from the purely literary critic and probed in his own way into the primitive and subtle "tragic sense of life." Taking from Scott Buchanan's book, *Poetry and Mathematics,* the statement that as poetry preceded theory so likewise the histrionic sensibility "undercut" all discursive thought, Fergusson borrowed from Burke a graph of the tragic rhythm in three phases—*purpose, suffering,* and *perception*—and made use of this in the analysis of great drama. His classic illustration he found in Sophocles' *Oedipus Rex.* And holding Sophocles and Shakespeare as his examples of the tragic art whole and crystalline, still in touch with ritual and mythic levels of understanding, he argued that the modern theater since Racine was a broken bundle of mirrors.

Purpose, suffering, and perception: the analysis was sharp and profound, but in one respect it was itself incomplete. In the course of the book, Fergusson referred often to Dante's *Divine Comedy* as containing the deepest and most elaborate development of this "rhythm" in Western literature—a view of some novelty, since Dante wrote for no theater and explicitly denied his poem the elevation of tragic style. Seeing that Fergusson was not only able but willing to explain more fully what he meant, the Seminar Committee agreed that he should do so before the Princeton company. This took care of the second series of seminars, after Auerbach, and shored up the seminar fund that year for the purpose of bringing Schwartz and Schorer to Princeton. Fergusson's readings in the *Purgatorio* began on the evening of December 1.

WHAT FERGUSSON was trying to work out could perhaps be stated in general terms, though in no single set of general terms. It was the task of getting an effective balance between works of reason and works of art; between the intellect and the life of feeling; between philosophy and poetry; between what Blackmur in his notes on Auerbach called "formula" and "performance," or between moral and critical categories and the actual, "the wrestling, swindling authority of life itself." Fergusson was a teacher who understood teaching as training and coaching; he knew something first hand about the primacy and efficacy of the histrionic sensibility in handling experience. Properly disciplined and deepened, it seemed to him prior to rationalization and beyond it, suppler and wiser, "fixated" neither upon reason nor feeling. The refinements each of these faculties had reached in severance from the other marked the modern era and its characteristic "split"—something even then being exemplified in Princeton, as has been seen. What Fergusson wanted and wanted to make available from the reading of Dante was precisely what Dante had wanted to give—help; and this intention, however sophisticated, made his work all modestly vivid.

Help for whom? It was plain from his introductory talk that Fergusson had taken thought not only for everyone in general, nor only for readers and students in general, but specifically for poets, practitioners of literary art. He remarked to begin with that the *Purgatorio* might be read both as poetry and as a demonstration of the process of poetry making. Auerbach had certainly considered his examples of Baudelaire with a view as to how they were made, in one sense, but not in the sense of the making "process." Now this unobtrusive point was something to perk up about. It moved the locus of interest in the seminars several degrees closer to home, as a writer must think it. Closer, for that matter, than if Fergusson had proposed to study the same "process" in Pindar, say, or Gongora, or Lord Byron. For the first poet of the age in fascination and influence, T. S. Eliot, had declared some time ago that contemporary poets could have no better model than Dante; and it had been possible to ignore but not to confute him. *The Divine Comedy* had, beyond doubt, a place in the admiration of English and American poets that no other verse written before 1500, and only the greatest written later, could rival.

"We have to recognize, as the source of our delight in poetry, a principle of sane growth in the mind." This sentence of I. A. Richards, summarizing Coleridge, Fergusson took as his epigraph, so to speak, for the reading of the *Purgatorio*. Dante had not only assumed such a view of poetry, he said, but in the *Purgatorio* had illustrated it in a thousand instances which qualified and amplified each other. Fergusson gave his attention first to the alternations of day and night, waking and dreaming, in this central *cantica* of the *Divine Comedy*, the one that follows the rhythm of mortal life in time. In each of the "night" passages he thought Dante had indicated "subtle relationships between dreaming, reason and *mythopoeia*, varied modes of action whereby the mind seeks to grasp the reality of its situation." The first illustration was from *Canto* IX:

> Ne l'ora che comincia i tristi lai
> la rondinella presso a la mattina,
> forse a memoria de' suo' primi guai,
>
> e che la mente nostra, peregrina
> più da la carne e men da' pensier presa,
> a le sue vision quasi è divina. . . .

The beauty of this, at which the reader himself might fall into a waking dream, it was scarcely necessary to remark. Fergusson explained it, or part of it. "By means of his allusive method, Dante fuses many ideas and images into one poetic whole in this brief passage: the mythic childhood of the race, the hour of very early morning, the ancient plaint of nature in the sounds of birds, the clarity of dream before waking, and the state of the pilgrim at that moment in his ascent. The second tercet specifies the pilgrim's psychic state more exactly: that in which the soul is most nearly free *both* of the flesh and of 'thoughts'—which I take to be the concepts of

54

discursive reason—and can therefore perceive with the most direct, unimpeded and prophetic clarity. This passage introduces the dream. It would serve (with qualifications) as an introduction to all the dreams, and it is also a premonition of the earthly paradise."

Now in speaking of the dream that follows, Fergusson suggested a whole scale of symbolic meanings, running from the purely medieval associations of the eagle with secular, ecclesiastical and divine assistance to the infantile erotic connotations, as Freud would have seen them, in the swooping bird, the ascent and the burning together. He felt sure, himself, that Dante meant these connotations, since the whole *Purgatorio* could be regarded as an epic of the transformations of love, and since the dream of the following night contained explicit eroticism, formed and adult. The dream in *Canto* IX, therefore, referring as it did to Ganymede and the young Achilles, was an analogue in the dream "mode of action" of the passage out of childhood, the stage at which the pilgrim in the poem had arrived in the night before his entrance into Purgatory proper. Upon waking, in the bright morning sunlight, he is told by Virgil, his guide, the "literal facts" of the nocturnal change: Lucia, Illuminating Grace, had carried him up the mountain while he slept. Fergusson's comment on this brought out the point that he wanted above all to make:

"Now that the pilgrim's mind is fully awake and in possession of the facts, does he understand his situation better than he did in dream? We must say, I think, that he understands it *differently*, but that neither visionary dreaming nor waking, neither *mythopoeia* nor reason, can present to him the reality of his situation at that moment in his development. Both are necessary, but neither is complete, and he cannot employ them both at the same time; they offer complementary perspectives. I am told that the theoretical physicists use what they call a principle of complementarity in the present state of their investigation of light. They need two theories to explain the facts they have about light; but the two theories are not only logically contradictory, but based on different experiments, and hence cannot be entertained in the same way at the same time."

Here was a direct appeal for the comparing of notes between the artist who would cope with psychic and moral realities and the physicist who would cope, in this instance, with the mystery of light. The question was how to estimate their respective ways of coping. It was fitting, then, that for his next discussion the lecturer should go straight to the center of the *Divine Comedy,* the middle cantos of the *Purgatorio,* where classic reason gets its fullest exposition. He recalled how on the second day of the purgatorial journey the pilgrim, guided by Virgil, had painfully mounted the rock face of the mountain from the gate of Purgatory proper through the terraces of the Proud and the Envious. In late afternoon the travellers, rounding the mountainside, faced the direct light of the setting sun—the light that as always in Dante is the analogue of intellect. It was at this point, Fergusson suggested, that the reader should see faith and obedient moral effort supplemented by a beginning of sustained intellectual effort and understanding. The pilgrim in fact got too much light in his eyes; he reached the next terrace, the realm of Anger, "bursting with unanswered questions." Fergusson went on to a detailed study of *Canto* xvi, using the method of multiple analysis developed in *The Idea of a Theatre.* His bold argument was that each canto of the *Purgatorio* had been designed as an "action" in the Aristotelian and dramatic sense—a *moto spiritale,* the working out through "purpose, suffering, and perception" of a particular mode of the soul's being; in *Canto* xvi the ostensible mode was Anger purging itself, and the canto was to be understood first of all as a moving image of the state of anger.

"All who have been angry," he said, "will recognize the darkness, the discomfort, the abrupt self-righteousness, and the feeling of congested rationality, as though all the reason were *inside."* The metaphor of the smoke and *buio d'inferno* in which the pilgrim plunges with his guide had been handled by Dante, he thought, in such a way as to illustrate that principle enunciated in *Canto* IV as to the possibility of the soul, though remaining free in essence, becoming so bound by one faculty that it appears deprived of other sensitivity. In this case, though the free soul was suggested by Virgil's presence and by the singing voices beyond the smoke, the pilgrim was so blinded, the soul so bound, that without benefit of direct perception it had to guide itself by discourse and ratiocination alone. The exchange of dialogue with Marco Lombardo, hidden in the smoke, further conveyed the "action" of the canto by its impatient and abrupt rhythms at the start: "the frustration," said Fergusson, "of having to communicate by speech and concepts, in the dark."

As to the long discourse of Marco on human freedom and responsibility, that was of course philosophy, and beautifully clear and cogent philosophy, in what Fergusson called "the revivified Greek tradition," but Dante's handling of that, too, conveyed in another way the single "action" of the canto. For it was philosophy in a context; it was dramatic utterance by Marco in his actual plight as a soul undergoing the purgation of anger, and it arose from the dramatic impulse of Dante's question, his "arrogant either-or formulation of the problem: determinism or free will." Fergusson pointed out very neatly that the correct dialectical answer as given by Marco—the soul is both free and bound—was of only theoretical help to Marco himself, who remained in the smoke. Likewise, the lovely image of the *anima semplicetta,* the created soul, though it suggested a release in memory, the memory of childhood, could not fully avail, since the pilgrim and Marco were caught in difficulties both actual and logical, which the simple soul of childhood could not even perceive.

"Thus we are led to the question of responsibility, or blame, in another and wider context: that of history and of the whole human community. Church and State each claim absolute authority, very much as the faculties of sense perception or thought which should guide the individual are overvalued and in this idolatry [of one or the other] divide the soul. Church and State, with perfect logic but on inadequate premises, each demand absolute power. So they quench their own and each other's light, leaving the human community and all the individuals that compose it in angry darkness. . . . Now we can grasp Marco's rationalization of the world he knew, contemporary Italy, and of the angry habit of mind he acquired there. . . . The end of the canto also completes, with the aid of a few brief concrete allusions, the picture of this timeless mode of human life, this state of the soul, which, though a moment only in the long process of development, recurs in every experience. . . . Marco and Dante, the pilgrim, part—Dante to proceed toward the new light which glimmers ahead, Marco to dive back abruptly into the smoke, like a man chewing on a sore tooth which he cannot yet extract."

Dante's picture of this timeless mode of life had obviously, in Fergusson's mind, an important relevance to the twentieth century. "We see," he said, "in a thousand forms the actual conflicts of authority, the logical impasses of rationalized attitudes and beliefs; the anger that goes with [this plight] and the implicit belief in the sole authority of the discursive reason on which it is based." He also thought that *Canto* xvi had a bearing on Pascal's *Pensée* concerning Force and Justice that had been the subject of Auerbach's first seminar.

"The style of this *Pensée*," he said, "as Professor Auerbach showed, is, ostensibly and in its beginnings, that of logical analysis and demonstration. But the logic . . . destroys itself, and the style of the passage . . . moves toward angry-despairing rhetoric. Professor Auerbach showed how the actual world to which Pascal refers, behind his logic, was in fact divided and darkened by conflicting claims of absolute authority, spiritual and temporal, much as Marco's Italy was. Pascal, I suppose, was at least as tormented as Marco by this darkness and these splits. But he seems, at least in this passage, to lack Marco's sense of a possible release—he has no sense of the innocent freedom of the simple soul, of childhood in a real world, nor, in the other direction, of the possibility of the soul's freedom and integrity beyond this mode of awareness but still in the world. For Pascal, the only escape from the darkened world of *La Raison* was by way of the blind wager—the leap of faith not sustained by any sense of analogies between modes of being."

Further and finally, "this part of the *Purgatorio* throws a good deal of light on the Age of Reason in general—notably upon the basic scheme of neoclassic tragedy, the tragedy of reason. Dante is apparently here concerned with a similar mode of life and is presented with analogous poetic, rhetorical, and philosophic modes of discourse. But he throws light upon it by placing it in a wider context. The seventeenth century didn't like the notion of gradual purgation, it took its own habits of mind, not as parts of a changing spectrum, but as absolute and final. But Dante the pilgrim proceeds on his upward path."

THE THINNING SMOKE—anger purged and dissipated—the sun's bright ball perceived, and the emergence of the travellers in *Canto* XVII were the prelude to a new *moto spiritale,* a fresh effort of intellect, now both loftier and wider of prospect, characterized at the start by the serenity and lassitude of evening. Fergusson recapitulated *Canto* XVII: Virgil and the pilgrim mount to the terrace of Sloth before darkness overtakes and strands them there; Virgil now takes up the discourse of Reason and in this and the following canto instructs the pilgrim in the transformations of love—an idea "much profounder than the noble moralism and impatient rationalism of *Canto* XVI" and indeed, as Fergusson had said, the very

59

subject of the *Purgatorio*. Yet here again the lecturer warned against taking these philosophic passages out of their context in another "action" that must end as the ascent continues. He described this action as "pleasurable contemplation of the Idea of Love, which turns out to be dynamite; and when the real force of love is felt, the contemplation is dissolved." His analysis was remarkably rich.

The discourse by Virgil that takes up about half of *Canto* XVIII is clearly in "the revivified Greek tradition." Its mode, Fergusson said, was Platonic and Aristotelian, the mode of philosophic contemplation, subsuming the rational under-standing or *epistêmê* of Mark the Lombard under the higher faculty of mind, *nous,* that intuits both the Idea and the varied instances of its realization in perception. He suggested the resemblance here between the teacher-pupil relationship of Virgil and the pilgrim, sharing Virgil's pleasurable explora-tion of the Idea of Love, and the relationship between Socrates as midwife and the eager minds of the Platonic dialogues. The first part of the discourse, he said, took up Marco's image of the simple soul moving toward what delights it, but in a wider perspective that envisaged love in all living things. Fergusson supplied an example that Dante might have used if he had known it: "if any of you have seen an amoeba under the microscope, flowing toward the food which attracts it, and taking the color of the food, you have a visual metaphor for the spiritual movement of love which Virgil is exploring." But the recurring question of Free Will made Virgil expound the specifically human appetites for spiritual and intellectual things. "Thus the human soul perceives a wider realm of being than the animal soul, desires more kinds of things, may fasten itself to ideas, true or false . . . and thus has a dangerous freedom from physical determination, a responsibility which animals lack." Its objects of desire may starve or distort as well as nourish. Fergusson pointed out that the soul's move-ment of desire, here in line 32 called *moto spiritale,* was what he himself was calling "action" and that the *Purgatorio* as he understood it was an "imitation" of this action in its varied forms.

He observed, as well—and again with obvious relevance to the whole poem—that by Virgil's account of it the "soul is in a real body in a real and common world. The only way we can see the shifting life of a human soul is by way of its sensuous effects . . . flushing and paling, tensions and relaxations, the words and sounds it utters, physical movement. So it is that we divine the life of the plant's soul through the vegetable swelling and unfolding of its leaves. . . . Thus the life of the soul is firmly anchored in the body, and in the world of common sense which we all in some sense share, whatever our metaphysics may be." And in this particular and precise sense Dante was a Realist, he said; but Fergusson did not say explicitly, as he might have, that there was something more to being a Realist in this sense than in Auerbach's sense of "existential seriousness." This omission interested the writer, and he will return to it. But Fergusson had a related point to make, concerning the "process of poem-making" that he had promised to consider.

Dante knew, he said, that just as one can only perceive "action" by way of its perceptible symptoms, so one could only *imitate* action by means of the sensuous or perceptible. "Thus Dante imitates the endless modes of action of the *Purgatorio* first by a mimetic response of his inner being, and then by manifesting it in appropriate sights, sounds, rhythms and modes of discourse. If he can give us so sharply the sense of Marco's personality, it is because he can, through sympathy, see the world through Marco's eyes, then feel what Marco feels, and then expound this anger-darkened vision in the style . . . it generates." This capability, psychological and esthetic, was evidently close to what Fergusson had meant all along by "the histrionic sensibility," and again one would have liked to ask, if one had been there, to what extent and why Dante had surpassed Flaubert, for example, in "imitation" so conceived. Fergusson only alluded to Dante's own famous description of his practice, in *Canto* XXIV:

> Ed io a lui: "Io mi son un che, quando
>   Amor mi spira, noto, ed a quel modo
>   che ditta dentro, vo significando."

And he concluded: "If one is to be truly faithful to one's direct sense of love's infinitely varied movements, they must be imitated in the modes of understanding and discourse—thought, symbol, sensuous imagery—in which they are naturally and necessarily communicated. In Dante's letter to Can Grande he says of his poem: 'the form or method of treatment is poetic, fictive, descriptive, digressive, transumptive; and likewise proceeding by definition, division, proof, refutation, and setting forth of examples.' This passage has puzzled commentators, and there has been a tendency to dismiss it as mere superannuated jargon. Curtius in his new book has found Dante's sources for these terms, and thrown some light on their meaning. . . . I think one may guess that, when Dante speaks of the *modes* of love's speech and the *modes* whereby he signifies it, he is not talking through his hat, but hinting at fundamental aspects of his extraordinarily resourceful literary art."

The last part of *Canto* XVIII Fergusson demonstrated to be a stunning example of this resourcefulness. For he noted that by the end of Virgil's great discourse the reader had been subtly prepared to see the intellectual delectation of Virgil and the pilgrim, even with the philosophy of love, as an instance of Sloth; yet when the shift occurred in line 76, "the effect is surprise, almost guilty surprise." For the moon here suddenly seen in the midnight sky, like a burning bucket, dimming the stars, "is the real moon we all know . . . that inspires the tomcats on the back fences to complain of *their* insatiable *amor*. . . ." Then "we see the passionately repentant slothful rushing by in the moonlight, calling upon classic instances of zeal; we see the Abbot of San Zeno, and then, dropping to sleep, classic instances of sloth. Zeal and sloth are here passed very quickly in review, perhaps to indicate the high awareness the pilgrim enjoys at the moment, perhaps also to give an impression of rather helpless and crazy speed— the rhythm of overstimulated daydreaming after exciting conversation. In general, the whole passage serves, as I re- marked, to break up the Idea of Love and the concentration of the pilgrim, thus ending the doting-slothful-contemplative action of the canto. . . . The Abbot of San Zeno tells of Alberto della Scala, who had doted upon his misshapen son. This picture resumes the image of love distorted in its object, and prepares for Dante's own dream of the Siren in the next canto.

"The only other passage I wish to call your attention to is lines 91–96, the comparison of the repentant slothful to the Thebans invoking Dionysus. Dante got the picture of the Bacchic or Dionysian rout from Statius, who has three or four lines on it in the *Thebaid*. But, as usual, Dante makes the image mean far more than Statius, as it seems to me, ever dreamed of. He uses Dionysus, at this point in the canto, to break up the rather Platonic idea of Love, and to replace it with a sense of Love's dangerous, creative, and unrational- izable power. Thus Dionysus performs exactly the same dra- matic role in this canto as the choruses of Greek tragedy, also traditionally invocations of Dionysus, do in the dramatic de- velopment of the plays. The parallel between this bit and the final chorus in *Antigone* is especially close. The chorus yells for Dionysus to make haste, to come leaping to help. In both cases the world of reason and ordered thought is suddenly replaced by the nonrational, the dark primitive dynamisms of the soul—including, I think, all that Freud means by the subconscious."

What was the news here? From the date of composition, it had been plain on the face of the *Divine Comedy* that the poet used, in deliberate balance and with precision in both, so did Milton. But Fergusson was showing that Dante had been able to grasp certain aspects of the classical heritage with a sophistication and depth greater than Milton's and equal to any understanding achieved since. *Canto* XVIII seemed an example of the Greek tradition "revivified" indeed—and by a poet who knew no Greek and no Greek tragedy. If Fergusson had been reading much Virgil he might have thought that the Roman poet could have been an intermediary in Dionysian lore as well as Platonist. But his interest was in these cantos as an example of poem-making—a wonderful example, as he demonstrated. The "histrionic" sense, Fergusson's cultivated gift, was his key. And by his allusion to the subconscious he invited again some interchange between the sense of life in Dante and the research of modern times.

IT WILL BE clear from these pages that in the writer's judgment Fergusson pretty well proved his point as to the dramatic quality of Dante's art. His succeeding papers in the seminar series did not—perhaps could not—add much to the proof. The rough drafts that the writer saw were somewhat less dense with original insight, less closely worked out. They were to be overhauled and greatly expanded in the course of the following two years, for Fergusson was writing his book on the *Purgatorio,* and his seminars were tentative sections. The one the writer went to was the next to last. Fergusson talked about *Canto* XXVII—in which the now rapid climb on the highest escarpment of the mountain brings the pilgrim at last to the wall of fire, the dreading plunge and passage through it—the purgation of lust. There could be no difficulty in seeing the dramatic, almost melodramatic interest of this canto, in which Reason itself (in the person of Virgil), with sadness but also with a kind of humor, had to appeal to the pilgrim in the name of a guide higher than Reason before he could be induced to enter the flame. In the opening succession of images, Fergusson saw something like a movie effect: the camera view hustling and shrinking down from the grand cosmic vista to a closeup of the pilgrim's little figure, rooted and hushed, facing his final trial. Auerbach was at the seminar, and amused himself by making fun of Fergusson's theory that every canto had the curve of dramatic action. Auerbach's shining question was, in effect, whether one could oblige Dante to follow the rule rigorously; and he poofed in simulated derision. Fergusson, warm but wary, only laughed in reply.

The truth was that at that time and later Fergusson was learning a great deal from Auerbach's own learned work, *Figura*—untranslated as yet into English—as to the "figural" interpretation of history, developed by the Church Fathers and of course fundamental to the *Divine Comedy*. Auerbach's seminars had been chiefly the presentation of thinking already done; Fergusson's were more like weekly notes on work he was then doing. Not a line in *Mimesis* was rewritten in consequence of the seminars; but Fergusson's book took shape in the course of the three years he directed them. His own evenings to some extent, and to a greater extent the long job he was always working on, provided an occasion for the kind of exchange of learning, taste, and aperçus that the seminar program had been set up for. Charles Singleton, of the Romance Languages department at Harvard, was a guest on the same evening as the writer, and Fergusson continued discussion and correspondence with this scholar, whose book on the *Vita Nuova* he very much admired. Singleton had undergone and survived, at Johns Hopkins and Harvard, the old-fashioned grind of philological training from which only an occasional Auerbach or Curtius ever emerged even in Europe; his scholarship, like theirs, served a sensitive reader and a mind alive to poetry. He was perhaps the leading *Dantista* in the United States. It was worth notice that between him and Fergusson—and to that degree between Harvard and Princeton—professional sympathy flourished during the years covered by this chronicle.

The fact seemed all the more striking that between Fergusson and Singleton's academic counterparts at Princeton no such relationship ever quite got going. The writer thought this odd as well as unfortunate. The head of the department, Wade, had shown so much stylistic intelligence in the talk about *Madame Bovary* that the writer would have assumed he would add a good deal to the Dante seminars; yet he did not attend them. Neither, in the following year, did he attend the seminars given by Jacques Maritain in which one of the principal subjects of inquiry was the significance of French poetry after Baudelaire. Wade gave Fergusson to understand, as to the Dante, that he remained away simply because he had never read the *Divine Comedy;* in the case of Maritain, he considered that he disagreed too intensely with Maritain's thought in general to be a helpful party to the discussion. These had the merit of being strong reasons, given with candor, but their oddity did not cease to impress the writer when the time came for him to put his mind on such matters. Professors Bonfante and McAllister, who taught Italian at Princeton, were acquainted with the *Divine Comedy* and attended the Dante seminars, but their interests, linguistic and historical, remained comparatively untouched. Over this watershed no canal was dug in these years.

On Fergusson's side, on the side of Dante as poet, there was however a considerable, even a stately confluence. Oates and Stauffer gave their blessing to the enterprise on behalf of the Classics and English departments, respectively; younger members of the departments came along; and in time the Temple Classics edition of Dante was even ordered by the university book store—evidence of the "revivification" among students and faculty of a culture that had rather lapsed since the days when Edmund Wilson studied the *Divine Comedy* with Christian Gauss. Blackmur looked into Dante again and seriously for purposes of discussion with his friend, and the effect was profound; he began finding things in Joyce that he had never seen before, and he and Fergusson engaged in a good deal of mutual instruction. This in itself was probably to be rated as an important result of the Princeton Seminars.

"A day when the historians left blanks in their writings I mean for things they didn't know."

The seminars of Delmore Schwartz on T. S. Eliot, which succeeded Fergusson's and ran from February 2 through March 9, must be treated here without ceremony simply because the writer neither attended them nor laid hold afterward of any notes upon them by Schwartz or others. Fergusson had, in a way, though very much in his own way and to independent ends, pursued, in his study of the *Purgatorio,* perceptions that Eliot had suggested; "Are not Homer and Dante dramatic?" Eliot had asked, for example in his "Dialogue on Dramatic Poetry." Schwartz's interest in Eliot and his work was different, and the writer would even hear it described as obsessive: the interest of a young man conscious of a potential place in his generation rather like Eliot's in his, and curious then to reassess for himself and his friends the achievement of his notable predecessor. Schwartz's gift for verse and fiction had been unmistakable since his first book in 1938, and he had written much criticism as an editor of the *Partisan Review* (1943-1955). He showed his degree of interest in Eliot's career when he went through the *Criterion* from first issue to last, after that handsome London quarterly ceased publication in 1939, and wrote a long essay on Eliot's editorship. The book on Eliot, biographical and critical, which he had planned for New Directions as early as 1945, could be expected to go beyond the careful and warmly defensive exposition by F. O. Matthiessen, since 1935 the standard work on the subject.

Schwartz had a keen social sense of literature and literary men—something that Eliot also most certainly had—and displayed it in his published essays, already mentioned, on Eliot as International Hero and Literary Dictator. The drift of these essays was that although Eliot's peculiar position and influence had been merited and invaluable under the circumstances of literary history, they had, by their very success in changing the circumstances, made other and more catholic attitudes desirable. Schwartz could handle these ponderous matters with ease; he was experienced in teaching and discussion; and altogether his seminars made a promising occasion. Perhaps too promising; for the performance did not seem, to many of the Princetonians, as impressive as they had thought it might be; and Schwartz's seminars were remembered by several as thin and even weak. The writer found it easy to imagine seminars otherwise lucid and expert appearing thin by contrast with Auerbach's or Fergusson's, and he reflected further, with melancholy, that an impression in itself as near to vacuity as this could be the thing retained by intelligent auditors, or at least the thing uppermost in their minds, rather than any of the illuminations offered or ideas advanced in the course of six evenings. It was not to be supposed that Schwartz had remained quite unconscious of his auditors' sense, though it were a vagary, of wanting more than they got. His continued delay in publishing the book, which was indeed never published, was perhaps traceable to this as well as to the discussions themselves, which, as he told the writer, convinced him that he would have to revise the chapters he had already done.

In this instance at least it could be said that the seminars had the effect of arresting publication, and one's opinion as to the utility or futility of this would depend on how great a value the possible publication might have had. The writer's general notion on this point was that there could be very little writing that would not be better published late than soon, if it fell into the category of the durable. He wished he had been on hand for Schwartz's evenings, for they at least must have called in modern verse for balance in a year otherwise devoted to "classic" writings in Auerbach and Fergusson, and to prose fiction in the final series in the spring.

Chapter Four

IN THE ENLARGED LIFE ❧
MARK SCHORER ON THE MODERN
ENGLISH NOVEL

N OW IN TURNING to the modern novel in English, Princeton's little conclave retained, one would suppose, the
recent impression of Fergusson's meditations on the *Purgatorio;* there was also, not so recent but still easily within grasp,
Auerbach's study of *Madame Bovary;* and to a mind putting
both in balance the new lecturer, Mark Schorer, had a good
deal to say.

Schorer had been teaching at Berkeley. His qualifications
as a critic included the valuable one of practice, for he had
written and published a number of stories as well as a book
on Blake and various essays. The most recent of these was a
piece called "Fiction and the Matrix of Analogy," printed in
the autumn issue of the *Kenyon Review,* an application to
fiction of that analysis of dominant vocabulary and imagery
that for twenty years or so had proved useful in the study of
Shakespeare and poetry in general. Schorer had only one
lecture written when he came to Princeton, and his seminars
were therefore, like Fergusson's and Schwartz's, examples of
work in progress, put into shape partly as the occasion and
company suggested. He spent each week rereading and pondering his chosen novels and then wrote out his reflections
in time for the evening session on Thursday.

Schorer announced his point of departure in a violent
quotation from D. H. Lawrence: Lawrence's remark that he

was "nauseated up to the nose" by the characters of Galsworthy because they seemed to have "lost caste as *human* beings and to have sunk to the level of the *social* being." The lecturer proposed to try defining the genre itself of the novel as a literary form that would hold together both the individual and the social being, both the movement of the spirit and, so at least the writer took him to mean, the pressure of others and of circumstances as seen by Auerbach, for example, in the *moeurs provinciales,* the bourgeois society, mirrored so without pity by Flaubert. Evidently Schorer felt as Lawrence had, not only as to Galsworthy's characters but as to a general blight they represented, for he remarked that Lawrence's feeling really defined "the human darkness that is modern social history."

When the time came for the writer to look over Schorer's neat manuscript, he found himself every now and then hesitating a moment, as he did now, in this case, to reflect that by the given terms *any* social history would be a human darkness in the sense that the psychic life of the individual would not fully appear in it, and he wondered if the point could not be made more clearly. It seemed to him related to his own opinion about Auerbach and so much other criticism formed under the immense load of historical consciousness peculiar to the time: fiction had been overinterpreted as documentary, underinterpreted as dramatic action in Fergusson's sense; and insofar as writers of fiction themselves had, as Galsworthy had, been affected by the disproportion, fiction had perhaps verged on "social history" and "human darkness." Schorer could put the case without lamentation, and did, when he added: "Isolate the individual consciousness and we will have pure lyric; isolate the social being and we will have pure narrative or 'history.' In neither will we find the kind of morality that it is the peculiar province of the novel to analyze, and in neither, then, will we find the full structural operation of what is called the moral imagination."

If the isolation of the social being were a defect in fiction, it soon appeared that this at any rate had occurred long before

Galsworthy. Schorer did not quote Lawrence on *Moll Flanders* but took that work as scarcely a novel, as marking the limit, rather, of the novel on one side of the gamut, the side of pure narrative without any more moral life than the heroine's interest in material security. The pathos of the book, he considered, lay in a paradox characteristic of the "middle class" in general—the illusion that values not subject to measurement could be created by the application of none but quantitative standards. Virginia Woolf, who as a connoisseur of personality was fond of Defoe, supplied Schorer with his terminal example at the other extreme: *The Waves* (1931), the ultimate result of Miss Woolf's desire for a form that would, as Schorer put it, "release the sensibility from social forms." That was precisely the trouble with it, Schorer said; it lacked social connection and therefore lacked the moral life. Moreover it exemplified what he called "the oldest of aesthetic fallacies: life has no design, therefore the designs of art are mere contrivances, untruths. Life has no plots, therefore novels cannot have plots. Life is evanescent, and the only way that evanescence can be expressed is in a novel that is itself evanescent." He ended with harsh words for the lovely writer in her misery dead: *The Waves* exhibited merely Virginia Woolf's sensibility; "that it was an arrant sensibility, without moral center, the struggle to write this kind of novel would in itself seem to demonstrate."

These preliminaries concluded, the lecturer took up for analysis and vindication the great principle of plot, slighted alike in Defoe's chronicle and in Woolf's lyric design. Here Schorer's formulations had an Aristotelian smack and vigor. "Plot, in the novel, as in the drama," he said, "is the first actualization of idea; if there is no idea larger than the events of the plot itself, we will have, at least, a novel; if there is a larger idea, we may have a good novel, depending on the quality of that idea and the force and accuracy of its actualization." There was an additional word, welcome to the critic of Aristotle, as to the necessary moral and imaginative and emotional urgency, in the artist, that would "push his story into being"—an urgency rather misrepresented by the notion of "technique" as something mechanical. With this addendum, then, accepting the plot as the soul of the work, the first cause, Schorer accepted also Fergusson's definition of action as "movement of the psyche" and of the tragic rhythm as a movement through purpose, suffering and perception.

"Plot at once implies," he said, "an intensification of the narrative method through an organization of action in *scene*. Thus the loose linkages of time are drawn together into more fully examined situations existing in *space*. Plot at once implies an identification of character and event. . . . Action in the novel can be subjective as well as objective; it can go on inside the character as well as outside; yet it is safe to say that if it goes on only inside the characters, it has passed beyond the limits of the novel and become either lyric poetry written in prose, or philosophy."

The vocabulary of criticism included other large terms, and Schorer proceeded to show his grasp of them. "Now as plot in the novel, as in the drama, implies an order of composition, a selection from experience arranged in a certain sequence in the service of an idea, a subject and a theme, theme being an interpretation of that subject, so necessarily it implies unity. This, it would follow, is a unity not of action alone but likewise a unity of view, since, however else 'view' may come to us in the novel, it must come first of all through that action which, organized, constitutes plot. But I should add that plot, in a great novel, is not first of all a means to demonstrate a view of life, but rather of forcing characters into positions where they will experience life at its fullest, its most intense and crucial, under the particular social circumstances. . . . Morality—shall we say *tested* morality—requires sustained *pressure* and *crisis*. . . . Plot is the occasion of such."

With this statement the lecturer passed to the consideration of two novels strong in "plot interest," *Bleak House* (1853) and *Jude the Obscure* (1895), the subject of each being the struggle of individuals in the net of social institutions. In

72

the Dickens novel a beautiful potential plot lay in the counterpoint between the "great repressive operations" of the
Court of Chancery and the effects, equally cruel, of social
idealism gone soft; but despite Dickens's art in thematic linkages and symbols the counterpointing pressures, Schorer
thought, never produced a coherent experience of "life at its
fullest." Dickens, he said, never held together his visions of
life as benignant and life as mean; "neither the benignity that
he respects nor the meanness that he abhors and that fascinates
him is large enough, the first being sentiment rather than
love, the second social crotchets rather than evil." To the
writer it did not seem necessary to reread *Bleak House* for
any confirmation of this lucid criticism; the superabundance
of Dickens and Dickens's shallowness of draft were in one's
sense of things from boyhood.

Neither, and for similar reasons, was it necessary to reread *Jude the Obscure*. In this case, as usual in Hardy, the plot
was a trap rather perfunctorily sprung to catch the creature
in whose feeble struggles the reader would see Hardy's un-
forgiving universe at work. Schorer again said well what had
been said before as to the sentimentality of the novelist's view,
and added, in justice to the novelist's imaginative scope: "It
would seem that in this novel Hardy was attempting something more than Dickens could even entertain—attempting
what the greatest novel, the greatest art, always achieves—
the individual being breaking through mere social allegiance
and understanding to a larger connection or revelation of
which human nature is capable—a genuinely cosmic tug. He
fails because he does not care enough."

THERE WAS NOW, at the beginning of Schorer's third evening, a brief digression ("We will expect of the good and the
great novelist simply what we expect of good and great men:
seriousness. I mean by seriousness not only an interest in
human value but a personal commitment to the necessary

task of discriminating between orders of human value.") and a sweep of the hand, so to speak, in resumption of the original points: "The characters of novels are not merely persons, they are also members; they are not only persons, they are *personae*. They are individuals, but they are also orphans, thieves, prostitutes, highwaymen, lawyers, doctors, fathers, mothers, brothers and half-brothers, gentlemen, ladies, servants, tradesmen and farmers. As social beings, the characters of a novel imply their institutional and professional and class connections." Schorer had also been meditating his definition of plot, and wanted to amplify that part of it having to do with the experience of life at its fullest. He submitted the revised version as follows:

"A great plot is a form of sustained pressure under which characters are forced to distinguish between their given social being and their hitherto unrecognized individual being." Here, Schorer said, was the basis of the discrimination of values in fiction, the basis of the moral subject, for the social and the personal in a novel were in constant interaction, and each was the means of testing the other. A novel, then, was simply a progress of events through plot; a good novel was a progress of characters, through events, in moral enlightenment or moral expiation; a great novel was a progress of characters in moral enlargement through events that consisted of moral expiation. Well, the writer thought Schorer had yielded a little here to the seductions of his own rhetoric. If only as a fellow pedant, the writer could note that the changes of subject in the sentence were a trifle heady, and that "expiation" was a bigger word than any of the novels so far considered could justify. These strictures could be the more willingly expressed in that the writer quite shared the sense of things, the general drift, in what Schorer was saying. And now the lecturer began a close analysis of Jane Austen's *Emma* (1816).

If, he said, morality in the novel lay not in spread but in scale, in the discrimination of values in scale and the proportion held between values within scale, Jane Austen was a serious novelist in the sense already understood. Because her passion had been expressed with such perfect clarity, most of her admirers were misled into thinking it merely charm. But Schorer, after a mode of examination that he held generally valid, had found in her style itself the needlework of her discrimination. "Jane Austen's style is, of course, remarkably nonmetaphorical, if we are thinking of explicit metaphor, the stated analogy, but it is no less remarkable in the persistency with which the buried or dead metaphors in her prose imply one consistent set of values. These are the values of commerce and property, of the counting house and the inherited estate." This vocabulary Schorer exhibited under five headings: Scale, Money, Business and Property, Number and Measure, and Matter. Her style began to call attention to itself, he said, when discovered in clusters where moral and material values were either juxtaposed or equated; and the effect of this texture—a world of peculiarly material values—underlying the world of refined sensibility and moral propriety on the surface of the action was the secret of much of Jane Austen's comedy. Every now and then these implied stylistic values "erupted" as Schorer put it into explicit evaluations, ironical illuminations of the characters in their special situations, as for example: "Emma perceived that her taste was not the only taste on which Mr. Weston depended, and felt, that to be the favorite and intimate of a man who had so many intimates and confidantes, was not *the very first distinction in the scale of vanity*. She liked his open manners, but a little less of open-heartedness would have made him a higher character [emphasis added]."

It was this texture of style, Schorer went on, that communicated the subject: not only courtship and marriage but the economic and social significance of courtship and marriage; the theme, or interpretation of the subject; and the tone, or the feeling of the author. Passing from style to structure, he discerned four intermeshing blocks of narrative, describable, so far as Emma was concerned, in the words of Knightley: "Your neighbourhood is increasing, and you mix more with it." There was, Schorer said, "a double movement in the architecture—the diminution of Emma in the social scene, her reduction to her proper place in the whole scale of values (which is her expiation), and the growth of Emma in the moral scheme (which is her enlargement)." The beautiful design was carried out by a severely limited method, "an alternation of narrative conducted almost always through the heroine's eyes, with dramatic scenes illustrative of the narrative material," but almost no direct statement of its significance. The whole thing depended on Jane Austen's irony transcending the ironic habit of mind of the heroine herself, and the quotation already given was an example of how she sometimes managed this: shifting her point of view a fraction away from her heroine's in the phrase "the scale of vanity," which could not possibly be Emma's, and then returning at once.

"For those who do not read while they run," Schorer concluded, "the range of Jane Austen's irony, from the gentlest to the most corrosive, will suggest that she was perfectly able to see with absolute clarity the defects of the world she used. . . . Emma is in many ways a charming heroine, bright and attractive and energetic, but Jane Austen never lets us forget that if she is superior to the Eltons, for example, the author (or, if you will, Knightley) is superior to her. . . . Emma's intellectual judgments do not relate sufficiently to her conduct; in short, she is immoral. . . . *Emma* is a complex study of self-importance and egotism and malice, as these are absorbed from a society whose morality and values are derived from the economics of class; and a study, further, in the mitigation of these traits, as the heroine comes into partial self-recognition, and at the same time sinks more completely into the society. . . . The problem, if we will risk being pompous, is nothing less than original sin—the dry destructiveness of egotism."

The novel that, appropriately enough, Schorer had wished to pair with *Emma* was *The Egoist* (1879) of George Meredith;

but he found that they scarcely made a match, indeed that his rereading of Meredith merely suggested further reasons for a high critical regard for Jane Austen. Like *Emma,* Meredith's novel had an egotist as its hero; unlike *Emma,* it was intent not on educating the hero but on routing him. Schorer found in it no active counterpointing through character; the egoist was the only egoist; and Meredith's attempt to make style alone perform the function of plot struck him, after Jane Austen, as disastrous. In the ensuing talk nobody took important exception to Schorer's really admirable work on *Emma,* but there was some dissent from his brevity with *The Egoist.* This took two lines that Schorer thought worth noting for future use: a question whether, treated in its own genre (not quite that of the novel as Schorer defined it but running to a tract with staged illustrations) the book might come off better; and Stauffer's scrupulous observation that in fact Meredith had made both Clara and Letitia declare themselves also "egoists" in the end, evidence that Meredith's characters were more responsible to his theme than Schorer had made out.

For his fourth seminar, Schorer had a little preface of some relevance to this discussion. He wished to say: "First, that, because it grows out of social concerns, the novel has become the peculiar vehicle for ideas in literature; second, that, because its impulses and its founding climate were secular, ideas tend to become the means to those expansions of feeling provided in other places by religious emotion; third, that mind and ideas are by no means the same and are often enemies, as T. S. Eliot observed in his famous remark on James, if we mean by 'ideas' the discursive power of the mind, and by mind itself the power of discriminating values: it is on the basis of such a distinction that one may assert that there is a finer mind at work in Jane Austen's *Emma,* a work devoid of ideas, than in *The Egoist* of Meredith, a work crammed with them."

The great novel that Schorer now confronted was *Middlemarch* (1871–1872), the masterwork of George Eliot. He began by inquiring where one might find the unity of this novel, in which he remarked that there were five stories and a mechanical plot, a plot that didn't begin until the book was half-finished and from which the major story interests and the major characters escaped almost entirely. The answer was partly in the unity of social scene and the intermeshing of almost all the stories in each of the eight "books," but more in what Schorer aptly called the unity of "moral scene," a consistent theme, in which all stories participated, of social idealism and love versus self-absorption and money. This statement of the case gave the writer, in his later pondering, another of his moments of hesitation. He had never read *Middlemarch* until led to do so by his interest in Schorer's seminars, but after reading it he felt uncertain as to what Schorer meant, for example, by the *five* stories. There was Dorothea Brooke's story, evidently the most important in the author's estimation; there was Lydgate's, next most important, and there was the story of Fred Vincy and Mary Garth. If Bulstrode's life, with its melodramatic crisis, were a fourth story, it did not begin, as Schorer noticed, until the novel was half over. To get a fifth, one could perhaps divide Dorothea's into two: the story of her life with Casaubon and the story of her love for Ladislaw. Or one might grant Mr. Farebrother a story. If one did, it would be easy to consider that Mary Garth had a story; there was indeed a story in Mr. Featherstone and his legatees. But then in this sense the novel was full of stories; Mr. Brooke's political venture was certainly a story; Rosamond Vincy had a story, so did Casaubon and Ladislaw and Mr. Garth and Harriet Bulstrode, at the end.

Schorer went on with an analysis that made this kind of captiousness seem justified. "Over and over, George Eliot reminds us of what she calls 'the entanglements of human action,' of the complexity of 'circumstance' and the consequent, sometimes excruciating difficulty of the moral life. For the book commits itself to this double proposition: that action is moral, an individual choice that entails individual responsibility; but also, that human life exists in interdependence. 'Any one watching keenly the stealthy convergence of human lots, sees a slow preparation of effects from one life to another, which tells like a calculated irony on the indifference or the frozen stare with which we look at our unintroduced neighbors.' It is through the great scenes of the book, then, where 'choice' and 'circumstance' (or if you wish, idealism and fact, love and money)—where these become 'enmeshed,' where the plot gradually closes down on the characters, that the book derives its real movement and life. At the same time, there is a larger, different kind of movement, expressive of the same theme—an opening and closing, serial movement, from social idealism to social fact—the breadth of aspiration versus the breadth of the community; a widening scene, and tempered values—as in Book I, for example, which starts with Dorothea's sublime hopes and ends with Fred Vincy's hopes of trading a horse. These gradual alterations of view, openings and closings down, each commenting on the other, form the larger pattern of the book."

The writer thought so, and thought the wonder of it was George Eliot's ability to represent, not in "five stories" but in the lives of at least a dozen extremely various characters adequately realized, the most acute pressure of entangling circumstances on moral choice and behavior. He felt no doubt of having encountered in *Middlemarch* the work of one of the strongest hands that ever wrote fiction, and it was a pleasure to him later to discover that it had been an important event in the fictional studies of Henry James. When James was twenty-nine he published a long review of *Middlemarch* that went from a properly guarded protest against its lack of "concentration" in design—the thing that James himself desired and honored—to such warm admiration of its actual powers that concentration in design seemed after all irrelevant. He thought the "old-fashioned English novel" could go no further—and surely it had not. James's review, in the *Galaxy* for March 1873 (pp. 423–428), was unsigned, and it was publicly identified for the first time, so far as the writer knew, in Leon Edel's book on James in 1953. Some of the statements in it were unimprovable, among them this:

> A work of the liberal scope of *Middlemarch* contains a multitude of artistic intentions, some of the finest of which become clear only in the meditative after-taste of perusal. This is the case with the balanced contrast between the two histories of Lydgate and Dorothea. Each is a tale of matrimonial infelicity, but the conditions in each are so broadly opposed that the mind passes from one to the other with that supreme sense of the vastness and variety of human life, under aspects apparently similar, which it belongs only to the greatest novelists to produce.

James complained that the episode of Bulstrode had a melodramatic tinge "unfriendly to the richly natural coloring of the whole," and apparently failed to appreciate George Eliot's formidable achievement of moral penetration in the study of Bulstode himself. Schorer, correctly in the writer's opinion, declared it to be one of her triumphs. "This is no caricature of hypocrisy; it is an irony that exempts neither the reader nor the human race, and thus it induces finally our compassion rather than our contempt." On the other hand, it was interesting, in view of one of James's great choices of subject later, that James had accepted George Eliot's portrayal of her heroine, Dorothea, as "a genuine creation, the great achievement of the book," while Schorer and some of his hearers clearly had difficulty in doing so. With respect to Dorothea's moral nobility they felt there were, as Schorer put it, "passages where the prose strains to ask us for more response than the facts of the material can justify." Blackmur noted that George Eliot's sympathetic irony in handling Dorothea seemed to fail after Dorothea was liberated from the trap of her marriage—a trap where humiliation, fear, and resentment baffled and qualified her virtue. Despite the lapse of irony and the consequent strain, however, the writer judged Dorothea's beauty of body and spirit sufficiently realized. James had professed not to know quite how this was done, and there was perhaps no way of telling except by reference to the undeluded and tenacious mind that created her. Apparently Schorer ended by accepting Dorothea on some such terms, for he concluded:

"I am quite ready to accept, on the evidence of *Middlemarch,* to accept, that is, as an aesthetic if not necessarily as a moral or a social fact, this observation [George Eliot's]: 'The presence of a noble nature, generous in its wishes, ardent in its charity, changes the light for us: we begin to see things again in their larger, quieter masses, and to believe that we too can be seen and judged in the wholeness of our characters.' For there is a wholeness in *Middlemarch* and we see it all in its larger, quieter masses, not in its fragments and its occasional agitations to taste."

IT WAS BAD luck for Thackeray that on Schorer's reading list *Vanity Fair* (1848) followed *Middlemarch;* the world of Becky Sharp might have been revisited less critically after the world of Moll Flanders. But Thackeray's taste for the eighteenth century was a historical fact that Schorer could ignore, and in placing his novel side by side with George Eliot's the lecturer gave a perfect example of the kind of revaluation that the critical study of fiction in recent years had brought about. Scholarship in these matters, as indeed in English literature as a whole, was scarcely a century old, and the project Henry James once imagined—of doing for English literature what Ste. Beuve had done for French—had perhaps only now become possible. Schorer had hoped, he said, to show that Thackeray was different from George Eliot but in his own way satisfying; but the hope was vain; he could do nothing to push Thackeray up that ladder down which he had most recently been pushed by the English critic, F. R. Leavis.

"I am even beginning to wonder," said Schorer, "whether there is any advantage at all in rereading books like *Vanity Fair* and *The Egoist*—the books that gave us our inadequate and youthful images of action and the wicked world." And the significance of this verdict passed easy measuring. There had been, within the lifetimes of the Princeton company, not a revolution but an establishment of taste with respect to the English novel.

"When the reader has finished *Vanity Fair*," Schorer said, "he is left to wonder what he is expected to contemplate, or upon what he can meditate. There is singularly nothing, because the novel is without theme. 'Vanity Fair' is of course intended as the theme . . . but I do not think that we can regard as theme, in the novel, an attitude that is merely imposed upon material, that is the same at the end as in the beginning, with no modification, amplification, or enrichment arising from our observing that theme demonstrably played upon in action."

He conceded that Thackeray's irony at its best was amusing but without the moral grip or undertone of Jane Austen or George Eliot. "When Becky gives us her moral survey, Thackery seems to write it off as hers, but there is nothing else in the book to suggest that it is not, as well, his: 'It isn't difficult to be a country gentleman's wife,' Rebecca thought. 'I think I could be a good woman if I had five thousand a year.' "

Schorer concluded: "I trust that I do not seem to be making one more appeal for what we are going to call, I guess, the 'well-made novel.' . . . *Middlemarch* is in no sense a well-made novel; indeed, it shows us what is too often lacking in the well-made novel. Not that, it is, nevertheless through the welding force of a coherent mind, a unity, and a great one. *Vanity Fair,* slipping back to the slackness of chronicle, is nevertheless more tidy in a mechanical sense; but it has no significant unity, it points to nothing. . . . The contrast is between the large and organizing mind, able to form its scattered materials into a vision of life, and a flabby and uncentered mind, that can do no such thing. And it is the first, George Eliot, that is able to seize upon the greatest theme of all, self-realization."

CONRAD'S *Chance* (1920) and James's *Portrait of a Lady* (1881) were the next examples. In *Chance* the lecturer might have remarked that an intention as large as Hardy's—to show the power of a "cosmic tug"—was, as usual in Conrad, pursued with a degree of passion that Hardy could scarcely sustain. Schorer quoted James's remark, with reference to this novel, that Conrad was "absolutely alone as a votary of the way to do a thing that shall make it undergo the most doing." The method of narration through Marlow served the purpose of bringing to bear on the ironic story a brooding speculative pressure that disclosed, little by little, its design and meaning. Though the novel might at first seem to claim special virtue for the individual isolated from a social scene, the fact was that the sea, though out of society in one sense, really intensified social pressure; as Marlow said, "the exacting life of the sea has this advantage over the life of the earth, that its claims are simple and cannot be evaded" (Part I, Chapter I). So that Captain Anthony, who thinks he hates the world, comes to represent the world, the persecuting world, to Du Barral, while at the same time Du Barral *is* the testing world to Anthony. The pressure, said Schorer, is here not alone in the events of the plot but in those events as Marlow's mind works over them, Marlow being the register of conscience for characters who are either without it or incapable of articulating it. "He is Ancient Wisdom, larger than even the best social sense."

These were lucid and satisfactory statements about the art of Joseph Conrad. It was unsatisfactory to describe the theme of the novel as "A chance to meet moral reality," but this glibness was only thrown off in passing, for Schorer later did justice to the epigraph of the book—"Those that hold that all things are governed by Fortune had not erred, had they not persisted there" (Sir Thomas Browne). He noted that Conrad's characters did not persist there, and that Marlow ended up by saying: "I am not afraid of going to church with a friend. Hang it all, for all my belief in Chance I am not exactly a pagan" (Part II, Chapter II).

A more serious lapse in Schorer's discourse on *The Portrait of a Lady* suggested to the writer the dangers of brevity in criticism. As Henry James said of *Middlemarch,* there are, in any work of art on a liberal scale, innumerable intentions; the critic must settle on a few, but it is well for him to bear in mind that his set is a selection and should be delicately proposed. When he came to James's beautiful novel, Schorer took hold at once and firmly but in one hand he held nothing, or rather he held he knew not what. Locating the underlying movement, the true plot, of the novel in Isabel Archer's progress toward self-realization, he referred to the rather early talk on selfhood between her and Madame Merle (Chapter 19), then to Isabel's long meditation in Chapter 42, from which he chose the following as an example of her now instructed thought: ". . . this base, ignoble world, it appeared, was after all what one was to live for; one was to keep it forever in one's eye, in order not to enlighten or convert or redeem it, but to extract from it some recognition of one's own superiority. On the one hand it was despicable, but on the other it afforded a standard."

Now the writer, observing that this was not Isabel's thought at all, but her representation to herself, in indirect discourse, of Gilbert Osmond's thought, had to ponder a certain enormity. Schorer himself seemed to appreciate the intent and value of the long first half of the novel in giving rondure to the character of Isabel. By Chapter 42 she had been so defined, by one touch after another on hundreds of pages, that one would have supposed it impossible to attribute the quoted sentiments to her. If they were hers, if that tone were hers, then Isabel became a bad dream, and so did the novel. Schorer was sensitive to the tones of prose; he must have been deafened by haste or headache when he picked this passage. And the writer was excited to wonder whether, of the innumerable artistic intentions in *The Portrait of a Lady*, Schorer had really understood the most important.

"The progress," he said, "is that of an apparently free individual being through a certain disciplining by the social world and at the hands of corrupted social beings into a true individual being, a truly free being, although free in the paradox of bondage." The schematic statement, unexceptionable in its way, seemed for the first time a trifle hollow in reference to this novel. James had after all asserted "the perfect dependence of the 'moral' sense of a work of art on the amount of felt life concerned in producing it." The range of felt life in *The Portrait of a Lady*, the loom and web of feeling, its great interplay and merging of shades, came before the mind to suffuse and overwhelm the bare statements of the lecturer. Auerbach had rather failed to derive a moral paradigm from *Madame Bovary;* here perhaps was the converse failure—a moral paradigm too quickly formed. Isabel's disciplining was complicated; the social beings who administered it were by no means all corrupt; and the novel would absolutely have lacked its specific beauty had not her progress depended in several ways on Ralph Touchett; had she not shared with him, in the end, in love, her learning and suffering.

Schorer went on to outline James's management of "point of view"—the way in which Isabel's is intermitted during the third quarter of the novel with such a heightening of effect. "Meredith keeps Clara, raging in her trap, and Willoughby, fidgeting in his, constantly before us; he cannot leave it; and it exhausts itself long before he has reached the point, in his plot, where, if there is one, the moral crisis occurs. James has the great art of backing away from his material when it is necessary, and backing entirely away from what is the very center of his book. For the first volume and the first eighty-five pages of Volume II we live intimately in the bright, open mind of Isabel Archer, as she at first is; and then, as abruptly as possible, we are pulled out of that mind, and we view its cold exterior, now that it is darkened. And when we come back into her mind, it is different." This was excellent, and true, though Isabel's mind, even when darkened, was not so different as to be indistinguishable from Osmond's.

There were faulty moments, and they have been noted, but none that gave warning of Schorer's final critical effort, on D. H. Lawrence—a surprising fiasco. To the writer it was worse than surprising, and like the estrangement of letters from science so recently exemplified at Princeton it indicated, on the humanist side, a weakness of which the humanists, more was the pity, seemed barely aware. The literary studies conducted up to this point in the Princeton Seminars had been various enough, and variously limited, but in general the well-disposed auditor must have found them comprehensible and clarifying. Styles had been minutely examined; in style surely some criteria had emerged. The meaning—the "feeling"—of moral progress, or *moto spiritale,* had been studied; surely certain moral criteria were understood. Close attention had been given to the mutual testing of social forces and personal aspiration in which great artists had represented the drama of life. Now Schorer, who had come forward with vigorous formulae and argument consistent with all this, seemed suddenly to abandon ship.

As to the intention of *Women in Love* (1920), he quoted one of Lawrence's letters at length:

> When I read Marinetti—"the profound intuitions of life added one to the other, word by word, according to their illogical conception, will give us the general lines of an intuitive physiology of matter"—I see something of what I am after. I translate him clumsily, and his Italian is obfuscated—and I don't care about physiology of matter—but somehow—that which is physic—non-human, in humanity, is more interesting to me than the old-

fashioned human element—which causes one to conceive
a character in a certain moral scheme and make him consistent. The certain moral scheme is what I object to. In
Turgenev, and in Tolstoy, and in Dostoievsky, the moral
scheme into which all the characters fit—and it is nearly
the same scheme—is, whatever the extraordinariness of
the characters themselves, dull, old, dead. When Marinetti writes: "It is the solidity of a blade of steel that is
interesting by itself, that is, the incomprehending and
inhuman alliance of its molecules in resistance to, let us
say, a bullet. The heat of a piece of wood or iron is in
fact more passionate, for us, than the laughter or tears
of a woman"—then I know what he means. He is stupid,
as an artist, for contrasting the heat of the iron and the
laugh of the woman. Because what is interesting in
the laugh of the woman is the same as the binding of the
molecules of steel or their action in heat: it is the inhuman
will, call it physiology, or like Marinetti—physiology of
matter, that fascinates me. I don't so much care about
what the woman *feels*—in the ordinary usage of the word.
That presumes an *ego* to feel with. I only care about what
the woman *is*—what she IS—inhumanly, physiologi-
cally, materially—according to the use of the word: but
for me, what she *is* as a phenomenon (or as representing
some greater, inhuman will).

The quotation was well chosen. What gave one pause
was to see Schorer accept it. Critical responsibility—responsibility to meaning itself—seemed never to have been so oddly
intimidated. "The intention in the novel," said he, "is so
tremendous, and so central to our lives, that I hesitate to raise
once more our really little thesis. (It grows littler, I would
be the first to confess, in the presence of a book such as this,
which seems simply to defy it.)" It came over the writer, as
he went through Lawrence's novel with this estimate in mind,
that he had lived a long time amid joy and woe. He had
understood Lawrence's exacerbation for twenty years, and

he understood why one would not wish to let Lawrence down in certain company. But this occasion had to be presumed more serious than that. It was easy—*anche troppo*—to share Lawrence's impatience with the moral conditions of life, but this did not dispel the conditions. Lawrence's dislike of the "old-fashioned human element" and the moral scheme in Tolstoy, Turgenev and Dostoievsky seemed, in 1950, only slightly less exhibitionist and vulgar—and dated—than Dorothy Parker's boredom with women who had breasts in front.

Schorer remarked the resemblance of *Women in Love,* in structure, to a dance, developing through the shifting allegiances of the members in a kind of "psychical dialectic," there being no plot "in the conventional sense" but a fluid pattern with some hallucinated dream effects. Well, either Schorer had himself defined plot in some other than "the conventional sense" or Lawrence's novel was open to strictures no less severe than *The Waves* for lacking it. The novel as genre was not the dance. Lawrence had indeed perceived something real and had insisted on it—the subtle and wild "dance" of sensuous relationships, the "knowledge of the blood"; but he insisted, as brilliant and disoriented people did in 1920, far too much. *Women in Love* was not tremendous in any respect. It seemed a shame that the word should be applied to this feverish and prolonged daydream in which no single individual was realized in the circumstantial life of a human being. And Schorer was really uneasy; he admitted that most readers had found it either a tiresome or a revolting novel. Nevertheless:

"It *is* a novel because, whether Lawrence would admit it or not, it retained enough at its very heart of the social reference to give these characters, whom he did not intend as characters, the wall off which they had to bounce. That is why I should urge particularly that you attend to the chapter called 'The Industrial Magnate' [Chapter xvii] and to all the references to the mines and to the social and economic works of man. It is a difficult novel to judge because it will not accept the discipline of plot. Oh, we know why; we will even believe Lawrence when he in effect equates plot as we have been discussing it with a morality that has lost its relevance, even its reality. But some new limitation must then be found, that will *contain* material such as this, and not force us, at so many points, to love Lawrence the man in order to forgive Lawrence the novelist. . . . Does the difficulty not lie in the attempt to do something here that the novel as Lawrence developed it and as we know it simply does not itself know how to do? I do not mean for a minute that it should not and must not be done. No novelist speaks more directly to us than Lawrence, and if we can't hear him, God help us, really. But he has not, in *this* novel, found the way to speak."

These reflections so embarrassed the writer that he could scarcely lay hold of a judicious word. The talk in the novel seemed to him pitifully of its period, an audacious make-believe, most of it, and never more so than in the chapter recommended. Lawrence had unquestionably been trying to break through like a "Futurist" to an original vision of life; but his fate had put him among the sun–bathers. Granted that there was a fine, harsh, and quick intelligence in Lawrence, he spoiled it, or let it be spoiled, in his sick and driven life, by quitting the business of an artist for that of a seer. It saddened one to see Schorer wobbling in the company of Lawrence's "disciples," forced to "love Lawrence the man" and to talk as if "the novel," a literary category, could know how to do anything. The writer could hear Lawrence quite distinctly, and he infinitely preferred the alternative source of help that Schorer had indicated. He had to note, for his chronicle, that the end was not yet.

"If we follow [Lawrence] on from *Women in Love,* through the next really shattered books, and to the end, we shall see that he took, finally, two ways: in his last two books, *Lady Chatterley's Lover* (1928) and *The Man* 'ho Died (1931), both, in my view, very great books, he divided the intention that in *Women in Love* is one. In *Lady Chatterley* he retrenches his claims a little—it is a novel in a solid and sustained social context, and it is a novel with a clear and happily developed plot, in which the characters function fully and the author lets them speak for themselves; in *The Man Who Died,* he made an absolutely undiluted claim for the sanctity of the purely self-responsible individual human being, society not more than a shadowy threat, and he gives us a real image of what he does not give us in Birkin, the wholly integrated man; but he writes in the form of the fable. And this is, perhaps, as far as we have gone with the novel."

No record remains of the interchange that evening, not even a jotting by Schorer, and it seems a fair inference that the company had offered no serious debate. Lapses of this kind would be inevitable in the seminars, for the spirit in such gatherings is precarious and will strangely fail; a couple of unlucky absences, a shade too much fatigue, a confusion of amiability and shock, even lack of preparation, would account for the missed opportunity. Of the lecturer's honesty and generosity there could be no doubt; moreover he had, it was true, distinguished forerunners, including most recently F. R. Leavis, in placing his estimate of Lawrence high. Nevertheless Schorer on Lawrence remained, in the history of the Princeton Seminars, a loose end and a dead end. It was not toward Lawrence's last fable, his cold Christ in the dream-temple of Isis, that the artistry of Jane Austen, George Eliot, and Henry James, to say nothing of Baudelaire, Flaubert, and Dante, would lead the student or the poet.

Schorer's evening in recapitulation was again excellent, resuming the strength of his approach to novel writing through the study of structure. It was a useful and professional kind of criticism in contrast to what he called "the watery world of the book review, where the novel is told that it must concern itself with the very finite 'truth' of one reviewer or another." He had indeed, as he claimed, explored fiction in a way that the best previous critics—Lubbock and Forster, for example—had rather neglected; and he had demonstrated something very recent in the study of stories: "the importance of language, especially of figurative language, as the first means to conception of subject and as the ground from which structure in the most general sense arises." He repeated his essential formula: a novel was a literary form that would hold together both the individual human being and the social being, standing thus between poetry and history.

Resurveying the novels he had discussed, Schorer found evidence of an increasing difficulty at the heart of this form. In *Emma* the two beings interacted, separable but not at odds; in *Middlemarch* the polarity was greater, as between Bulstrode and Dorothea, but still balanced; in Hardy the individual was defeated, in Conrad isolated; in James the difficulty showed in the "rarity" of his social scene (this seemed to the writer a good perception); in Lawrence, the individual was shown "struggling to leap beyond the social boundaries entirely," and in Woolf the individual usurped the whole scene and social responsibility disappeared. "It is," said Schorer, "this newly developed relationship of the individual and the social interest in the twentieth century, this relationship in which the two are characteristically at violent odds, that has brought the genre itself to its present state of outmoded or confused aims, and possible extinction."

Great men had said the like. Extinction, however, was not the business of the artist, nor, in their secondary way, of the Princeton Seminars, and there was virtue for both in what seemed, from Schorer, a reminder of other and perennial possibilities: "The greatest novels are, actually, an account of how individual being transcends its limitations in an enlargement of the moral life through social conflict. It is in this enlargement, where individual being comes into self-realization and self-responsibility through an active social engagement passionately registered, that the novel overcomes its purely secular origin and achieves—not, perhaps, religious feeling—but the intensity of moral seriousness that we expect of any work before we can . . . regard it as art. The novel's business seems to be the refinement of will, and in the enlarged life, the reader takes his share."

THE STURDY SLIP ❧ ROBERT FITZGERALD ON THE PROGRESS OF THE SEMINARS

ONE WHO, like the chronicler, had nothing but the glimpses and sketches hereinbefore recorded could easily see the principal charms and peculiar difficulties of the seminar project. It was like a pilot laboratory attached to the university for special research, in which the university was investing no great amount of risk capital—because the university as such could allow itself only moderate faith in the project. The enthusiasms of academic as of other corporate bodies are reflected in their budgets. One might suppose, in the abstract, that the sturdy slip that the director of the Institute and the heads of two academic departments wished to graft on to Princeton would be lavishly tended and its appropriate fruitage taken for granted; but in the American plan these things must prove themselves—and prove themselves over and over. The director was expected to write an informal report at the end of the year on the "progress" of the seminars; he did so, discreetly observing that it was still too early to assess the "results," and adding that, granted the uneven quality of the talk, the success of each series had been partly a matter of the profit derived by individuals and "the slow building of a group with certain values and ideas in common."

Nature, surely, would insist on its being slow. The writer admires speed, being himself a slow workman, but believes in growing things full grown and the price in time that they exact. On the part of severe Princetonians, there was at times what would later seem to the writer an unreasonable expectation that the discussion of a particular point on a particular evening could be framed and conducted with that purposive logic that leads to decision. Blackmur wrote as though he wanted something like that; but in practice, nobody talked more as the spirit spiralled than he did. If a question raised on a certain evening were profound enough really to interest, it would probably be knotty enough really to perplex, and the untying could take weeks or months in anyone's mind. So with Fergusson's thought on the text quoted by Auerbach from Pascal. He could not give his considered comment until it had been considered, and this required its reference to the central bureau of Fergusson's interests for correlation with his thinking on Dante. Such an intellectual operation may indeed happen in an instant, but then again it may not, and it cannot be commanded. As has been observed in the account of Fergusson's own seminars, he apparently had not even by that time fully considered the differentiation of Flaubert's "realism," Auerbach's and Dante's; perhaps he never did. These things take time.

How to build a group, insofar as that lay in the power of the director and his friends, would continue to be a problem. Building implies addition; but the "temporary addition" is not, in architecture, a feature of beauty. For the fourth and concluding series of seminars in the first year, Fergusson had to engage a man who had not attended any of the seminars preceding. The only reference—at least the only recorded reference—to Flaubert in the course of Schorer's discussion of the English novel was a quotation from T. S. Eliot interjected by Blackmur—to the effect that Flaubert and George Eliot had been alike in their kinds of seriousness. Yet Schorer's whole argument implied important corrections of Auerbach's very interesting submission on Flaubert. Again, if Schorer had taken part in the evenings when Fergusson was talking about the action of the *Purgatorio,* he might have yielded less easily to the wisdom of the blood in D. H. Lawrence, or he might at least have been forced in the direction of more stringent critical judgment. Such were the disadvantages of a budget that could not begin to support four seminar leaders in residence throughout the year.

At the same time, it was true that the little group of faithful seminar-goers had an opportunity to sift together and weigh up the varying messages of the year insofar as they bore on common questions. This of course each member did for himself as his interests prompted him. Unconscious and sharp divergences might well have been the most stimulating for these people; Schorer's discussion of action and plot in the novel, for example, for just the reason that it was presented in ignorance of Fergusson's work on the *Purgatorio,* must have reminded everyone forcibly that Fergusson was using the term "dramatic action" in a special sense: as the singular movement of the psyche *in the protagonist,* considered apart from any such "sustained crisis of events," within and revelatory of one whole set of characters, as Schorer posited for the novel. Might not a formal occasion of some sort be provided for clarifying these differences and pulling the year's work together?

In his year-end report, Fergusson noted gratefully that Auerbach, by grace of residence at the Institute, had been a steady participant in all the seminars. He noted hopefully that the director of the Institute continued to be interested in the seminars; that he continued "his policy of appointing one or two men of letters per year who, like Professor Auerbach, may wish to collaborate with us." Fergusson and Oppenheimer had in fact been making a good many efforts. For the year 1950-1951, they had successively asked I. A. Richards to come from Harvard, William Empson to come from Peiping, and Marcel Raymond to come from Berne; but Richards felt obligated to do his work at Harvard, Empson felt obligated to stay in Peiping, now Communist, on behalf of the British Council; and Raymond was ill. Nor would Eliot come.

95

It looked as though 1950-1951 would have to be planned without the assistance of any appointee at the Institute, and in these circumstances the university came to the rescue. The University Research Committee granted the seminars $4,000 for the coming year. With this fund the Seminar Committee did a very sensible thing. It arranged with the departments concerned—English, Classics, and Modern Languages—to lift part of the teaching load from three young and able teachers who had been following the first year's seminars, and it provided an equivalent stipend for two other men—Joseph Kerman, a musicologist at the Westminster Choir School, and David Sachs, of the Rutgers Philosophy department—in order that all five should again be in attendance through the year and should then, to make the final set of seminars, collaborate on a symposium. The idea was to get men from several "fields" to form a working nucleus throughout the year's program and bring it all to focus at the end.

Fergusson also pressed into service the admirable Jacques Maritain, who agreed, after twenty years, to put his mind again on the matters treated in *Art and Scholasticism* and thus to make the third series for 1950-1951. For the first Fergusson counted on the writer; for the second he went on searching. Of all this the writer of course knew nothing at the time. He spent the summer in Connecticut and read, among other things, a good deal of Thucydides. The deliberation and edge of this writing moved him much as Flaubert had done: the formal irony, grand and at times terrible, with which Thucydides placed in succession the elaborate talk of generals and statesmen and the narrative of what they did and what happened to them.

Chapter Five

FROM REASON TO ROMANCE ❧ RENÉ WELLEK ON THE TRANSITION IN LITERARY CRITICISM

T HE WRITER found Princeton delectable in late September 1950. Since his family was firmly established elsewhere, it had been arranged that he should compress his teaching into a weekly visit, from Wednesday noon to Friday afternoon; and Blackmur and Stauffer got him elected to the Nassau Club, where he took a room. A breeze from backyards and trees came in crisp or warm through his open window; and he took pleasure, too, in the fragrance of frayed carpet in the hall, of pine soap in the shower. The town, he felt, had not outgrown the scale of human settlement nor got out of touch with the past. Ancient black waiters moved softly in the Nassau Club dining room, and at dinner Blackmur introduced him to the eldest, whose name was Washington. With Blackmur the writer sipped bourbon downstairs in the little bar and talked about much that they mutually remembered. As it turned out, he had leisure to savor his weekly visits during the fall, for Fergusson had put off his seminars until December. The first series was now to be given by René Wellek, professor of Slavic Languages and Comparative Literature at Yale. The meetings were to be on Wednesday evenings for Wellek's benefit, for he could only come down from New Haven for that night.

This meant beginning the year again with a scholar of high degree. Wellek had been born in Prague, of French and

Bohemian parents; his learning was supernational, but he had old ties with Princeton, for he had taken his Ph.D. in English there in 1930 and had begun his teaching in the Modern Languages department as an instructor in German. He had then taught English literature at the Charles University in Prague and had gone to the University of London in 1935 to lecture on Czech language and literature. During the war he was a professor at Iowa; after the war at Yale. Wellek was thoroughly a professor, a man of systematic learning, a haunter of the world's great libraries, a master of the stacks, as none of the previous seminar leaders, even Auerbach, had been. But he represented—and with great ability—a class of thorough professors who were sincerely sympathetic to the profession of letters. While at Iowa he had collaborated with Austin Warren, one of the most sensitive of scholar-critics, on a book called *Theory of Literature,* published in 1942. It interested all the humanists and was a revelation to the writer in more ways than one.

The writer had never in his life so much as opened the famous *PMLA* in which the literary scholars of the United States gave to print, month by month, their choicest papers all a-twinkle with footnote digits. He recognized later, when he did, that the Warren-Wellek book was like a *PMLA* on a grand scale, a *PMLA* to end all others. Methodically, topic by topic, it took up all the abstract questions that could arise in the study of the world's literature, commented on all the principal "contributions" to these matters by the world's scholars, and concluded or recommended with all apparent sanity and concision. Numbered notes (to the number of 556) followed and a bibliography of about 800 titles supported the trenchant text. It was a packed and impressive book. Ostensibly and no doubt in intent, it was a plea for the ventilation by living criticism of old-style scientific and historical scholarship; in essence, it was a formidable display of just such scholarship; in implication it obviously called for a little more scholarship—that is, accurate background knowledge—in living criticism. Now it happened that this accorded with some recent searchings of the heart among critics, including those at Princeton. The *cause célèbre* that had given them pause was a published exchange between William Empson, the most celebrated and ingenious of textual critics, and a scholar named Rosemond Tuve. Miss Tuve had shown some of Empson's ingenuities on the text of George Herbert's poem, *The Sacrifice*, to have been possible only to ignorance. All that autumn Blackmur had this sharp lesson on his mind, as the writer noted from his friend's frequent musing, at the most unlikely moments, on the word *improperia*—a term from the Good Friday liturgy to which Miss Tuve had referred in the course of skewering Empson.

Though it took a high and judicial tone, *Theory of Literature*, closely read, yielded a significant professional animus or two, and one of these was to the work of George Edward Bateman Saintsbury. The significance was that Saintsbury's three-volume history of criticism and taste in Europe was a work that Wellek thought should be supplanted and intended himself to supplant. He had published in 1941 the first volume of a history of English literary criticism, promising a second; now he had abandoned this enterprise and planned a history of European literary criticism in two volumes. For the Princeton company he proposed to discuss the period from Johnson to Coleridge, basing himself on chapters already written. Since this was the period of transition between the Age of Reason and the Romantics, Wellek might be expected to fill in the great gap between Auerbach's talks of the preceding year. If any connections were to be made, however, the Princetonians would have to make them, for Wellek had neither attended Auerbach's evenings nor did he, to judge by a single reference to *Mimesis* in *Theory of Literature,* find himself much enkindled by Auerbach's work.

Wellek's style, in fact, turned out to be rarely aglow; it was the level, exhaustive kind that comes from a lifetime of lecturing to people who are expected to take notes. At dinner with Blackmur, Fergusson, and the writer, he talked with relish of university affairs and appointments, of teachers' insurance, of the critical acumen (doubtful) of the London *Times Literary Supplement;* but one noted, not for the first or last time, that a man whose life was devoted to reading could go through dinner in like company without ever talking happily about something he had read. The gray but boyish man, strong and agreeable, could have been a lawyer or a doctor just as well; he lacked what Blackmur had once called the stigmata of the professional writer. So much the better if he is on our side, the writer thought. And his range of knowledge, his enlightenment—that was very great.

WELLEK began with neoclassical critical theory, and it appeared at once that his attitude toward the past was not questioning but declarative. The empathetic imagination that softens judgment rarely softened his; he was not what he himself would have called a historical relativist. The sense of literature that lived with greatest refinement, on the Continent, in the work of Voltaire he firmly called "one of the most special tastes the world had ever seen"—one that could have few claims to approval from the critic who looked before and after. The documentation was very full; it was evident that Wellek's method required this and in fact consisted largely in quotations with comments. As to Dr. Johnson, Wellek was almost as severe in his way as Johnson had ever been in his. He announced that Johnson was "one of the first great critics who has almost ceased to understand the nature of art, and, who, in central passages, treats art as life. He has lost faith in art as the classicists understood it and has not found the romantic faith."

Johnson's fondness, in drama, for domestic tragedy—his praise, for example, of Catherine's speech on the death of Wolsey in *Henry VIII* (IV, ii)—involved a suspicion of "fiction" and a belief that literature should be "a just represen-

tation of things actually existing and actions really performed."
Wellek recalled with amusement Johnson's grumbling at Milton's *Lycidas:* "Passion plucks no berries from the myrtle and
ivy, [etc.]" and remarked that the sincere grief that Johnson
wanted to require of Milton would by implication do away
with three-quarters of the world's literature. He was just as
positive about the second great principle of Johnson's criticism, "moral truth." Without disputing the merit of didac-
ticism properly safeguarded, Wellek thought that what
Johnson often wanted was mere moralizing, "a selection from
nature which frequently runs counter to his own principle of
reality." Johnson, he said, went so far as to share the taste
of the general public for a happy ending to *King Lear.*

At this point one felt for a moment that there was perhaps
more to say. Johnson had indeed approved the happy ending, and had added: "I was many years ago so shocked by
Cordelia's death, that I know not whether I ever endured to
read again the last scenes of the play till I undertook to revise
them as an editor." The writer remembered this sentence
very well for he had happened to read it that morning. He
had wondered if what Johnson meant was not that he wished
King Lear otherwise, but that he had been too much moved
by the play to reread it; in that case his approval of the happy
ending was less a criticism of the play than a concession to
his own and others' weakness. The sentence in question should
at any rate have been quoted.

There was indeed in Wellek's whole discourse on Johnson
a tendency to wash out the flavors and shades of that great
man's critical moods. Wellek was too intelligent not to realize
the danger of this; in speaking of Johnson's opinion that
Rousseau was "a rascal who ought to be hunted out of society," he observed very justly that Johnson at the time was
needling Boswell, who had made a pilgrimage to Switzerland
to see Rousseau. If in some other contexts Wellek was less
acute, this did not perhaps affect more than the edges of his
general picture of Johnson as critic. The central points were

well taken: that Johnson's realism and moralism were uneasy companions and each in its way inadequate as a critical principle; that the first was also in conflict with his neoclassic demand for the general and the universal in art; and that Johnson never seemed aware that these criteria, which he used by turns, did not hang together.

Wellek nevertheless could not but credit Johnson with having broken through the narrow neoclassic limits in several respects. His love for Shakespeare gave him an enormous advantage over Voltaire, for example; and Johnson could reject the rigid "unities" of time and place and defend the mixed genre of tragicomedy. Wellek thought that in these arguments Johnson had correctly grasped what modern aestheticians would call "aesthetic distance."

With the "tumour and bombast" in Shakespeare's language, his ambiguities and "quibbles," Johnson of course had less sympathy; and Wellek rated Johnson very low in appreciation of metaphorical language, citing the well-known adversions on Gray's cat and Denham's Thames. Here again someone sympathetic to Johnson might have heard more overtones of the mock-solemn and wayward than Wellek did. He noted Johnson's view of genius as *ingenium*, "a mind of large general powers, accidentally determined to some particular direction"—a definition without any trace of romanticism. Though Johnson had literary sense enough to praise Pope's "invention" in *The Rape of the Lock,* Wellek thought that basically "he did not like or understand highly imaginative art unless he could reinterpret it as a picture of truth."

The concluding remarks were well balanced. "He did not and could not very well see that he himself stood almost at the end of a great tradition. The stirring of the new seemed to him only the odd, perverse, and, at the most, partially successful revival of old and worn-out things. . . . Johnson, while holding firm to the main tenets of the tradition of neoclassical criticism, constantly reinterprets them in a spirit for which it is difficult to avoid a term he would have hated: 'liberal.' "

What chiefly saved this treatment of Johnson from seeming merely competent, though decided, was the sense of Wellek's *copia;* the sense that he had, in his fashion, command of not only this subject but of a whole world of subjects on one and the other side of it, as his big pile of typescript and his sureness of manner attested. Literature was very large, life was very long, and this man surveying the largeness and length was able to keep Johnson in a perspective whose grandeur Wellek's own reasonable style could not suggest; one had to divine it. No one did at once, but it became possible certainly on the third evening. For now Wellek moved on to the Germans with whom as a Continental-born and as a scholar of a certain type and training he was very much at home. Here too he kept his judicial interval, but warmed a little to his work.

"LESSING," he said, "has an enormous reputation as a literary critic, but a clear account of the reasons for his prominence in a history of European criticism is hard to find." He noted that Lessing was the first great man of letters in modern Germany, that he was a dramatist, theologian, philologist, and aesthetician who "speculated importantly" on the limits of the arts and the differences between poetry and painting (in *Laokoon,* 1766; finally, a literary theorist and critic. "All these varied activities are held together by the power of an obviously straightforward, honest personality and an individual style of wonderful clarity and sobriety which it is a joy to meet in reading German." It was not easy, though, to get at Lessing's literary criticism, and Wellek said one could understand Saintsbury's remark that (as there was always something Clarissa Harlow preferred to truth) there was always something Lessing preferred to literature. In *Laokoon* the detailed criticism of Homer and Sophocles was still ponderable, and there was the claim, "astonishing for the time and place," that Shakespeare was a much greater tragic poet than Corneille. Much of Lessing's criticism concerned German literature that is no longer of interest except to specialists. Wellek here mentioned something of interest that Saintsbury overlooked—characteristically, Wellek found it in one of Lessing's letters. Writing to one Gerstenburg on a play called *Ugolino,* he disparaged the theme of passive, innocent suffering as undramatic. It was a kind of criticism that one found later in Yeats's dismissal of such a theme as unfit for poetry— quite another matter—when he rejected the poems of Wilfrid Owen. But by and large, Wellek concluded, "like most professional critics, Lessing could not really relish the taste of a new generation," and his pronouncements "do not add up to a corpus of sensitive evaluation or close discussion of great works."

Wellek now summarized Lessing's work as a theorist of literature in *Laokoon.* Beginning with his hardheaded objection to Winckelmann's wooziness about the "composure" of Greek art and literature, Lessing had slowly worked up to the celebrated dictum: "Subjects whose wholes or parts exist in juxtaposition are called bodies. Bodies with their visible properties are the peculiar subjects of painting. Subjects whose wholes or parts are consecutive are called actions. Actions are the peculiar subject of poetry." Here certainly there appeared a flute note from the past introducing Fergusson's great critical preoccupation; but the meaning was more abstract still than Fergusson's. Lessing in consequence condemned "history" painting and descriptive poetry. Quoting Ariosto's elaborate "enumerative" description of Alcina to prove that it did not enable the reader to visualize her, he praised Homer's method in *The Iliad* of suggesting Helen's beauty "by its effect." To have recalled this, as Wellek did, without referring to the importance that this "method" had in the practice of great fiction writers from Flaubert to Hemingway seemed to the writer very curious. But Wellek was interested in the *theory.* And he thought it correct.

"Lessing's main distinction between the arts of space and time, though debatable, is basically sound. His objections to static description in literature were not only salutary in their time, but, if properly qualified, are applicable even today. Lessing is certainly putting his finger on the issue when he points to the difficulty of our forming a whole from an accumulation of traits, and is also right in opposing the stress on visualization in literature. Literature does not evoke sensuous images, or if it does, does so only incidentally, occasionally, and intermittently. In the depiction even of a fictional character the writer need not suggest visual images as well. We can scarcely visualize most of Dostoevsky's or Henry James's characters."

There was a kind of roughness here, one thought. Wellek was possibly entitled to ignore that school of twentieth-century poetry that called itself Imagist, but he was on doubtful ground in denying the visualizing power of Henry James. One could be deceived by James's writing, but the images slowly formed of Gilbert Osmond or Mme. de Vionnet, for example, were of great sensuous richness and detail. Wellek had perhaps been overpersuaded by Lessing on this point. On other points, however, he made the proper objections, in particular to Lessing's notion that drama was the highest and central part of literature. Part of this was due, he thought, to Lessing's equation of "action" with drama, part to the "insensibility of Lessing and his contemporaries to the lyric, which to modern readers seems the center of poetry"; there was also the fact that Lessing himself wrote plays, and there was the example of Aristotle and the central position of tragedy in the *Poetics*.

Wellek, as usual, made no attempt to discuss contemporary work or theory, but he soon showed the difference between the criterion of "the dramatic" in Burke or Fergusson and the theoretic elevation of the same in Lessing. Here he had a definite addition to make to current knowledge on his subject—a document that he believed had never been quoted in English before. In a letter to Friedrich Nicolai on May 26, 1769, Lessing qualified the thesis of *Laokoon* to the extent of admitting that painting was not actually confined to "natural signs" nor poetry to "arbitrary signs," but "the more painting gets away from natural signs, or mixes natural signs with arbitrary signs, the more it gets away from its highest point of perfection; while poetry approaches perfection the more nearly, the more its arbitrary signs approximate natural signs." Now this approximation would be nearest, so Lessing seemed to have thought, in the "natural" language of dramatic poetry—natural because spoken by living and breathing characters. It was a curious idea. Lessing also thought that the language of poetry could approach the condition of the "natural sign" through meter and metaphor. "As the power of natural signs consists in their similarity with things, metaphor introduces, instead of such a similarity, which words do not have, another similarity, which the thing referred to has with still another, the concept of which can be renewed more easily and more vividly."

Wellek considered this a strange theory of imagery, since it "reduced" metaphor to the comparison of unfamiliar with familiar objects; nor did he think it established the claim that metaphorical language was natural and not arbitrary. To several of the company this seemed a trifle too literal a reading of Lessing, and in the discussion afterward they tried to open speculation as to the insight, possibly quite valuable, that Lessing might have been groping toward. The new letter which Wellek had translated fascinated them, for they recognized in the notion of poetry as "natural sign" a forecast of Mallarmé, of MacLeish's lines, "A poem should not mean/ But be." Wellek would point out again Lessing's apparent understanding, but he would not be drawn far into impromptu speculation. He answered questions temperately, a little vaguely, but he had not Auerbach's ready flair for talk; he never got up to sit on the edge of the table; he tended to stand pat on what he had already said, or rather read. He was reading fast now and sometimes skipping great fistfuls of typed pages to get through on time.

He finished off Lessing with an exposition of Lessing's interpretation of the *Poetics*—a very keen and sane one for his time, agreeing with Butcher's later interpretation of Aristotle, according to which "the dramatic action must be so significant, and its meaning capable of such extension, that through it we can discern the higher laws which rule the world." The trouble, Wellek said, was with Lessing's view of these higher laws, for his universe corresponded with the eighteenth-century one—an ethical cosmos in which all was for the best. Here was the limitation of neoclassicism. By this limitation, Wellek observed, "tragedy is deprived of its connection with sacrifice, with the grandly heroic, the marvelous and divine, the *mysterium tremendum,* and is reduced to an object lesson in humanitarianism." The criticism seemed as profound as it was sharp, crowning the scholarly study that had produced it. Wellek drew his severe conclusion: "Thus Lessing illustrates the same failure of his age to grasp the nature of art which we found in Dr. Johnson and in Diderot. Along with them, he prepared the conception of literature underlying the psychological and social realism of the nineteenth century."

WITH HERDER, Wellek came to a figure whom Saintsbury had, he thought, dismissed "without proper examination"; and indeed Saintsbury's wit had found congenial exercise in the relations between Herder and what Herder called "the dear Goddess Ennui." Wellek admitted the "wooliness" of Herder's writing, but he had read it just the same (as he thought Saintsbury had not), and he found it obvious that Herder's ideas were the great quarry for the German romantics. Herder had been, moreover, the fountainhead of universal literary history and the most influential force for stimulating interest in folk poetry. In this last respect his influence in the Slavic and Scandinavian countries—regions that Wellek knew a lot better than Saintsbury did—had been immeasurable.

As early as 1767, Wellek said, Herder was saying—against the whole neoclassic position—that the critic should "submit" to the author; he conceived criticism mainly as a process of empathy, and practiced "that criticism of beauties rather than faults of which Chateaubriand is supposed to be the originator." He wanted living reading, "heuristics," and went so far as to say, "Criticism without genius is nothing. Only a genius can judge and teach another."

"These were important sayings," Wellek declared, "salutary in their time for their stress on understanding, but they also contain the germs of much that is worst in criticism since Herder's time: of mere impressionism, of the idea of 'creative' criticism with its pretension to duplicate a work of art by another work of art, the critical errors of excessive attention to biography and to the intention of the author, of mere 'appreciation,' of complete relativism." The little catalogue was chilling in proportion to its brevity; one could imagine the zealous critic toiling to free himself of these flagrancies, like the pilgrim on the tiers of Dante's Purgatory. There was one example, too, whom Wellek had doubtless not forgotten. George Saintsbury had been large in his revels but not always punctilious; he had mentioned none of Herder's works by name, and Wellek rather pointedly did so: from the early *Kritische Wälder* of 1769 to the late *Briefe zu Beförderung der Humanität* (1796).

He thought the first, in which Herder tried to refute Lessing's *Laokoon,* one of Herder's most impressive and coherent performances; in the second, Herder declared for the "natural" method of criticism, that is, his own, which would take pains to see every work as part and parcel of its *milieu,* fulfilling its moment, and scarcely to be judged but only savored. This Wellek described as a development of the historical sense more extreme than any before, but obviously much echoed afterward. Of another title, *Abhandlung über den Ursprung der Sprache* (1772), Wellek might have noted that its premise greatly resembled a favorite theme in the later criticism of T. S. Eliot: that "the genius of a language is also the genius of the literature of the nation." He might have but did not. Nor did he bother to draw the contemporary parallel for another of Herder's tenets: that "what we know, we know from analogy, from creature to us and from us to the Creator." There was no other key to the interior of things than imagery, analogy. Poetry was not an imitation of nature but "an imitation of the creating, naming Godhead." Here surely, Wellek might have said, was the late romantic imagination in embryo. That he did not say these things was typical of his austerity; it left the obvious to the hearer. And it kept the subject, Herder's thought, distinctly to the fore.

To Herder, as to Vico and Fontenelle, an age of imagination had ended, and poetry perhaps belonged to the past. It required contact with nature, emotion, and spontaneity; and these things modern civilization was stifling and killing. Herder did not quite draw the fatalistic consequences. Young Goethe, Herder's personal pupil, seemed to justify his hope, until Goethe turned to what Herder considered sterile classicism. But his fondness for the past, even for prehistory, and the implication that, as Wellek put it, "the origins of poetry describe its nature," foreshadowed that fashion of explanation by genesis that the nineteenth century would take up and work to death. It was a Herderism in this sense to neglect the study of contemporary poetry in favor of the study of Anglo-Saxon.

Herder thought the German language "peculiarly aboriginal" and thus superior as a source of myth and poetry to the clarity of the French. At the same time, Wellek said, Herder constantly held up the examples of the other nations to the Germans and tirelessly translated, collected, and described the wealth of the world's literature. His *Volkslieder* (1779), now best known under the title given to them by J. G. Miller after Herder's death, as *Stimmen der Völker in Liedern,* was the first comprehensive anthology of world literature, animated by a conception of folk poetry that was extremely broad. "Folk," said Herder, "does not mean the rabble in the streets which never sings and creates, but roars and mutilates." What "folk" did mean was inclusive enough for Genesis, The Song of Songs, the Book of Job, the Psalms, Homer, Hesiod, Aeschylus and Sophocles, Sappho and the *Greek Anthology*, Chaucer, Spenser, Shakespeare, and the contents of Percy's *Reliques*—even Dante and of course Ossian.

Saintsbury had called Herder "one of the very few leaders in the conversion of Europe at large to a catholic view of literature." Wellek had higher if more judicious praise. "The view that poets such as the Troubadours or Chaucer or Dante were in any way popular seems to be totally mistaken," Wellek said. "Herder certainly has a very one-sided conception of Shakespeare or Homer; he overrated or started the over-rating of all kinds of folklore, without being able to distinguish genuine folklore productions from artificial derivatives and even fakes such as Ossian. His criticism of much neo-classical literature seems to us grossly unjust. His conception is too indulgent toward the purely naïve, the mere lyrical cry, the merely spontaneous, and too inimical to great art, which may be intellectual, sophisticated, ironical, grotesque. But we must realize that Herder was struck with the novelty of his discoveries, which were fresh and appealing on the background of a decaying neoclassicism, while we are inured to many romantic charms by a century and a half of their trivialization."

Here again, as in the case of Lessing, critical justice seemed achieved, and Wellek finished by saying handsomely that in spite of the excesses of his primitivism and lyricism, "Herder no doubt had a clearer and truer conception of poetry than all the critics we have discussed hitherto. His conception of poetry is certainly true: he is right in his stress on the role of metaphor, symbol, and myth in poetry, and he believed in its essential function in a healthy society."

THE EXAMPLE given in Auerbach's seminars of providing each evening a particular passage of "text" on which to center discussion had not been followed, strictly speaking, in any of the subsequent series. Fergusson had come closest to it by announcing beforehand the canto or cantos of Dante that he proposed to take up; Schorer had "assigned" two novels each week; and it was a matter of seminar routine that books of special importance in the eyes of the seminar leader should be put on reserve in the Princeton library reading room. All who wished to attend the seminars were supposed to prepare or refresh their minds by looking into these documents. In the case of Wellek's seminars, the writer could not do this for two reasons, each practically conclusive: first, he knew no German; second, he did not get to Princeton until noon of the day, Wednesday, when each seminar would be held, and he went to work as soon as he got there. So far as he was concerned, Wellek's lectures were lectures indeed, occasions of pure instruction. Since this was their character anyway, the writer's pupilage was appropriate. The Wellek papers were not written as discussions or to induce discussion; their purpose was to convey information, intelligently sought and evaluated.

Now the question could, and did, arise as to whether this was a proper end for the seminars to serve. Fergusson and Blackmur had not precisely had it in mind. The university itself no doubt existed chiefly for instruction, mediating between the learned and the unlearned; the seminars were to be an opportunity for men presumed learned enough to work out what their learning meant. Wellek was covering his subjects in great detail (significant samples only are here reported), and each evening he unloaded upon his submissive hearers a harvest wagon of research. The display had great scientific interest, as it were; it was knowledge, and it was generally sound; but the rumble of falling facts continued to echo in the discussion periods, and very little good talk got started. Wellek's work in fact was beyond the discussion stage, and therefore not at the point of maximum utility for the seminars; Fergusson had invited him to present it nevertheless for its intrinsic interest. He had failed in three previous attempts to get work in progress from other men, and Wellek was "filling in" at the last minute.

What made up for this disadvantage, at least in the writer's later judgment, was the value of admitting to consideration in the seminars the period of German literary creativity. The culture of the Continent, of which Americans in the new age were inheritors and reviewers, would be seen in considerable disproportion if the Latinate literatures alone were remembered. Such was the writer's own tendency, corresponding to his disability, but he was far from unique; since 1916 or at least since the end of the Weimar Republic, North Americans of amateur standing had turned less frequently in cordiality toward things German. This was blindness; and to have heard Wellek on Lessing and Herder opened or reopened one's eyes to a part of one's patrimony. It was established that in the second half of the eighteenth century the *éclairage* of imaginative art that the English-speaking identified with Wordsworth, Coleridge, and their successors had already struck in Germany. One recognized the paternal culture of Auerbach and Curtius, the strong impulse that, turning to philology and *Wissenschaft,* had made Germany in the nineteenth century so preeminent that training in German, even now in 1950, remained the old school tie of the inner fraternity of scholars. Fergusson, incidentally, could wear it, for he had studied at Heidelberg in his youth and eaten strawberries on the hillside during the ritual student duels.

As for Blackmur, it counted as opportune for him to hear Wellek, for he had only lately received from London his three volumes of Saintsbury; he was getting up the history of criticism in order to give a lecture course in it at the university. It was directly useful to him to have Saintsbury corrected where Saintsbury no doubt stood in need of correction. One need not, though one inevitably would, contrast the irrepressible warmth and humor of Saintsbury's writing with Wellek's level tones; or if one did, one might have to take one's wounds from it gladly. Saintsbury for example had called the whole of German literature from 1750 to 1830 "a sort of *Seminar* . . . a kind of enormous and multifarious Higher Education movement." *Obiter dicta* like this were not, after all, intended to endear the Edinburgh connoisseur with the masters of graduate study in the United States or indeed with academic humanists anywhere.

It had been decided by this time that the subject of the year's final series of seminars, to be conducted as a relay by the five young men already alluded to, with a summing up by the director, would be the late novel, *Doctor Faustus* (1947), by Thomas Mann. Wellek's examination of German pre-romantic and romantic aesthetics had its relevance to this future occasion. It would not be absurd, either, to say that both might cast their distant light on what the French called "the German problem," as that problem re-emerged on the Continent of Europe—one of the most puzzling and even, again, dangerous political questions of those years.

IF SAINTSBURY had scanted Lessing and Herder unjustly, he had been positively unkind to Schiller, in Wellek's opinion (he had as a matter of fact treated Schiller as an unfortunate prig), and had ignored "almost all [Schiller's] important ideas."

"With Schiller," Wellek said, "we enter into a very different and new atmosphere of critical theory: that of dialectical idealism. Its main sources are in the epistemology and aesthetic theory of Kant, but Schiller himself cannot be described as a mere disciple of Kant. He drew much of his terminology and some basic assumptions about man's double nature, sensuous and free, natural and moral, from Kant's teachings; but he sharply modified them. In some respects he picks up the thread of neo-Platonic aesthetics derived from Shaftesbury and the followers of Leibniz in Germany. Schiller's theories proved to be the fountainhead of all later German critical theory. In a changed form, his method continues in the writings of the two Schlegels, in Schelling and Solger;

it comes to England through the mediation of Coleridge; and it culminates in Hegel, who in turn deeply influenced many later nineteenth-century critics such as Belinsky in Russia, De Sanctis in Italy, and Taine in France."

He recalled that because Schiller, in his writings on aesthetics, came to recognize the distinctness and "apartness" of the aesthetic realm, he had been thought a progenitor of the "art for art's sake" position—notably by Irving Babbitt in his book, *On Being Creative*. Wellek said this was a gross misinterpretation of Schiller's actual point of view. Schiller's term "play-urge" (*Spieltrieb*) for aesthetic activity had nothing to do with the lack of consequence, the frivolity and unreality of a child's game; it designated the artist's freedom from immediate practical purposes, from utilitarianism and moralism—his creativity. Schiller saw the artist as mediator between man and nature, between intellect and sense, "between the *Stofftrieb* (the urge to assimilate the world of the senses) and the *Formtrieb* (the urge to subdue the world to the moral law). Art thus assumes a tremendous civilizing role, described by Schiller in his *Letters on the Aesthetic Education of Man* in 1795. Art heals the wounds of civilization, the split between man and nature, and within man himself between his intellect and his senses. Art makes man whole again, reconciles him with the world and with himself."

According to Wellek, Schiller had expected from his speculations a complete regeneration of his own art as a dramatic poet, but in the end he decided it was a "question whether the philosophy of art has anything to say to the artist." He admitted that he would give "all that I and others know about abstract aesthetics for a single empirical advantage, for a single trick of the craft." This alone should have made Schiller memorable to the Princeton company, for as has been seen and will be seen again, the same question and the same impulse occurred often to its more gifted members. "Philosophy and art," Wellek quoted Schiller as saying, "have not yet comprehended each other and interpenetrated, and one misses more than ever an *organon* which would mediate between them." For Schiller to try to remedy the deficiency was, as Wellek put it, hardly utopian or unimportant; indeed the importance had become ever clearer since Schiller's time, and it was no premise of the conversations at Princeton that such an ambition, perhaps the most difficult that could be conceived for literary criticism, was utopian.

Wellek thought Schiller's most important critical work was his treatise *On Naive and Sentimental Poetry* of 1795-1796. These categories were Schiller's improved versions of the "ancient" and "modern" sides of the celebrated *querelle*. Naïve poetry was natural, written with the eye on the object, realistic, objective, impersonal, plastic. Sentimental poetry was reflective, self-conscious, personal, musical. Clearly the term "sentimental" as understood in English in 1950 had little to do with it. The sentimental poet confronted a gulf between reality and the ideal. He had a choice of attitudes toward it. He could stress the distance between, look down from the height of the ideal to reality and thus take the attitude of satire. He could mourn the loss of the ideal and write elegies. Or finally he could imagine the ideal as real in the past or future and write idylls. There could be an elegiac drama such as Goethe's *Tasso* (1790), or a satirical tragedy such as Schiller's own *Robbers* (1781). All three sentimental "modes" could be found in *Paradise Lost* (1667).

Naïve poetry was primarily that of antiquity and especially Homer; sentimental poetry was modern poetry—the poetry of an age in which the poet was in conflict with his environment and divided within himself. Intellect and feeling were divorced, the unity of apperception had been destroyed, the "dissociation of sensibility" (Wellek here referred to Rémy de Gourmont and T. S. Eliot for this phrase) had been accomplished. But the historical distinction, Schiller realized, was not clear-cut. There were sentimental poets in antiquity, Horace for example, and there was at least the possibility of naïve poets in modern times. Schiller meant Goethe, whom he admired and envied—most of all for the "classical" efforts that Herder mistrusted and posterity forgot.

"The difficulty of combining a typology of literature with a philosophy of its history and a concrete critical application to particular figures and ages was not completely overcome," Wellek said. "It is easy to point out that there never was a purely 'naïve' poet or a purely 'naïve' age, that Schiller thinks too much in terms of oppositions, pure types, and sharply set off ages. But with these reservations, the theory gives a profound insight into the process of literature and the peculiar situation of modern literature." He discerned in Schiller "a feeling, for his time extraordinary, of the alienation of the artist from his age." Schiller considered that poets of the naïve type could not come out of modern society; they might appear from time to time "like strangers whom we gape at." Such a poet, indeed, he said, "must become a stranger to himself; must extricate the object of his fervor from his individuality." And he thought the popular poet who would not pander to the taste of the masses should attempt the much more difficult task of satisfying the taste both of the connoisseur and of the people.

Wellek went at some length into the history of Schiller's appreciation (on the whole poor) of Hölderlin. After this digression on Schiller's critical faculty in practice, he reverted to Schiller as theorist, now on the subject of satire, which Schiller broke down into two categories: punitive, as in Juvenal, Swift, and Rousseau, of which the requirement was that it must be sublime; and laughing, as in Cervantes, Fielding, and Sterne, of which the requirement was that it must be beautiful. Mere invective was not poetry, and neither was mere pleasantry, such as Voltaire's. Wellek thought that modern theories of satire had not gone much beyond this classification and these judgments.

The surprising thing was that Schiller at first discussed both tragedy and comedy in the context of satire; he even exalted high comedy as the genre that allowed the greatest freedom to the poet's mind. After reading Kant he came closer to grips with the theory of tragedy and thought that the victory of moral law over natural law accounted for our pleasure in tragic works. Joy in mere purposiveness, even if it were purposive malice, explained the interest and pleasure we take in the machinations of villains such as Iago. In another work on the same subject in the same year he remarked that at the highest point of tragedy all dissatisfaction with fate disappears and "loses itself in an intuition and even better in a clear knowledge of a purposeful coherence of all things, a sublime order of a benevolent will." This was like Lessing's view of tragedy as theodicy. But a year later Schiller had changed, saying, "the highest aim of art is to represent the supersensuous, and tragic art, in particular, achieves this by sensualizing man's moral independence from the laws of nature in a state of passion." Wellek observed as to this that moral freedom in Kantian terminology was supersensuous. Tragedy then, for Schiller, had ceased to be apologetics for the world order and had become rather the representation of free will defying the universe; and Schiller returned to the old Stoic interpretation of *katharsis*.

There was another matter of great and general interest. "In experience the poet begins with the unconscious," Schiller had said, "and he must consider himself lucky, if the clearest consciousness of his operations allows him to find again the first dark total idea of his work unweakened in the finished labor. Without such a dark, but powerful, total idea which precedes everything technical, no poetic work can arise. Poetry, it seems to me, consists just in this: to be able to express and communicate that unconsciousness, that is, to transfer it into an object." Wellek thought that this was a remarkably clear statement of something to which T. S. Eliot had given classic formulation in his phrase about the "objective correlative" for the poet's emotion. Here again the file cards, or memory, had deceived Wellek somewhat, for Eliot was not talking about the "poet's emotion" but about the emotion imagined by the poet as felt by a character in a play. But Wellek was right in praising Schiller's statement. If Schiller had said nothing else, it would have sufficed to establish his importance as a critic—which Wellek suspected had been obscured and overshadowed by his tremendous, though transient, national and international success as a playwright.

Schiller, he said in conclusion, offered a theory of literature that held firmly to the essential truth of neoclassicism without the handicap of adherence to the "rules," the didactic fallacies and pedantries of the official version. He held also an extraordinarily fruitful theory of modern literature and of its relation to modern specialized and mechanized society. His theory of the "modes of feeling" was at least moving in the right direction toward a modern genre theory that would abandon mere external classifications without rejecting all distinctions as Croce did. He seemed to Wellek to have correctly understood both the "apartness" of the aesthetic realm and its relations to morality and civilization.

"Schiller's influence," Wellek observed, "has not been recognized in its whole extent. This is, in part, due to his unfortunate personal relations with the Schlegels. Actually, his impact on Friedrich Schlegel was enormous: the very distinction between the 'classic' and 'romantic' is a modified restatement of Schiller's theory of the 'naïve' and 'sentimental.' Coleridge, either through Schelling or directly, echoes many of Schiller's leading ideas: for instance, the view, central also to Coleridge's theory, that art 'is the mediatress between, and reconciler of, nature and man.' . . . Hegel in his *Lectures on Aesthetics* has freely acknowledged the importance of Schiller's aesthetic ideas for his own system. Even if, with the decline of German idealism, Schiller's direct influence has waned, one can observe his indirect impact even today. . . . Carl Jung's types of 'introvert' and 'extrovert' correspond to Schiller's two types very closely. . . . The final aim of art is, according to Sartre, 'to recuperate this world as if it had its source in human liberty.' This is pure Schiller except in its pragmatist and skeptical reservation, 'as if.' "

THE WRITER had to miss Wellek's final evening, and the manuscript for it was not among those that Wellek supplied to him a year later when he engaged himself as scribe for the seminars. It was his impression that in trying to cover the ground—the Schlegels and Coleridge—Wellek felt that he had had to skip and attenuate too much; and some at least of the seminar company were discontented with the result. One reason for their discontent might have been their general sense that in Wellek's opinion there wasn't much in Coleridge's criticism that didn't come out of Germany or hadn't at any rate appeared there before. It was an old and famous question, and one on which Wellek was likely as usual to be decisive. But Fergusson and Blackmur had been reading Coleridge and Richards on Coleridge, and Stauffer was about to edit a one-volume selection of Coleridge, and there were others present who held Coleridge in affection or in awe. Wellek's doctoral dissertation of 1931—*Immanuel Kant in England*—had contained a long and closely studied chapter on the question, and he had probably literally forgotten more about it than most of his hearers ever knew; but a neutral treatment of Coleridge's "ideas" was not likely to appeal to them.

In any case, the chief value of Wellek's seminars was in the link they admirably supplied between the Age of Reason and the Romantic Period, a link embodied, if in any one man, in Schiller as Wellek had presented him. Wellek told the writer that the discussions had in some cases induced him to modify his position or at least to change his phrasing, and he had obviously greatly enjoyed his visits. Manuscript for his history was still piling up a year later, and two years later the Oxford University Press had not yet announced a publication date. The Princeton company had therefore had a preview far in advance of what would certainly be a work of great interest and value when it appeared—and would have to be read along with Saintsbury, if not in place of him, by all who hoped to know with accuracy the history of literary criticism.

AS GOD HAS OTHER INTERESTS THAN RELIGION ❧ ROBERT FITZ-GERALD ON THE BRIDGING OF THE CREATIVE AND THE DISCURSIVE

Some of Blackmur's personal and literary quality came of being saturated in the noblest English styles of modern times: James, Adams, Yeats. The title of the paper that he gave, in the fall of 1950, before the English Club of Princeton, was taken from Isaiah by way of Yeats's poem to Von Hügel, and the writer found this paper, "The Lion and the Honeycomb," relevant to the seminars, to the Princeton group, and to what he himself thought of offering for discussion. The *organon,* in Schiller's words, that would mediate between philosophy and art: this was still to seek, and Blackmur seemed to propose that it be sought on the critic's side. He proposed at any rate that literary criticism construe itself afresh for a new effort and a larger growth.

The "New Criticism," which had meant, in the hands of Eliot, Tate, Empson, Yvor Winters, John Crowe Ransom, and Blackmur himself—to mention stars principal only—loving and expert attention to the formal and verbal characteristics of poems, had so decisively won its point that by the time it was named, in a book by Ransom in 1941, its proponents were tasting the ashes of success. The title, of course, rather bored them all. And they had almost all, even by that time, escaped the category of New Critics by other means than by growing *older.* But Blackmur was thinking of them and of the fashion that had followed upon their zeal; of Miss Tuve's instruction, and of his own capacious and recently intensified interests; he was thinking of the next phase, and he wanted it original and fruitful, as before. He could see it grinding into a self-centered methodology in Ransom, in Empson, and particularly in the "grammars" of Kenneth Burke, and an analogy from ancient times served him: "Rhetoric," he said, threatened to absorb the other "modes of the mind," as it had done in the centuries between Plato and Quintilian. His paper was a plea for the restoration of "dialectic" and "poetic" as such to the repertoire of the professional writer, the complete literary man.

One had seen how Blackmur affected the university; here perhaps was an instance of how the university, and the idea of a university, had affected Blackmur. A certain pollen for his bloom of discourse could be traced to the physical and friendly proximity, at Princeton, of the Classics department and its energetic chairman Whitney Oates, who worked down the hall and around the corner. The writer had now seen how this worked; it worked by joint recourse to coffee in midmorning at the little library cafeteria two floors above. In these conversations as in those at the Nassau Club, one noted Blackmur's versatility of interest; he had a mind "of large general powers," in Johnson's phrase. Oates was a Platonist whose finest recent work had been done in prefacing and editing the big "Basic Writings" of St. Augustine for Random House. He had noted the kinship of Plato and Augustine in what he called, on Plato's part, the "intense desire to keep his philosophical inquiry alive and not permit it to crystallize into a series of verbal formulae," and this "openness" of "dialectic" was evidently part of what Blackmur, too, understood in that term.

"The Lion and the Honeycomb" also clearly owed something to the example of Dante, as Fergusson had interpreted him, and to the *Poetics* of Aristotle, reviewed likewise in the light of Fergusson's work. Blackmur even suggested that as

121

I. A. Richards had written his most vivid book *On Coleridge and the Imagination* (1934), he might take in a further range in a book called *On Aristotle and Imitation*. He recommended, indeed, to all concerned that they inhale the air of these large worlds in Aristotle and Coleridge, getting into relation with other than literary objects—with theology, history, politics, and personal experience.

After hearing this essay read to a roomful of teachers, each with his glass, in the Nassau Club bar room, the writer's exhilaration outlasted the evening. Not that he failed to appreciate in his friend's delivery, and in some turns of phrase, that touch of the proconsular—the calm of the small compact silver head—that, as he realized by this time, had kept Blackmur's popularity decently incomplete among the professors.

The writer was not a New Critic nor indeed a critic of any title at all, though he had for some years put his mind on books and written about them for a living. He disliked specialization and liked the various employments of being alive. He could not see any such magic rings around accurate study, reasonable discourse, or the making of verse as should deny a human being serious occupation with all three. He took Blackmur's essay as a statement on his side—only the latest and most deliberate, indeed, for Blackmur had extolled the amateur before.

One other Princeton occurrence weighed on the observer's mind. John O'Hara, then living near Princeton, had been brought by Meredith to one of Schorer's evenings of the previous spring. When introduced to Schorer after the seminar, O'Hara was heard briefly to express a story-writer's attitude toward criticism in general and Schorer's in particular: he observed that The Novel was obscenity; obscenity The Novel, he advised. Though Schorer kept a pleasant face at this declaration of war, he must have recognized in his viscera the contempt of the creative for the discursive that had emerged as one more "dissociation" of the twentieth century. The writer thought that amenity if not amity should be possible between them. Here again the mediation, the *organon* that Schiller desired, remained, in spite of Coleridge, still to be sought.

ONE MIGHT try apprehending, or renewing the apprehension of, certain existential and essential roots or principles. When Blackmur talked about Aristotle, he had not gone very far into what he was talking about. "The Lion and the Honeycomb" contained almost no references to any Aristotle except certain key terms in the *Poetics,* and these a trifle oversqueezed after Blackmur's manner when he embraced lexicography. The paper was a rounded proposal, distinguished and humane, but the center from which Blackmur had striven to write it remained inadequately realized.

The focal illumination of Aristotle's thought, if it were to engage the attention of the artist, seemed to the writer very clearly in the *De Anima,* and he opened his seminars on December 8 with some reflections on that work. His point was not only that the *Poetics* could not be understood unless one understood the philosophy in which it was a subsection, but more emphatically that the nature of intelligence and of the real and their relationship were the first concerns of literature, and had been looked into by Aristotle to a depth not often appreciated since the fourteenth century. The seminarist wanted to see what the *De Anima* might supply toward defining that center of operations that he had found implied but diffusely in Blackmur and expressed but with barbarism by O'Hara.

He began with lame and elaborate preliminaries, covering his nakedness of professional scholarship as best he might. He had discovered that *sophia,* the word for the object of philosophy in the original sense, had been used both in Plato and in Aristotle almost interchangeably at times with *technê,* the word for "craft," and thus he dropped the suggestion that wisdom might not be the proprietary end of the discursive thinker but was in fact precisely what the artist sought. He ventured to say that until *sophia* were restored as the reigning affection of the university, the university would be unworthy of its name. He remarked that criticism had begun as an offshoot of philosophy or Greek general thought, and if it were to satisfy general intelligence would have to acknowledge the trunk that bore it.

The Aristotelian quality *par excellence,* he thought, could be called simply a power of close attention. Since vagueness and anomaly concerning the "soul" were prevalent elsewhere, and since the "soul" had, for the humanist, matchless importance in relation to "the dignity of the individual," he proposed recovering Aristotle's grasp of the soul as an intelligible factor in an intelligible world. He then gave an outline of hylomorphism and the Aristotelian theory of causes, and ran as rapidly and clearly as he could through Aristotle's description of what the human soul is—a description that he thought would never lose the power to shock with its plain wakeful precision, its freedom from any dreaminess whatever. The soul perceived as the form of the body, and also as the cause of the body, efficient, formal and final—that was individual dignity for you, it seemed to the writer.

Aristotle had remarked, as to "perception," that each of the senses had the power of receiving into itself the sensible forms of things without the matter, and had proceeded to note that "when that which can hear is actively hearing and that which can sound is sounding, then the actual hearing and the actual sound are one." It followed that in all cases, in order that such things should become actual, sense perception was necessary; and this entailed not merely a sense organ but a soul capable of perceiving by means of a sense organ—the soul being "that for the sake of which" the bodily organ existed. One could infer that the "sensitive soul"—the soul insofar as it had sensation—was endowed therefore with quite a lot of dignity, since if there were no sensitive soul the sensible forms of things in the universe would remain forever unactualized. "There would be, for example, no actual star-light, no actual light at all. There would be a real universe, but it would lack this admirable feature, which it now includes because it includes us and because light is a product of our interaction with other real things." This seemed an interesting reassurance as to the cosmic status of the sensate—for so long, in modern times, denied high standing.

Between sense perception and intellect Aristotle had remarked the analogy: mind is related to what is thinkable as sense to what is sensible, and actual knowledge is identical with its object just as the act of hearing is identical with sound. As to the objects of knowledge, Aristotle had said: "What actual sensation apprehends is particulars, what knowledge apprehends is universals, and these are in a sense within the soul." The seminarist tried to give clearly but briefly the great discovery of "universals" as refined by Aristotle over Plato and by St. Thomas over Aristotle. It was not to be supposed, however, that he could walk the razor edge of Moderate Realism invulnerably; and his interpretation was simplistic. Universal concepts, begotten in us by the essences or intelligible forms of real things, constituted weak but faithful knowledge of the forms; strictly speaking it was the form, not the universal, that could be said to have independent existence.

What the writer wanted was an inkling of the cosmic status of the intellect, and here, as with sense perception, he thought Aristotle hit the right measure of esteem. As his text for the evening, he had had mimeographed the following passage from the *De Anima:* "Mind is in a sense potentially whatever is thinkable, though actually it is nothing until it has thought . . . (and mind so understood) is what it is by virtue of becoming all things, while there is another which is what it is by virtue of making all things: this is a sort of positive state like light. . . . Actual knowledge is identical with its object: in the individual, potential knowledge is in time prior to actual knowledge, but in the universe as a whole it is not prior even in time." Aristotle's dry manner of being awesome would not distract the meditating auditor, the writer thought, from seeing the equipoise here: on the one hand the *nous poetikos,* "a positive state like light," making all things in the sense that it seized their forms into universals so that mind became them all; on the other hand the mind, imperishable in some sense, acknowledged as momentary in a perfectly ordinary sense—"actually it is nothing until it has thought"— so that confidence in the mind and its work must be subject to enormous qualification.

"Here," he said, "I believe Aristotle had forestalled centuries of scientific rationalism, the arrogance of reason from which we have suffered: that arrogance by which the full and necessarily humble intelligence, the intelligence that includes that of the artist, or in a word 'wisdom,' has been discredited and the love of it desiccated." He then produced a series of numbered propositions designed to drive home what he meant by "necessarily humble"—propositions that opened up, as it were, spaces or "distances" between things, notions and words. He especially dwelt on the faint and provisional nature of universals, of all abstractions, in their character as signs, their original transparency toward the real.

"It will be evident," the writer hopefully concluded, "that there are many apparent conflicts and indeed agonies of thought from which we may be delivered by remembering these things; and to remember them is perhaps a requisite for practicing that mode of thought known to Plato and Aristotle as dialectic. The best definition for this that I can think of at the moment is 'the criticism of abstractions through the contemplation of reality, and the exchange of corrections made necessary thereby.' Surely *sophia* cannot be rightly sought or nearly approached otherwise; *sophia* has therefore absented herself from entire civilizations. In the idolatry of scientific reason, the idolatry of knowledge, the artist whose labor always is in the criticism of abstractions could never fully

126

take part; and by the idolaters his intuitive and making intelligence has been denied the name of intelligence."

THE WRITER'S emphatic exordium met no decided opposition that evening, whether because the company was im-
pressed or because it merely felt taken aback. Berryman
remarked to him afterward, with congratulatory alarm, "No
one attacked you!" Oates had in fact gone out of his way to
back him up in his general interpretation of Aristotle and in
the high value he had placed on the *De Anima,* a work that
nevertheless Oates as an avowed Platonist could not quite
accept. It appeared on this occasion, as it would again later,
that the head of the Classics department at Princeton was a
man of admirable humanity. Nine out of ten men in his
position would not have refrained from indicating that position, however politely, in commenting on the submission
of anyone with such slender credentials in learning. But Oates
had no "side" and neither was he faking anything; his interest
was as real as his generosity. At least a hint of attack, however, came from a "left wing intellectual" friend of the writer's,
Irving Howe, who entered the discussion briefly to inquire,
in effect, what earthly use all this epistemology could be;
asking, with innocent practicality, what the seminarist wanted
to know that he didn't already know about the table he was
sitting at. It was a surprising and not very welcome diversion,
and Howe did not elaborate the pragmatic line; but on the
second evening the writer found occasion to discuss the table.
    He wanted to press on into the *Poetics* and had first to
swing his sights around more squarely on the implications,
for the literary art, of what had gone before. He recalled the
reserve of artists like James and Joyce toward "ideas"—evidence of the anticonceptual bias provoked in wakeful souls
by the immodest claims of rationalism. He harked back to
Auerbach's quotation from Pascal and pointed out in that

bitter fragment the use of "justice" and "might" in a series of logical antitheses as if they were geometrical abstractions, amenable to a process of demonstration, instead of being, what they were, rougher kinds of abstraction amenable only to dialectic: Pascal's error having been to ignore what the writer called distances between modes of thought and between all modes of thought and their object. He quoted Valéry's remark that philosophy as understood in modern times was "defined by its apparatus and not by its object"—wherefore Valéry declined the title of poet-philosopher. Yet when Valéry, a poet, stated that the man of intellect "must knowingly reduce himself to an unlimited refusal to be anything whatsoever" he had shown an Aristotelian understanding of the mind—the mind that is nothing actual until it has thought. The conclusion was clear, and the writer drew it, that philosophy in the original sense—the use of the whole and therefore humble intelligence—was better exemplified in modern times in the distinguished work of poetry than in philosophy so-called. He noted how inadequate therefore was the word "aesthetics"—derived from the Greek *aesthanomai*, the verb for feeling—a word that came into use only after rationalism had arrogated intelligence to itself. He quoted Wellek and Warren in their *Theory of Literature* as saying of the critic: "He must translate his experience of literature into intellectual terms, assimilate it to a coherent scheme which must be rational if it is to be knowledge. It may be true that the subject matter of his study is irrational or at least contains strongly unrational elements. . . ." This implied that the experience of literature was not in itself intellectual, coherent, rational or knowledgeable—an implication at the wildest variance with the facts and an example of the unwisdom that had opened a chasm between scholarship and art.

The writer knew that in leaning so heavily away from the point of view expressed by Wellek and Warren he had seemed to swing past the point where many of his friends would cling—that is, the notion of art as "work of the imagination"; and having been thus provocative, he turned to inquire into the linkage between mind and imagination. He had brought along St. Thomas's commentary on the *De Anima* and read several passages of gloss on Book III, two in further clarification of the *nous poetikos* or *intellectus agens*— since several of the company professed themselves still baffled by this—and one that ran as follows:

> It must be admitted that the intelligible things of our intellect have their being in sense impressions, and this is true just as much of what are called abstractions, like those of mathematics, as it is of the states and feelings of sensitivity. And because of this fact no man can learn anything in the way of newly acquired knowledge, nor know anything in the sense of using knowledge already acquired, without the sense impressions. No; when a man is actually thinking speculatively, he must at the same time form for himself some phantasma or sensible image. . . . It is plain that Avicenna was wrong in laying it down that the intellect has no need of sense after acquiring knowledge.

With this the seminarist got down to cases with the question of the table, introduced by Howe. He analyzed as thoroughly as he could the perceptual and conceptual situation occurring in contemplation of the table and pointed out that although the study of the object by means of abstract notions derived from it could proceed indefinitely—one notion after another—the object remained inexhaustible and absolutely unpossessed. The humble status of conceptual knowledge thus established should free the soul, he suggested, for a mode of thinking that he proceeded to exemplify in the concrete by making up a little reminiscence for the table to speak—a dramatic monologue telling of how a tree was felled, sawn, seasoned and built into a piece of furniture. This poem, or micromyth, as he called it, served to bring out two points previously left in abeyance: first, that full contemplation of reality would be contemplation of something happening, some action, or *praxis;* second, that the full being of anything would not be comprehended except in terms of what had happened and what was possibly still to happen—"the being is the full tale of the becoming."

"Aristotle's statement of this," the writer observed, "in his own particular set of abstractions from the real, is that reality—everything that is—may be found as form, potentiality, and the actual in which continually the two are joined. The larger the lens of intelligence, the more it will take in of all three. This is why, in the *Poetics,* Aristotle said poetry was more like *philosophia,* more weighty and significant, than history—because 'the poet's function is not to tell what has happened but the kind of thing that might happen and is potentially capable of happening.' . . . The potentiality of the piece of wood is not only to be a heap of charcoal but to have been a part of a tree. The point, again, is that this potential being comes in, according to Aristotle's understanding, as a real aspect of the actual present being; in fact no part of reality fully exists, or is at all presentable as existing, except in all that it has been and all that it will be. Therefore the Muses are daughters of memory and therefore both in art and in action wisdom implies awareness of the past and divination of the possible future to an extent that will permit, in Robert Bridges's phrase, 'masterful administration of the unforeseen.'

"Now, if this account—rough as it is—squares with the facts about the life of the intelligent soul, let us ask what, in consequence, is the status of pure thought as it is called and what the status of poetry or the myth composed in *phantasmata.* In our context as established the answers should come fairly readily. The humble nature of abstractions requires that we esteem any discourse like the present one as a necessary convenience, but only faintly representative of the process by which it is achieved or the reality to which it refers. The process itself, even in the case of original mathematical thought—and I have verified this with a great living physicist [the writer had in fact badgered Oppenheimer about it] is rich in *phantasmata,* the gifts or deliverances of the senses and of memory. Insofar as these are present in the myth or poem, the myth or poem may represent more fully the work of the intelligent soul and the world in which it finds itself. In any case, it will add, or rather restore, to the *intelligibilia* of the mind a taste of the sensed penumbra out of which they have been seized. There is here no necessary conflict nor ground for anything but courtesy between the workman who limits himself to abstraction and the workman whose bent is for mimesis in phantasmal material. Neither may think the other *per se* disrespectful of the reality both should love; each may recognize in the other, as Aristotle recognized in both, an aspect of *philosophia.* We will have noticed in the *Poetics* that Aristotle thinks of mimesis as a kind of representation from which people learn something, and since to learn something is a delight, he accounts in this way for the popularity of Homer and dramatic poetry. It is well to bear this in mind when we come to interpret his praise of Homer for having taught other poets 'how to tell lies properly.' The great myths of Homer no less than the micromyth I made up a while ago about this table have qualities that Plato stigmatized as lying— the qualities of being arbitrary, conventional, and at a distance from the real. But Aristotle understood more clearly than Plato did that precisely the same can be said of ideas. One may learn something, but not everything, from truth-telling discourse in the order of truth. One may learn something, but not everything, from the fiction properly constructed in the order of art. And we are unfortunate if we cannot see these orders as mutually complementary—for example, in one of the great dialogues of Plato."

The writer thought he had decently succeeded on this occasion, had explained in his given terms—the Aristotelian—that center of understanding in which Schorer and O'Hara could be reconciled and from which the kind of work

Blackmur desired could be done. The discussion, however, was not much concerned with this feat, which had perhaps escaped the notice of the company; at any rate the *De Anima* was still sticking in several craws. The writer found himself under interrogation by Harold Cherniss, the classical scholar from the Institute, a pleasantly skeptical, weathered and seasoned Hellenist whose life work was a study of the relationship between Aristotle and the Academy. Cherniss had evidently surmised that the interpretation given of *nous poetikos* lacked any underpinning from the great Arabic commentators. The writer indicated that the support was there, though slender, and invited Cherniss to strengthen it, whereupon the direction of the wind became noticeable as Cherniss remarked that he hadn't come to "give a speech." It looked as though some of the seminarist's large and positive statements concerning scholarship and the universities had been, regrettably, annoying.

ON THE WRITER's third evening he began by trying again with his little message, accented somewhat differently: that the actual, in this world, is forever what we have and where we are, and that Aristotle's close attention may direct ours to it, alerted and trained down fine; that actuality is precarious, that as the mind barely escapes being nothing actual so does everything else; that if we take to this near nonentity as ducks to water that is because we can exist only in it, but we are not ducks and can realize this much about it. That actuality nevertheless overbrims our concepts, they but faintly embody it, yet we may think how faintly; that one respect in which they are inadequate is in their grasp of those important constituents of any actual thing or person, the potential or possible forms—those that have been, those that are to be fulfilled, and those that neither have been nor are to be. That the fictional or poetic art, the subject of the *Poetics,* may supply us with at least a *homoioma,* a likeness, of such potential or possible forms, and so bring home to us their presence in the given actual thing. That in this way one might locate within the context of Aristotle's general thinking his well-known estimate of poetry as more like *philosophia* and more meaningful—wider and finer in its reference to reality—than the chronicle of actualized particulars that Aristotle understood as History. That, finally, it would be thus that the representational arts gave instruction—not didactically, as later pedantic understanding would have it—but by being what they are.

What the writer wanted to do next was to bring the *Nicomachean Ethics* into the discussion. He was able to illustrate, in this case, too, the division he had talked about between departmentalized philosophy and departmentalized literature; it happened that Bertrand Russell on the one hand and Ezra Pound on the other had written recently about the *Ethics* and had each, without paying much attention to the *Ethics,* gratified his vanity as "philosopher" or "poet" at the expense of that work. The writer also noted the opinion of the English Aristotelian, W. D. Ross, expressed in 1923, that the method of dialectical reasoning pursued in the *Ethics* had lost validity, since "the way of science" was the better way. One had to observe that the way of dialectic and the way of science were not in fact alternatives of which the latter was superior, but that each was a way, and the only way, appropriate to its own form of inquiry in its own degree of abstraction about its own kind of subject. The text mimeographed for the evening contained Aristotle's own explicit statement as to this at the outset of the *Ethics:* "Precision is not to be sought for alike in all discussions, any more than in all the products of the crafts."

The seminarist proceeded to follow Aristotle's dialectic in Book I. It pleased him as he went along to correct by reference to the text the familiar and indeed almost canonical exaggeration by which Aristotle is supposed to have been aware of no larger social unit than the city-state, even though he lived in the time of Alexander. In the text Aristotle, oblivious of his fate, was remarking how much better it would be to attain the highest good for a nation, *ethnei,* and for cities in the plural, *polesin,* than for a single individual. There were other interesting incidentals. The philosopher had taken note of the differing and even opposite values that could be given identical acts in differing times, regions and peoples, so that it "almost seemed" that good actions were not such by nature but by custom; and he had observed the ironies by which good things such as wealth or courage could be the undoing of men. Since life was like that, he had concluded, the student should be content "in speaking about things which are only for the most part true and with premises of the same kind to reach conclusions that are no better." In ethical matters, the writer suggested, most people would welcome conclusions "for the most part true" if Aristotle's lived up to that description.

Starting with the received belief that "happiness" was the final good or the very best thing for everyone, Aristotle defined it broadly as *eu prattein,* doing well and getting along well; then he examined and rejected various opinions as to what that meant: honor, excellence, wealth, and a doctrine he attributed to the Academy—"participation in The Good." The close and famous formula he arrived at was that happiness was activity of the soul—the function proper to a human being—in accordance with excellence, in a fulfilled life. This, however, would presuppose a minimum of physical and external good things: a man on a rack, or a friendless man, could scarcely qualify. The question arose as to whether the external prerequisites of happiness and thus happiness itself did not depend upon luck, or god-appointed destiny. The writer here noted Aristotle's avoidance of further discussion on this point and the desirability of such discussion, since if god-appointed destiny made happiness possible in some cases, by the same token it made it impossible in others. As to the "fulfilled life" Aristotle accepted Solon's saying to

134

the effect that no man should be called happy as long as he is still living; after his death he may be said to have been happy, if he was. The philosopher ended with curious remarks distinguishing between things that are praiseworthy and things worthy of honor. Praise, given in words, would appropriately celebrate virtues that had their value not in themselves but as contributing to happiness; honor, not a matter of words, would be reserved for happiness, the end in view. We might honor the happy gods but to praise them, Aristotle said, seemed funny because it implied some reference to or comparison with ourselves.

Now the writer abruptly started reading passages from "Today Is Friday," Hemingway's funny dialogue of the Roman sentries on the night of the Crucifixion. By this reference the seminarist was doing again, but in the ethical context, what he had done before with "epistemology" and "imagination" in the case of the table. He wanted to confront one kind of dialectic with another—a fictional dialogue—and see how each came off. He found that the fictional situation, concrete and particularized, gave a measure of the degree of abstraction or generality in Aristotle's discourse. It also made apparent the degree of aspiration that the philosopher permitted himself. The Roman soldiers, types of common men, did not even aspire to happiness; they aspired about as far as the things Aristotle said were preconditions of happiness. One of them was certainly ready to honor as an absolute a certain degree of fortitude—though Aristotle would have said that fortitude was merely to be praised, as a contributory excellence. It was the best thing the soldier knew, however; and it looked as if, to him, happiness or unhappiness would be relatively unimportant. The soldiers also made it evident that luck or god-appointed destiny, which Aristotle had avoided discussing, were mysteries much to the fore with *hoi polloi*—and the fact was that *hoi polloi* included everyone at least part of the time. The poetic work, in short, vis-à-vis the *Ethics* supplied a *homoioma* or useful reminder of what life

135

was like, in a limited example but not a false one. In its turn it received some elucidation from being exposed to the terms used by Aristotle and to the light of his definition. Neither the work of dialectic nor the work of art, the seminarist concluded, suffered from being looked at together.

THIS well-meant meditation provoked expressions of feeling too sharp for dialectical development; the writer could only fend and marvel. From the back of the room Sachs asked Fergusson in measured tones if the director considered the submission just heard relevant to literary criticism, because he, Sachs, did not; and Berryman protested against what he regarded as first-grade stuff, saying that after all everyone present was a big boy now. Cherniss was not even there. Sorrowing, but unpersuaded to apologize, the writer got some support from others, including Fergusson and Blackmur, who granted that there was literary interest in the evening. On the following Thursday night the writer, who was coming down with grippe and felt disagreeable, quoted the late Archbishop of Canterbury as saying that God seemed to have other interests besides religion; he suggested that literary people might find in this some sanction for extending theirs. He remarked that if literature and literary criticism were to be discussed together they would have to be discussed from some standpoint not exclusively that of either, and that he had been laboring to expound such a standpoint. He added that valuable as literary criticism could be, there were pursuits more valuable still, the making of literature being one and the pursuit of wisdom another; and as to the priorities involved he asked whether Sophocles or his audience had suffered any great disadvantage from lacking literary criticism, which did not then formally exist.

Speaking as gadfly-in-chief, Sachs had complained of hearing no criteria for judging a work of art; so this evening the writer offered one. He took the neoclassic notion of "clarté," Voltaire's supreme criterion, and pointed out its derivation from *claritas;* it was then possible to show that the first was a thin translation of the second, and thin because merely literary, cut off as Voltaire and his century so largely were from the philosophy in which the term had full significance. An effort to recover that significance could be quoted from Joyce in whose *Stephen Hero* (1944) *claritas* was interpreted as *quidditas* or *splendor formae*—an interpretation by which the work of art as *homoioma*, likeness, was understood to share the nature of reality, to be primarily neither an "idée claire" nor composed of "idées claires" but something from which such ideas could be abstracted. The writer then applied this to the poem of Baudelaire upon which so much ingenuity had already been spent in Auerbach's seminar and produced an exegesis that he thought at least as coherent as any. He added for good measure a further criterion for judging, in themselves, general statements occurring in poetry: they would be the more valuable the more nearly they conformed to reality in the way in which Aristotle's general thought conformed to reality—a criterion by which Yeats's line, "Things fall apart; the centre cannot hold," if understood ontologically, he judged inferior to Robinson's "Love builds of what Time takes away."

Hoping that this would hold Sachs and Berryman at bay, the seminarist now briefly completed what he had wanted to say of the *Ethics,* praying the company to bear in mind that if he seemed again to depart from literature he did so in order to prepare for a reading of *Oedipus Rex.* Aristotle had distinguished the excellences proper to the soul thinking from the excellences proper to the soul acting, the first chiefly to be had from instruction and the second from exercise, or *assuetudo,* as William of Moerbeke put it in Latin. As to these latter excellences or virtues there was no precept adequate for any particular occasion but judgment must be left to the "practical wisdom" of the individual; nevertheless in general the moral virtues could be destroyed either by deficiency or excess. "He is talking about the soul now," the writer noted, "and having listened to him on the soul in *De Anima* we are in a position to know what he means; he does not mean the body or a body. But our quantitative notions come from our perceptions of bodies. Deficiency and excess are abstractions drawn from the world sensuously perceived. He is applying them to the soul, *dei gar,* he says, *tôn aphanôn tois phanerois marturois chrêsthai.* "We have to take visible things as witnesses of invisible"—a point that W. D. Ross in his translation failed to convey and obviously failed to understand.

"Then what is neither in excess nor deficient is the proportionate or, as it is later called, the intermediate. This would be the midpoint on a line between two termini representing excess and deficiency. But it is very important to notice that Aristotle places excellence not at the midpoint absolutely but at the midpoint relative to the given individual in each case. The line is infinitely divisible, there is an unlimited number of points on the deficiency side and on the excess side—this, as I see it, is why he says that evil or off-centeredness belongs to the class of the unlimited—and there is one right point between. Hitting it accidentally is not enough; one must choose to hit it and know what one is doing and it must be in one's character to do so. And now we have our definition of moral excellence: it is a disposition concerned with choice and is at the midpoint relative to us. It seems to me that when you have tested this general statement, as qualified, in every way you can think of, it will stand. The "mean," with its connotations of mediocrity, is a poor translation of *mesotês;* we ought rather to have a word that would bring out what John Burnet in his edition insists on, the sense of tunedness or being in tune. Excellence in the soul acting is beautiful. And this is in the nature of things.

"We ask whether there are moral principles; of course there are, and this is one, but in order to understand it we must understand what I've been driving at from the start, which is the distance at which the abstraction, the valid abstraction, is found from the actuality of which it constitutes knowledge. One way of putting it is to say that the true principle is always the same but the application is never the same in any two instances. . . . The perpetual danger about principles and holding principles and the people who hold them is that they will not understand how important the perception of the given case is. But it is given cases and perception, isn't it, out of which intelligence makes literature. Here then is a special instance of what I said some time ago to be one of the values of art: art as a criticism of abstraction. Of this particular value nobody could have been better aware than Henry James. What is the whole point of that delicious masterpiece, *The Ambassadors* (1903)? To represent for us in all its mystery the *case* of the man of principle engaged in an action in the course of which we realize that the more he compromises with his principles the more he is exemplifying a principle superior to those he thinks he holds."

The writer finished by reading the climactic scenes in Forster's novel, *Where Angels Fear to Tread* (1905), for a violent presentation of action in which parody principles were contrasted with true principles and these subjected to the ironies of perception through human passion and weakness. In the discussion period he finally got around to his fourth text, the last scene in Thucydides' narrative of the Athenian débâcle in Sicily—a passage that served as ironic comment on the virtuous man, Nicias, who brought disaster on himself and on a whole army. The writer had forgotten, but Stauffer reminded him, that this awesome passage had been quoted by Longinus as an instance of the sublime. He was glad to be reminded, for it bore out his choice of the text as a link between the *Ethics* and the tragedy of Sophocles that he had reserved for his final evening.

"I COULD TAKE THUCYDIDES," the writer began, next time, "only in one aspect, though that one an important one and

139

one that I believe people have rather slighted—his aspect as
an ironist, a contraster of word and deed: the style all energy
and elevation, the nearest thing in Greek to Flaubert; the
attitude toward the general, Nicias, a little like Flaubert's
toward Charles Bovary—an elaborate compound of exact,
even sympathetic, justice and majestic contempt. The *aretê*
or virtue by which he says Nicias regulated his life would be
the sophist's version, which is always with us, a *sophrosynê*
that runs to smugness; and Thucydides seems to say that the
fatal thing about this when it is conducting crucial affairs is
that simply by being self-centered it cannot see into the realm
of what's possible. Thus it hampers that excellence of the
mind which Aristotle called practical wisdom and which is
absolutely central to his whole discussion of all the excellences, moral and intellectual.

"Thucydides has a very interesting word for what we
call The Future: he calls it *to aphanes,* the invisible. This can
be found also in Hamlet, who speaks of Fortinbras 'making
mouths at the invisible event.' It is the nature of this part of
reality to be always previsible, so to speak, but as I tried some
time ago to make clear, it is no less real for that. . . . Let us
take only one example of how unrealistic, in this sense, Nicias
is. His second speech in the debate with Alcibiades in the
Athenian assembly is disingenuous; he does not say what he
thinks but tries by enlarging on the *cost* of the Sicilian ex-
pedition to dissuade the Athenians from undertaking it. The
effect, Thucydides notes, is just the opposite of what he intended. Now it would have been impossible for Themistocles, Pericles, or Brasidas—three statesmen whom Thucydides
respects—to be so obtuse to possibility. Therefore one must
not infer that Thucydides thought the 'difficulties of a states-
man' insoluble. At Salamis, Themistocles divined what was
possible, acted on it and won—and he didn't do this by keeping his mind on himself. Nicias, hampered by kidney trouble
and self-esteem, did not grasp the potential in the actual and
by one mis-step after another led the Athenian host into un-
mitigated misery and slaughter.

"The experience of pain and savagery without mercy as conveyed in that tale and in the excerpts I read out of Forster has had to enter this discussion in order that the full conditions and possibilities of human being be recognized. And lest Aristotle be accused of sophistry in ethics—that sophistry that is always vanity and evasion—I had wanted to notice how in *Ethica Nikomachea* VII, after covering the formal nature of moral excellence and excellence in the mind (Truth is the excellence of the mind, as I may not have mentioned) he turned again to consider the difficulties of life, as if they had been bothering him in the meantime; to consider what stands in the way of achieving happiness through the discipline of excellence. What stands in the way, of course, and what threatens *aretê* at every moment, is the whole congeries of things that happen to a man; not the acts that he chooses, wills, and performs but the conditions assailing him and able to check or overthrow him. Aristotle names as *akrasia* the state of being unequal to these conditions; Ross's translation is 'incontinence' in which the original Latin meaning is now rather sunk; what the Greek means is weakness of grip. It may precede or preclude choice, as when the passions govern—passion being in Greek *pathos*, a suffering—for we suffer emotions in the sense that we cannot help feeling them, we have no choice. An instance of *akrasia* is Philip Herriton's inability to withstand the physical pain inflicted on him in *Where Angels Fear to Tread*. He has chosen well and acted bravely but what immediately ensues for him is not happiness but torture. There is, then, *praxis* or action and *pathos* or suffering and with this progression we are at once within what Francis Fergusson calls the 'tragic rhythm.' "

The writer did not propose to talk about tragedy or "Greek tragedy" as such but to confine himself strictly to the *Oedipus* plays and mainly to the *Tyrannos*. He began with Sophocles' language, giving instances of the epigrammatic mastery of wordplay, vowelling, and syntax that made his verse so beautiful, a quality in the very marrow of the work. Aristotle had spotted this and in the *Poetics* had called it *hedusmenos logos*—

"language given sweetness or savor"—something that By-
water's translation, "language with pleasurable accessories,"
utterly misrepresented. The writer's next point concerned the
motive of poetry in general, which he defined as the impulse
to pay tribute to the qualitative fullness of being, actual and
potential. Further, that "what the poet *qua* poet discerns as
the formal and final cause of the poem is a *poetic* potentiality,
or rather a number of them: those possible qualities, movements, modulations, meanings, figures, elegances or mere
breaths of style that come to him and compose his 'vision.' "
He added that the relation in which this vision stood to the
real was that of a *homoioma*, a likeness; that the action of
which the tragedy was a mimesis would be an action conceived in the mind, a mythos reminding the spectator of the
fullness of the real.

"In the case of the table myth," he said, "I hoped it would
remind us first that contemplation of reality would always
be the contemplation of something happening, that is, of
action and suffering; second, that the full being of anything
is the full tale of its becoming, all that it has been and all that
it will be, whence the Muses are daughters of memory and
perhaps also mothers of prophecy; third, that no existing
thing can be understood apart from the context of the real,
the other reality, to which it is related. Of these general truths,
the *Oedipus Tyrannos,* a dense particular, in all its sweetness
of speech, will remind us in its particular way."

The writer thought that the received version of Oedipus's
solution to the Sphinx's riddle was remarkably childish,
though this fact had passed unremarked by the commentators
from Dikaiarchos to Dindorf. He now offered a less childish
interpretation that had come to him one morning on the
Pennsylvania Railroad. "Let us imagine the effect of the word
man on the conceivable Sphinx. We may see her complacently
switching her great tail, making bread with her enormous
paws. She arches her perfect eyebrows and looks limpidly at
the hero. 'If you don't like my periphrasis, all right,' we may

hear her say, 'you can put the riddle in one word if you like; but now do go on and give the answer.' Oedipus does not give the answer, he lives it. It seems to me likely that in the *Oedipus* plays Sophocles proposed nothing less than a kind of answer to the riddle of man, the answer being in terms of dramatic poetry. . . . Oedipus the great king in whom so many excellences are met is to demonstrate for us first of all the *akrasia* common to men—their inability to withstand passion. There is his rage against Teiresias, there is the remembered rage in which he killed his unknown father, there is the fear that begins to sicken him, I think, even before he brawls with Creon, and which possesses him more and more until the *katastrophe;* and there is his regal passion for Jokasta.

"In the Habimah Theatre production, some of the meaning came across at her entrance. Up to that point—through more than a third of the play—we have had only men on the stage and combats between men; now in her soft flowing chiton enters the woman to whom all eyes turn—the only woman in the play, intensely seductive by contrast; and she chides the children. The mystery is almost too dense for analysis, but we may understand perhaps that what is being done with her is to concentrate in one figure at one time all that a woman naturally is at different times—prize, wife, and mother at once, just as in Oedipus there is a concentration of son, hero, husband, and father *at once.* The being is the sum of its becoming; the past action is now present, or to be made present, in one terrible rush of revelation. And we apprehend that Eros, sexual passion, is at the heart of mortal existence, creating incalculable worlds.

"But we are not finished with passion. Teiresias too suffers it—the blind clairvoyant, servant of the truth, gives way to anger in the cause of truth. I have talked about *sophia* and made a beginning perhaps of understanding what it is. So has Oedipus evidently made a beginning; he is renowned for it when the play opens. We are unfortunately prone to associate wisdom with mellowness—ruddy, with a twinkle. It is far from that in Teiresias, and it will be far from that in Oedipus when he gets over his assurance. He must be blinded to approach it; and in the *Colonus* he will himself be like Teiresias: holy and terrible because of what he knows, and like Teiresias capable of passion in the service of what he knows. And this beginning of wisdom is better stated in terms of another revelation: the beginning of wisdom is the fear of God. What is learned in *Oedipus Tyrannos* is that there is an absolute disproportion, an absolute incommensurability, between God's power and man's, between God's justice and man's. Oedipus is doomed from the start to demonstrate this, and one of the things he realizes before the end of the play is that he has been especially designated. What is providence? What is luck? We inquired of Aristotle, who said that luck or chance might deprive us of the preconditions of happiness. There is a reply in the *Physics* that goes like this: 'Chance is an efficient cause of the kind called incidental . . .' but ' . . . no incidental cause can be prior to a cause per se. Spontaneity and chance therefore are posterior to intelligence and nature. Hence, however true it may be that the heavens are due to spontaneity, it will still be true that intelligence and nature will be prior causes of this All and of many things in it besides.' In the *Poetics* ix there is a guarded sentence about the possibility of seeing design in chance. In *Oedipus* you see it—indeed you see chance and design as one, or the presence of a reality to which both words seem applicable and both inadequate. . . . Such, or such in meagre outline, is the answer lived by Oedipus to the Sphinx's riddle."

The writer had one more point. He wanted to notice that an explicit answer was also stated in the play—in the chorus following the moment of recognition and *katastrophe*. He had quoted these lines as the mimeographed text for the evening: "Alas, generations of men, how near you are to nothingness; even as you live I set you down as naught." Now the writer observed the import of the chorus: on some scale that man could grasp, he saw himself as nothing. He thought it worth noting that this, the supreme insight stated in the play, accorded closely in meaning with the supreme insight of the lover of wisdom, Aristotle, in his work *De Anima*. At the same time he had to add that the chorus was a chorus in a play, speaking the thought that, as Aristotle in the *Poetics* would say, suited the situation and was consonant with it. And having brought the discussion back to where it began, the writer made an end.

He had been trying, as Blackmur had proposed in "The Lion and the Honeycomb," to get at what Schiller had called the *organon* that would mediate between philosophy and art. His texts were all Greek, but he had essayed to make the most of them, and now that he had finished there seemed to be less dissatisfaction in the company than he had found earlier. The final discussion, at least, was well-fed and amiable, as if however the scholars might judge his submission they now conceded its relevance to literature and literary criticism. Blackmur was amused by his version of the Sphinx and her riddle and referred to it in a paper he was getting up for delivery to an art association. As to what the writer might do with his own papers he remained for a long time undecided. He thought of giving them professional form as a book; he even thought of translating and editing anew the *Poetics* and *Ethics,* since he found the available English insensitive. In the end he settled for such currency as his notions might get in the retrospect of the present narrative.

Chapter Seven

A MAN WRITES WITH HIS WHOLE BODY ❧ JACQUES MARITAIN ON POETRY AND REASON

A T THIS JUNCTURE, the end of 1950 and the beginning of 1951, an excursion into Thucydides had its topical point, for the Communist Chinese had just entered Korea and smashed American divisions advancing in the north. It seemed to the writer that critical toil often came of the necessity, while treating one thing, to keep other and coincident things in view; so, now, the freezing infantry in the distance took his eye along with his immediate subjects in Greek. But the distraction, if it could be called that, was general at Princeton just then. Though the Korean business had started badly in the previous summer, it had never appeared in the long run hard to handle. With the Chinese engaged, however, the United States might be in for a dangerous war. The university administration reckoned on losing perhaps two out of five students to military service in the course of the next year. Hopes for the cultivation of peaceful arts were bound to shrink accordingly. The university made new investments in physics, but it planned to retrench in the humanities—a distribution of interests already evident at the Institute, as has been seen. The public case was clear enough. If Western society could not defend itself it would fall, and free activity would cease in the arts as elsewhere; therefore plenty of electronics was desirable. The man of letters, being free, was still free to ignore electronics and to express himself on the causes that narrowed his future; so Blackmur and the writer could muse, in the coffee hour, over the fact that the university now contemplated no assistant or "resident fellow" in the writer's place next year. No job for him who might be back in the Navy, anyway. Alba Warren, one of the men who had been counted on for a paper in the spring symposium on *Doctor Faustus,* now in fact disappeared from the scene, called back to active duty with the Army. Here was the shock of the quilted Chinese, passed back in a shunting series from the Asian hills to Princeton.

Jacques Maritain did not attend the writer's seminars because he was too busy preparing his own—thus illustrating another type of obstacle to the continued dialogue that Fergusson and Blackmur had wanted. In this case the dialogue lost something in explicitness—for Maritain, too, came at poetry by way of Aristotle—but perhaps gained something in dramatic contrast. The writer's offerings had suffered from rashness in composition, boarding big galleons and cutting away at too many pikes. Maritain could go further, and with more professional control, even though he worked, as the writer had, against a weekly deadline; each Thursday night when he sat down to read he opened a sheaf of papers freshly written in his cobwebby serene hand.

Thirty years had elapsed since the Catholic philosopher had first written on the art of poetry; he had sketched his *Art et Scolastique* in Paris in the year after the Treaty of Versailles. The writer took this book with him to a snowbound Swiss village in the winter of 1931; in the winter of 1932 he found an English edition of it in T. S. Eliot's hands at Harvard. It is the multiplication of such particulars that makes a work "historically important"; the value of this one lay in its equal, and equally intelligent, ardor for scholastic thought and for French verse after Baudelaire. At the same time the writer remembered it as somehow esoteric and out of relation with the classic order in art—an order ever present, by comparison, to the mind of Valéry. Now in the intervening years no philosopher could have failed to acquire a context for the School of Paris. Except for three years as French ambassador to the Holy See (1945–1948), Maritain had lived in the United States for ten years or more. He had thought over an expanse of subjects from the causes of the French débâcle in 1940 to the metaphysics of Leibniz, his class subject just then at Princeton. He had read English and American poetry; friends including Fergusson and Allen Tate were able to advise him where to find the best of it. His most recent book treated of political philosophy, and he had a work on ethics in hand. But it was clear that he had put his mind with great intensity on his subject for the seminars—the perennial subject, "Poetry and Reason."

He began, his first evening, with "Art as a Virtue of the Practical Intellect," and the mimeographed texts were two quotations from *Ethica Nicomachea,* three from Aquinas, and a remark of Oscar Wilde's. These were "suggested to help focus the notions to be discussed." In this use of the mimeograph Maritain differed from Auerbach as from the writer, and the difference would grow more striking as time went on. Opening with strict Aristotelian common sense, he recalled that *homo poeta* rode on the shoulders of *homo faber:* among works of intellect there were the speculative and the practical, and all art belonged to the sphere of practice. To be distinguished within the practical were *factibilia* (works of making) and *agibilia* (works of acting), and it followed that art, dealing with *factibilia,* was concerned with the good of the work, not with the good of Man. Thus Aquinas: *Dicendum est quod ars nihil aliud est quam ratio recta aliquorum operum faciendorum: Quorum tamen bonum non consistit in eo quod appetitus humanus aliquo modo se habet; sed in eo quod ipsum opus quod fit, in se bonum est. Non enim pertinet ad laudem artificis, inquantum artifex est, qua voluntate opus facit; sed quale sit opus quod facit.* But as to this Maritain had a further reflection: "Art breaks into human life and human affairs like a moon prince or a mermaid into a customs office or a congregation; it will always make trouble and arouse suspicion. But art exists in a human being—the artist. As a result, though the fact of a man's being a poisoner is nothing against his prose [as Wilde said], the fact of a man's being a drug addict can be, in the long run, something harmful to his prose. . . . Once a man is through, his art is through also."

Now the philosopher touched on a conception that the "revival of learning" had bruited about a good deal, in literature as in architecture: the "rules" of art. Imagine, he said, the first boat ever invented; in that case the only rule was to make something buoyant on which to cross the river. For the second boat there were already two rules: the first one and another, the newborn rule of making a raft. For the third there were three: the first two and the newborn rule of improving on previous work. The primary obligation remained, and would always remain, to rule number one. But "even in the useful arts, the rules are not ready-made recipes, taught by professors in schools and museums, but vital ways of operating discovered by the creative eyes of the intellect in its very labor of invention." In the fine arts this would be doubly true. Concerning them, Maritain seemed to go back to Plato and the *Symposium* for a statement that he would amplify and modify later, to his purpose: "Left to the freedom of its spiritual nature, the intellect strives to engender in beauty." For the present he accepted this as "the first ontological root of the artistic activity" and went on to say, dealing with the notion of usefulness in the fine arts, that beauty was of no use and was "as transcendental and infinite as the universe of the intellect. . . . Thus the very end—transcendental end—intended pertains to the realm of the intellect, of its exultation and joy, not to the world of utility, and the intellectuality of art is in the fine arts . . . at a much higher degree than in the arts of the craftsman." This being the case, it seemed that the rules in the fine arts "must be perpetually reborn . . . with respect to beauty to be participated in; and beauty is infinite, and the mirror the artist holds up to it is no bigger than his own heart. He is bound to go hunting a new analogue, a new typically different participation in beauty; and this new participation in beauty will involve and require new ways of making—either a new adaptation of the fundamental and perennial rules, or the use of rules not hitherto employed, which are simply new, and which at first disconcert people."

In this argument Maritain had been using intellect and reason almost as interchangeable terms, and in a sense that to the modern ear was already very capacious. Now he made a further distinction: "The intellect or reason which plays the principal and royal part in the arts is not conceptual, discursive, logical reason, or even working reason. It is intuitive reason, in the obscure and high regions which are near the center of the soul. . . . The working reason plays an essential and necessary—though secondary—part . . . not only secondary, but merely instrumental. As soon as it gets the upper hand, the work is but a corpse of a work of art—a product of academicism." He ended by saying that in his opinion Valéry and Stravinsky, great artists who took pleasure in describing themselves as mere engineers in the manufacture of artifacts, were purposely not telling the whole truth.

This arrival at "intuitive reason" reminded the writer that he, too, had insisted on that category and that neither he nor Maritain had referred to any Aristotelian locus for it. Of the talk that followed all he could later remember was that he had tried to make up for the omission by recalling the passage in the sixth book of the *Nicomachean Ethics* in which Aristotle named intuitive reason as one of the virtues of the intellect, that which grasps the first principles on the one hand and the concrete existent thing on the other. It seemed to him that this belonged among the texts for the evening.

THE TITLE for the second meeting was rather elaborate, a double title heralding something new: "Art Bitten by Poetry

Longs to be Freed from Reason. The preconscious life of the Intellect." The mimeographed sheets this time were two, bearing quotations from André Breton, Plato, and Aquinas. The point of the Breton manifestos was precisely to illustrate the fact that—despite Valéry, and avowedly in the surrealist case—the arts in the recent age had longed to be "freed from reason." Maritain applied himself to interpret this. In the first place, he said, art felt itself threatened by "modern reason— a so-called reason, as afraid of looking at things as it is busy digging in all the detail around them, and as fond of illusory explanations as it is insistent in its claim to recognize only statements of fact—the reason of those who believe that poetry is a substitute for science intended for feeble-minded persons." So much for positivism, whose traces the writer had found in Wellek and Warren's *Theory of Literature*. But Maritain went on to say that the longing in question had to do "with a typical aspiration of art in its own line and inner life, insofar as it has become conscious of itself during the last century to an unprecedented degree, and has found, at the center of this self-awareness, poetry, naked and wild poetry." In the effort to get free from the intelligible and logical, an effort of which surrealism showed one extreme, the philosopher thought that art had in fact obeyed that intuitive reason of which he had spoken—something prior to logical reason. But in surrealism the effort was not only extreme but aberrant. He described it as "a deliberate and systematic craving to deny the supreme autonomy of a power which is spiritual in nature, to reject everywhere and in every respect both the control of conscious reason and, even in its preconscious life, the superior intuitivity of the intellect, and to let loose the infinite powers of the irrational in man." The result, he said, wherever the surrealists truly achieved automatism, was not freedom but only dispersion, though at the same time surrealist poetry was being required "to provide man with deceptive and flashy substitutes for science, metaphysics, mysticism, sanctity."

What could be said, then, for the movement of which Breton's dated manifestos were a reminder? "We must recognize," Maritain concluded, "the importance of the task achieved by surrealism in calling attention to many *invidiosi veri* which the rationalist bias of our everyday dealings, our classical teaching, our industrial civilization, and our moral prudery would prefer us not to see. The surrealists were right in unmasking the part (not principal, but real indeed) played by the workings of the automatic or animal unconscious in the soul of the poet, and in emphasizing . . . the longing for the world of the marvelous, the availability of sensitiveness to all the allurements of chance."

By this path Maritain reverted to Platonism for the dissent that everyone had been expecting. The mimeographed quotations, from the *Ion* and the *Phaedrus*, both insisting on the "madness" of the poet, now took their place in the context of discourse. Plato, he said, like the surrealists, though for opposite motives, had totally separated poetic inspiration from reason. "The myth of the Muse signifies that the source of poetry is separate from the human intellect, outside of it, in the transcendental eternal fatherland of subsisting Ideas. A conception which is akin, in the realm of art, to the Averroistic conception of the separate Intellect in the realm of knowledge, and which is responsible for that detestable idealism which has for so long spoiled the theories of philosophers on beauty." Maritain's solution was very direct—to make the Platonic Muse descend into the soul of man as creative intuition. "My contention, then, is that everything depends, in the issue we are discussing, on the recognition of a spiritual unconscious, or rather preconscious, of which Plato and the ancient wise men were well aware, and the disregard of which in favor of the Freudian unconscious is a sign of the dullness of our times." Not that Freud's lively region could be disregarded. "The notion of the psychological unconscious was made into a self-contradictory enigma by Descartes, who defined the soul by the very act of self-consciousness. Thus we must be grateful to Freud and his predecessors for having obliged philosophers to acknowledge the existence of unconscious thought." But the Freudian unconscious, an animal or automatic or deaf unconscious, "the unconscious of blood and flesh, instincts, tendencies, complexes, repressed images and desires, traumatic memories," would not accommodate the Muse, whose seat must rather be "the spiritual or *musical* unconscious or preconscious of the soul."

The principle invoked here was of course a great one in Thomist philosophy: logical, formal and indeed causal priority belongs to what is superior in grade of being. The unmusical cannot account for the musical. In the present case, "the universe of concepts, logical connections, rational *discursus* and rational deliberation, in which the activity of the intellect takes definite form and shape, is preceded by the hidden workings of an immense and primal preconscious life. Such a life develops in night, but in a night which is translucid and fertile, and resembles that primeval diffused light which was created first." Now the philosopher ran through the Aristotelian and Thomist "psychology" concerning the formation of concepts—giving with assurance and authority what the writer in his seminars had struggled to extract from the treatise *De Anima*. The necessity of explaining how phantasms and images originating in sensation could yield abstract concepts had obliged Aristotle to posit the *nous poetikos* or *intellectus agens*—an "Illuminating Intellect" which would permeate the images with its spiritual light and actuate or awaken the potential intelligibility in them. This had been a postulated process totally escaping experience or consciousness. "Well," concluded Maritain, "if there is in the spiritual unconscious a nonconceptual or preconceptual activity of the intellect even with regard to the birth of the concepts, we can with greater reason assume that such a nonconceptual activity of the intellect, such a nonrational activity of reason, in the spiritual unconscious, plays an essential part in the genesis of poetry."

IN THE READING of this fragile and intent aging man, with his tired eyes and white chin tuft like a snowy Mandarin, there was an astonishing quality of energy. It would have been rather pat to call it spiritual, but watching the seated figure—a gray scarf hung down over his lapels in the mode of a scapular—half rising from the chair to make his decisive points like blows, the writer was reminded of Rémy de Gourmont's saying that a man writes with his whole body. One became aware, too, in one degree or another, that the level of discourse was now rising toward something superior, some revelatory largeness and accuracy. In discussion people were brief and subdued; even Sachs put neutral questions in quiet tones. It was interesting to see Blackmur's reserve; the writer guessed it to be the outward sign of inward activity, as the caverns of reference within his friend were sounded. Maritain's thought, like Maritain's faith, Blackmur would be resisting as a matter of irreducible temperament; but not openly, not just now. On the other hand, the writer felt no discontent, but thought he saw the *organon,* the desired mediation between philosophy and poetry, taking shape as these seminars proceeded.

Next time there were three mimeographed sheets with a rich variety of examples: ten in all, some rather long, ranging from Melville through St. John of the Cross to Max Jacob. The philosopher now made use of the blackboard as well. He drew on it a diagram of three pendent and concentric or converticate cones, an illustration for his own remarks *de anima* and *de anima poetae.* His subject for the evening was triple: "Poetry and the free, nonconceptual life of the intellect, at the single root of the soul's powers; The subjectivity of the poet and the creative intuition; Poetic knowledge." As for the cones, it appeared that the exterior and broadest but shortest represented the intellect, the next and narrower but longer represented the imagination, and the central, narrowest and longest one represented the life of sensation. Within these bells a shaded core was sketched—the automatic unconscious—reaching up through the volume enclosed by each to meet the preconscious of the spirit, which entirely filled the volume from the vertex downward about two-thirds of the length of the cone of intellect. The rims of the cones represented the loci respectively of formed concepts, explicit images, and sensations. Within the total volume one was to understand a circulation both up and down through all phases of sentiency and thought, conscious and unconscious and preconscious life; in particular, "all things seized upon by sense perception, all treasures of that sapid and sonorous and colorful Egypt, enter and make their way up to the central regions of the soul."

All this made it abundantly clear that, besides conceptualizing, intellect had another kind of life for Maritain, which he called free—"I mean free from the engendering of abstract concepts and ideas, free from the workings of rational knowledge and the disciplines of logical thought, free from the human actions to regulate and the human life to guide, and free from the laws of objective reality as to be known and acknowledged by science and discursive reason." In this "root life" poetry was born. And since it was born where the powers of the soul were active in common, it implied an essential requirement of totality or integrity. "Poetry is the fruit neither of the intellect alone, nor of imagination alone . . . it proceeds from the totality of man, sense, imagination, intellect, love, desire, instinct, blood and spirit together." In what sense, then, could poetry be called a form of knowledge? The philosopher's statements here had a certain beauty. "The poet," he said, "knows himself only on the condition that things resound in him, and that in him, at a single awakening, they and he come forth together out of sleep." "The knowledge would not be conceptual but through connaturality or affective union. Knowledge through connaturality," Maritain observed, "plays an immense part in human life. Modern philosophers have thrown it into oblivion, but the ancient Doctors paid careful attention to it and established upon it all their theory of God-given contemplation. I think that we have to restore it." As to the poet, further, "his intuition, the creative intuition, is an obscure grasping of his own Self and of Things in a knowledge through union or connaturality which is born in the spiritual unconscious and which fructifies only in the work. So the germ tends from the very start to a kind of revelation, virtually contained in a small lucid cloud of inescapable intuition, both of the Self of the poet and of some particular flash of reality in the God-made universe."

Poetic knowledge therefore had the characteristic of tending to a work. It was at this point—a placement that the writer admired—that Maritain first spoke of the artist's emotion as entering into the work of art, and his statement was memorable. The essential emotion, he said, was not an emotion to be expressed but an emotion *which causes to express.* Behind this great discernment lay an acute reading of what a number of intelligent artists, Baudelaire and T. S. Eliot, for example, had had to say about emotion in art. The emphasis these men put on the work itself was an emphasis that Maritain wanted to keep. In the work alone would poetic intuition come to be objectivized. Therefore the work must preserve its consistence and value as an object. "But at the same time it is a sign, both a direct sign of the secrets perceived in things, of some irrecusable truth of nature or adventure caught in the great universe, and a *reversed sign* of the subjective universe of the poet."

Here the precarious nature of the whole business was recognized. The work, as sign, could be malformed from birth; it could lose touch with the intuition. "At the initial moment of the operative exercise, another process can take place. Then the poetic intuition becomes a craftsman's creative idea, losing its inherent transcendence and descending, as it were, into the mechanical noise and the merely intellectual concerns for manufacturing. This phenomenon comes about when man, in a hurry to display his own energy and to produce something great, or because poetic intuition is weak in him, goes *beyond* poetic intuition, and, instead of listening to it, endeavors to supplement it in his own way." But if the intuition were "listened to" faithfully, there would be more of it. "It is with the steady labor of intelligence intent on the elaboration of the form that the virtuality contained in poetic intuition actualizes and unfolds itself all along the process of production. And then the very exercise of artistic science and intellectual perspicacity, choosing, judging, cutting out all the nonsignificant, the fat, the superfluous, causes— precisely because it is always listening to creative emotion and appealing to it—new partial flashes of poetic intuition to be released at each step of the work. . . . As the mystic suffers divine things, the poet is here to suffer the things of this world, and to suffer them so much that he is enabled to speak them and himself out. . . . The degree of creative strength is proportioned to the degree of depth of his attentive passivity."

The presence among the mimeographed material of a poem by St. John of the Cross suggested a relation between this study of the genesis of poetry and Maritain's study of the "Dark Night" in *Les Degrés du Savoir*. What continued to impress the writer as he listened was the sensitiveness and adequacy of Maritain's vocabulary, of the terms drawn from Christian philosophy and Christian spiritual experience, to the matter in hand. Wellek had recognized, with entire justice, the importance of a statement by Schiller that ran like this: "In experience the poet begins with the unconscious and he must consider himself lucky, if the clearest consciousness of his operations allows him to find again the first dark total idea of his work unweakened in the finished labor." That was true; yet how much truer, so to speak, the same insight became when it had been all unfolded and refined by Maritain's distinctions, his delicate tracing of the process step by step.

DURING the first seminars, Auerbach's, Maritain had made one notable interposition. It came after Auerbach's analysis of Baudelaire's style as a fusion of high and low, when in response to Curtius's question as to whether Baudelaire had any psychological importance Maritain answered with a distinct affirmative. Poetic experience, he said, was a form of knowledge deep in the consciousness; Baudelaire discovered his own knowledge deep in his own "denuded human nature" and expressed his poetic intuition of it in a manner that Maritain would not dispose of as merely "style." No, Baudelaire discovered something new, and once for all, in the very sources of poetry. Now in Maritain's fourth seminar Baudelaire was apparently going to occupy the center of attention along with St. Thomas, each represented in the texts by a passage about Beauty—Aquinas with the famous definition, "Ad pulchritudinem tria requiruntur" (For beauty three things are required), and Baudelaire with *Hymne à la Beauté*. These passages and eight others, among them Rimbaud's equally famous prescription for the "déreglement de tous les sens," were mimeographed under the title: "Beauty as permeated by intelligence. The dismissal of Beauty and the craving for knowledge, magic, and (black) mysticism."

If there was one word that the Princeton circle had contrived to avoid in the course of thirty sessions on literary art, it was the word "beauty"; the writer has noted the quaint sound it had when pronounced by an Italian visitor one evening the year before. This shyness might never have existed for all the notice Maritain took of it. He had often alluded to beauty; beauty was now his subject, and beauty he would discuss. St. Thomas's three requisites for beauty were first, wholeness, or perfection; second, due proportion, or harmony; third radiance, or clarity—a requisite elsewhere defined, said Maritain, citing St. Thomas's *opusculum de divinis nominibus* (little work on the divine names), as "the splendor of form." Now this definition of *claritas* had been hit upon also by James Joyce, as the writer noted when he offered it as an artistic criterion superior to that faint derivative, *clarté*.

But Maritain's gloss deepened the whole thing still further: "If we were able fully to realize the implications of the Aristotelian notion of *form*—which does not mean external form but, on the contrary, the inner ontological principle which determines things in their essences and qualities, and through which they are, and exist, and act—we would also understand the full meaning intended by the great Schoolmen when they described the radiance or clarity inherent in beauty as *splendor formae,* the splendor of the form, say *the splendor of the secrets of being radiating into intelligence.* Thus the very words we are obliged to use—clarity, radiance, light, splendor—could be terribly misleading, if we came to forget that being is intelligible *in itself,* but not necessarily *for us,* and remains most often obscure to us, either because its intelligibility in itself is obscured in matter or because it is too high and too pure for our intellect. Descartes, with his clear ideas, divorced intelligence from mystery. Modern science is making us aware of his mistake. The Schoolmen, when they defined beauty by the radiance of the form, in reality defined it by the radiance of a mystery."

These notions were not univocal but analogous. "The beauty of a bunch of flowers or of a landscape is not the same as the beauty of a mathematical demonstration or the beauty of a generous act or the beauty of a human being—though because of the analogical community involved in beauty, they may happen surreptitiously to evoke one another in our minds—hence an ambiguity by which the poet will profit." Likewise, beauty being a transcendental was not enclosed in any class or category because present in any thing whatsoever; in the eyes of God all that exists is beautiful, to the very extent to which it participates in being. But this, said Maritain, was not the beauty which our sense perceived; aesthetic beauty was rather "a particular determination of transcendental beauty, confronting not simply the intellect, but the intellect and the sense acting together." Hence, for our senses, the category of the Ugly existed, but art "endeavors to imitate in its own way the condition peculiar to the pure spirits: it

draws beauty from ugly things and monsters, it tries to overcome the division between beautiful and ugly by absorbing
ugliness in a superior species of beauty."

Was beauty, then, the object of poetry? Had poetry any
object at all? Here the philosopher acknowledged that *art* had
an object, for in art as in science the creativity of the spirit
was subordinate to an object—in the case of science, Being
to be known, and in the case of art, the object to be made.
By way of parenthesis he added that in this case the intellect,
as in the Kantian system, created its own object—but an
object to be made, not an object to be known. But poetry
itself, the life of creative or poetic intuition, had no object
and was free. Beauty was not its object; it was rather "the
end beyond any end." Poetry therefore, said Maritain, "tends
toward beauty, not as toward an object to be known or to
be made, or a definite end to be attained in knowledge or
realized in existence, but as toward that very life of yours
which is in the one whom love has transformed into another
yourself. . . ." This was what he had meant when he declared
earlier, of the fine arts, that "left to the freedom of its spiritual
nature, the intellect strives to engender in beauty." And he
reinforced the point with a powerful negative: "To the very
extent to which the fine arts make beauty their object, they
recede from beauty, and tend toward academicism—the
proper perversion of the fine arts."

Now to state matters in this way drew attention at once
to certain possibilities of fright as well as glory, for a transcendent end is beyond human ease. Maritain had in fact been
thinking of Baudelaire, and of Baudelaire's successors, when
he placed Beauty as he did, modifying now after thirty years
the argument of *Art and Scholasticism* in which he had been
content to regard beauty as poetry's object. He quoted one
of those passages of Baudelaire that Auerbach would certainly
have called horrible:

> Tu marches sur des morts, Beauté, dont tu te moques;
> De tes bijoux l'Horreur n'est pas le moins charmant,

Et le Meurtre, parmi tes plus chères breloques,
Sur ton ventre orgueilleux danse amoureusement.

"Baudelaire was aware," commented the philosopher, "too aware, of the kind of transcendental indifference which beauty, as the end beyond the end of poetry, enjoys with regard to human things. He knew that beauty is one of the Divine Names. But the fact with which his own experience was obsessed and which his extraordinary power of perception made clear—and this event has a crucial significance for poetry in modern times—is that now this Divine Name is detached from God, and reigns separate in our human heaven."

Among poets who followed Baudelaire in suffering this condition, Maritain distinguished between those who nevertheless opted for God—Hopkins and Claudel, for example— and those who opted against Him, as did Mallarmé and Valéry. The choice made by these latter "taught modern poetry the experience of the void—and also, as concerns Mallarmé, a faint hope in magic." But the main point was that modern poetry could not be judged and understood in the perspective of classical aesthetics and mere literature—as well ask a butterfly hunter to catch an octopus or a whale. For when literary art was conceived as an assault on the absolute, in the phrase of Jacques Rivière, great new adventures and confusions came about. Maritain here alluded in passing to the notion of the Artist as Hero—a notion encouraged by Goethe and Byron and made colossal and ironic in the cases of Gide and Mann. He quoted an "astonishing sentence" of Rousseau: "I shall come to appear before the sovereign judge with this book in my hand." Said Maritain: "The poor man! A book in his hands." More concretely: suppose poetic knowledge not only became conscious of itself but took itself as its own aim? The result appeared in Rimbaud, who wanted poetry to be absolute knowledge, that is, a science—something contrary to its nature. Suppose that the poet elected to be a myth-maker in the religious sense, to create his own metaphysical myths. The effort was contradictory, since having invented them he

161

could not believe them. "A man lost in the night might as well invent an imaginary moon because he needs to have his way lighted." Trying the way of magical gnosis, surrealist poetry had become an empty perceptivity. Yet Maritain ended with a balancing perception:

"Let us not forget that all these shifts and swervings are accidental disorders which thwart, conceal, and obscure in modern culture the great essential fact: the spiritual advent, not of the self-centered ego, but of creative subjectivity. Given the misery of the human condition, these disorders appear as a ransom paid to our weaknesses for the invaluable advance achieved in the self-awareness of art and poetry." Memorable, all the same, were the preceding criticisms, in particular concerning the poet as "myth-maker," a solemn absurdity too much in fashion at the time.

FOR HIS FIFTH seminar the philosopher reserved certain other things he had to say on the limits of poetry. The temptation to Mallarméan or surrealist "magic" could be escaped, he suggested, only if the poet renounced any will to power— "even and first of all in relation to the evoking of inspiration"—this in contradiction to a well-known statement of Baudelaire's—"and if there is no fissure in the poet's fidelity to the essential disinterestedness of poetic creation." Maritain at this point was touching, in reference to the "will to power," an aberration of art that could be, in the measure of the soul exposed to it, both profound and terrible—as before the end of the year the seminars would have occasion to consider. He suggested what the writer had also tried to suggest—the recovery of wisdom in a rational understanding of the modes of the mind: "that poetry become self-aware can restore its normal state of stability and autonomy in the universe of the spirit only if the allurement of magic is counterbalanced for it by the attraction of a rational knowledge which itself has refound the full scope of its domain and a true reflective understanding of its own degrees of vision." There were, for example, in the "universe of the spirit," two principal undertakings with which poetry might seem to merge but from which it should be clearly distinguished: mysticism and metaphysics. As to the one, "poetry is from the very start oriented toward expression, and terminates in a word uttered, or a work produced; while mystical experience tends toward silence, and terminates in an immanent fruition of the absolute." As to the other, "metaphysics enjoys its possession only in the retreats of the eternal regions, while poetry finds its own at every crossroad in the wanderings of the contingent and the singular. The more real than reality, the superreal (I would not give up this word to the surrealists), the superreal which both seek, metaphysics must attain in the nature of things, while it suffices to poetry to touch it in any sign whatsoever."

The reason that these clear demarcations could so easily be blurred lay, of course, in the double nature of poetic activity—related on the one hand to mysticism through the ineffable quality of its source in poetic intuition or inspiration, and on the other hand to discursive thought through the rational virtue of art. Inspiration, Maritain added, "cannot *give form* without that operative reason which it transcends and uses as an instrument. Inspiration's power is the power of a source—not only a source which is at the beginning, as the source of a river is, but also a source which is, or should be, as far as the human condition permits, simultaneous with the entire process, from beginning to end, as is the eternal source on which all the moments of time depend. No instant in the making of the work should escape it. . . . Thus inspiration requires of necessity the steady attentiveness of a purified mind. . . . To claim to have inspiration expel intelligence and take charge of the work alone is an illusion similar to that of the *illuminati* in the order of mystics."

There were now some words of commiseration for the poets in their plight: "They are obliged to be at the same time at two different levels of the soul, out of their senses and rational, passively moved by inspiration and actively conscious, intent on an unknown more powerful than they are which a sagacious operative knowledge must serve and manifest in fear and trembling. No wonder they live in inner solitude and insecurity." And further words of counsel or prophecy: "We may believe that the conquest and discovery of the immense fields contained in poetic knowledge, and revealed by its becoming self-aware, will make the fortune of poetry, if the poets are thus quickened in their *work of creation,* that is, if their spiritual experience is deep enough, and their operative reason strong enough, to turn self-awareness into a superior sort of simplicity, through an *esprit d'enfance,* of disinterestedness, and of voluntary poverty. For the virtues required of the modern artist—I mean, in the very sphere of art, as aesthetic, not moral, virtues—are, as Max Jacob put it, evangelic in nature. 'One must be a very great poet to be a modern poet,' he said."

With this little salute to one of the saints of poetry in Paris between the wars, Maritain turned his attention now to the question of "poetic sense"—a question that more immediately involved the auditor or reader of poetry. Here the philosopher's position was already qualified and extended by what had gone before; the poetic sense would have other components besides the logical or intelligible sense. "The poetic sense is an immanent meaning made up of meanings: the intelligible meanings of the words (carried either by concepts or by images)—and the *imaginal* meanings of the words—and the more mysterious meanings of the musical relations between the words, and between the meaningful contents with which the words are laden. Thus the intelligible sense, through which the poem utters ideas, is entirely subordinate to the poetic sense, through which the poem exists."

This formulation seemed the neatest yet made on the subject—and there had been a number of efforts in the course of the seminars, beginning with that early exchange between

Maritain himself and Curtius, when Curtius declared that the words of poetry made "shapes of beauty" merely and Maritain was concerned to maintain that they also made sense, their own kind. As to the intelligible sense and the manner of its subordination, so to speak, the philosopher now wished to examine a variety of possibilities: more or less "clear" poems (with respect to the intelligible sense) and more or less "obscure" poems. His examples were all modern rather than classical work and therefore all in some degree affected by the new awareness of poetic sense and its primacy. Among "obscure" poems he found another distinction necessary—a distinction long since familiar in the best modern criticism— between poems obscure only in appearance, like Valéry's or Tate's—in fact better called "hermetic" or "difficult" by reason of concentrated intelligibility—and poems obscure in essence, like those of St. John Perse, in which "the intellectuality of the word is treasured only as a richer and more pungent vehicle of the subconscious rush of poetic knowledge." Baudelaire's poems were not obscure but clear; Yeats's *Sailing to Byzantium* (1928) was clear; the philosopher read it aloud, now, with affection. He read some verses by Apollinaire. He noted that, in poems like these, "discursive or oratorical development and liaison has been replaced by allusive streaks" but that "the intelligible sense is *explicit*." Then he read passages of Dylan Thomas, Henri Michaux, and Hart Crane, noting that in these poems, obscure by essence, "the intelligible sense dawning in the images is only *implicit*."

Further, "sometimes this implicit intelligible sense is still *determined,* I mean pointing to an object," like certain lines of Crane in *White Buildings* (1926) that "pointed to" the mysterious big city; "sometimes the implicit intelligible sense is *undetermined,* I mean pointing to no object, and only pushing our intellect in a certain direction . . . we see nothing, yet we feel there is something to be looked at." He quoted three fragments of Wallace Stevens, Jean Cocteau, and John Peale Bishop. "Our intelligence is aware of the existence of a signification, but the signified remains unknown. And it is enough for the poem to have radiance, as a black diamond has, and for the intellect to receive a delight, still more insidious perhaps as the signified is unknown: since the fact that what is signified by a sign is unknown is almost the fact that the sign signifies the unknown." He ended by reading the "Lady of silences" passage from *Ash Wednesday* (1930), a complex example of the "radiance" referred to.

Now, that specific interest that Fergusson, rather than Auerbach, had introduced into the seminars—the interest in poetry-making as a process—had moved, with Maritain, into the forefront of things, and Maritain in the course of five discussions had arrived at contemporary particulars—stanzas by Yeats and Thomas, for example—such as no seminar had yet coped with. Yet the strange thing was that even here, and despite the intensive or indeed expert familiarity, on the part of several of those present, with the matter in hand— the texts—almost no memorable interchange took place between the philosopher and his listeners. Why? To the writer, who gave ear to Maritain with that contentment that one feels when truth is spoken, the irritants that make for controversy were lacking; but could this be true in other cases? It must have been, rather, that the amplitude and open texture of Maritain's thought made it porous to the smaller though rugged components of the critic's or scholar's mind; that the discursive at this level of generality, however sharp its distinctions and however brilliantly applicable to the particulars under study, did not mesh with the discursive at the level of purely literary concern. The writer had tried approaching poetry and criticism from a point of view which would be that of neither, and had brought down a little storm on his head by so doing. But Maritain's authority was so great and his success so unqualified that the auditors seemed to rest in the light they received.

They were rewarded in the final seminar with a discourse of great richness. The philosopher finished his analysis of the inwards of the poetic process, treated of the reading or reception of poetry, and came round at last to taking account of classical poetry—a context that up to now he might have seemed to neglect in his seminars just as he had neglected it in *Art and Scholasticism*. He ended with a discussion of metaphor that seemed a stroke in the definition of genius. But his first subject for the evening was "The Internalization of Music."

"A remarkable fact, on which I should like to lay stress, is the fact that the very first effect, and sign, of poetic knowledge and poetic intuition, as soon as they exist in the soul—and even before the start of any operative exercise—is a kind of musical stir produced in the depths of the living springs in which they are born."

This inaudible "musical stir" had been attested to, the philosopher thought, by Coleridge and Mallarmé; it might now and then take place at the same time as the outpouring of words and their arrangement on the paper. "Yet my contention is that these two stages in poetic expression are distinct in nature, and that the transient expression through those *natural* signs which are the imaginal and emotional pulsions comes first, and precedes in nature the expression through those *social* signs which are the words of the language." Here, though Maritain said nothing about it and nobody picked up the point, the two terms used recalled Lessing's "natural" and "arbitrary" signs. It would have been worth a digression to clarify the difference between Maritain's and Lessing's meaning. But Wellek, who might have helped to do this, was of course by this time thoroughly out of range in New Haven. Once more, in a special but interesting matter, the seminars failed to flower into the kind of dialogue they were meant to be.

"Already in the first stage," Maritain went on, "intelligence is on the alert, only, I mean, to listen to poetic intuition, and to what is given by it, the music of imaginal and emotional pulsions; and it may happen, now and then, that at the same time the first line of the poem is given." In the second stage, "creative intelligence is also at play as working reason, accomplishing a properly so-called artistic task, applying the secondary rules of making, taking care of the arrangement of words, weighing and testing everything. Here all the patience and accuracy, all the virtues of craftsmanship are involved, and intelligence works and works again, takes up the task anew, uses all that it knows, displays the most active sagaciousness to be true to its own superior passivity, to the indivisible inspiring actuation received—poetic intuition and wordless meaning or melody—to which it does not cease listening. And this effort of supreme loyalty can be resumed even after years."

His description of the poetic process being now complete, Maritain turned to his second subject, "The Transmission of Poetic Intuition through the Poem." "Here I should like to observe," he said, "in quite a general way, that the poem is essentially an end, not a means. An end as a new creature engendered in beauty; not a means as a vehicle of communication. . . . The poetic intuition demands to be objectivized and expressed in a work. It is enough that the work exists, that this kind of a world is created. The fact that it makes the poet communicate with other human beings, even the fact that it is seen, or listened to, is in itself an effect of superabundance, terribly important for the poet, for he is a man, but additional with respect to the prime essential requirement of poetry.

"Yet the function of conveying something to men, as additional as it may be, plays, in actual fact, a secondary but crucial and necessary role. And it is absolutely essential from the point of view of the reader, or the listener. What is it which is thus conveyed? Since the work is the final objectivization of poetic intuition, what the work tends finally to convey to the soul of others is the same poetic intuition which was in the soul of the poet: not precisely as creative, but as cognitive, both of the subjectivity of the poet and of a flash of reality echoing the world. Any poetic work is a revealer. A good work delights the sense and the intellect, but the radiance, in its beauty, is first of all the radiance of the ontologic mystery grasped by the intuition of the poet; thus, when the work strikes the eyes of another, it causes a communication of intuition, a passage from creative intuition to receptive intuition.

"Of course a great many things, and often the most important, the dearest to the poet, are lost and wasted in the process. Furthermore, because of the ambiguity essential to existence and to any great existential achievement, the significance of the work is larger in one sense, and more diversified, in the minds of men than in the mind of its author. . . . What matters is that something be perceived of what was contained, even virtually, in the inexhaustible intuition from which it proceeds. . . . A mere external contemplation of a work, appreciating its qualities even with trained intelligence and aesthetic discernment, but from the outside, remains on the threshold of poetry. We must listen to the interiority of the work and to the poetic sense, be open to what it conveys. . . . What we receive, though it may be partially or deficiently, is an *intellectual gift,* a participation in the poetic knowledge and poetic intuition through which the poet has perceived a certain unique mystery in the mystery of the world; then, it is true, since poetic intuition is knowledge through emotion, we receive a participation in the poet's emotion—not in his feelings, I mean, but in his spiritualized and intentional emotion, in his emotion as *causing to see.* We receive a transient and incomparable knowing, a vision, a fleeting revelation."

It was time now to consider more closely the different ways in which this revelation could be conveyed, and the philosopher gave his attention first to the classical—the category, as it might be put, of those poems that one was learning by heart before one ever heard of Crane or Cocteau. "In classical poetry, when it comes to the second stage in expression, the expression by words—the creative impulse enters the sphere of authority of conceptual reason, and conceptual reason claims its rights to sovereignty. The intuitive content which puts pressure on the poet must be translated into concepts, and this . . . must comply with the absolute primacy of the rational connections and the logical objectivity to be expressed through the signs of this social instrument which is language. . . . The reader is confronted with a work of words which signify, through concepts subjected to the sovereignty of rational connections and logical objectivity a definite set of things, standing as objective realities before the mind—for instance a lamp which is shattered, a cloud scattered, a lute broken, and a love forgotten—or the fact that a girl named Rose Aylmer had all gifts and died. Well, if this were all, where would be the difference between poetry and a piece of information—a piece of information which, moreover, would let the essentials escape? It is not this definite *set of things* that the poem is intended to signify, this definite set of things is only a means, an intermediary, even an obstructive intermediary.

"Far beyond it, what the poem signifies is the flash of reality to which the poetic intuition points, and which it has captured obscurely in the mystery of the world, for instance the unique pity of Rose Aylmer's death as intuitively grasped by Walter Savage Landor, or the frailty of love as intuitively grasped by Shelley. Thus, in reality, the reader is confronted with a work of words which signifies, first, as an intermediary, and through concepts subjected to the primacy of logical connections, a *definite set of things* standing as objects of thought—and, second, as the final aim, a mysterious *flash of reality* which has been grasped without concept and which no concept can express. How can the reader be made aware of this signification, the true signification of the poem? Only by being brought back toward the original intuition. And this can be accomplished only through a magnetic, supra-conceptual power, which is the *music of the words* (including that of the proffered notions and images) strong enough to overcome the obstacle created by the intermediary signifi-cation, the definite set of things, and to put the eyes of our logical reason to sleep, and to lead us, captive, to a partici-pation in the poetic intuition which was born in the spiritual night of the preconceptual activity of the poet." Here he read the poem of Landor and the stanza of Shelley from *Lines* (1822). "Thus it is that the music of words is of absolute necessity for the classical poem, and together with the music of words, the rhyme, and all the prosodic requirements of a regular form. All these laws and exigencies are but the in-struments of liberation of the poetic sense."

The case of the modern poem could then be briefly put by contrast: "the supreme law of expression is no longer the law of rational and logical connections, it is the law of the inner connections between intuitive pulsions. . . . Even in the clearest modern poem, in which the expression develops along pure rational channels, the secret law which commands everything remains the law of obedience to the movement of intuitive pulsions, the verbal expression remains ceaselessly sustained and permeated by the experience of this inner emo-tional and imaginal movement . . . now the poem is a *free form,* I mean not logically bound. . . . The reader is con-fronted with a work of words which does not signify first a *definite set of things*—the wall of separation has fallen. The poem signifies only the unconceptualizable flash of reality obscurely grasped in the mystery of the world by the intuitive emotion of the poet. . . . Now . . . the music of intuitive pulsions appears in the foreground, it is revealed in full, it has become the royal instrument of poetic expression. The reader immediately listens to it."

He then read some passages of modern verse, dividing them according to the "pulsions"—for example, "Sous le pont Mirabeau coule la Seine/ Et nos amours"; "I am gall, I am heartburn/ God's most deep decree/ Bitter would have me taste/ My taste was me" and finally Yeats's poem, *After Long Silence,* of which he gave a somewhat more complex analysis in the same terms. The blackboard served him again for indicating diagrammatically the structures typical of modern and classical poetry respectively, considered as "engines for making us pass through or beyond things." Before he finished with this discussion he reemphasized his point that modern poetry was not to be understood as merely affective and sensory, not to be understood, either, as empty of concepts—they might indeed be explicitly present and used with their full intellectual meaning.

Now the philosopher pressed on to make one of his most brilliant and useful distinctions—between two typically different ways of using images metaphorically. "On the one hand, there is the way of logical thought. We know a thing in a concept: for instance the fragility of worldly felicity. Then, in order to illustrate or clarify this object known, and definitely formed or expressed in our mind, or to make it more easily communicable, we look at our inner world of ready-made images . . . and we pick up among these images another thing which participates in the same common idea of fragility, say glass, the fragility of glass. And we say that the first thing is like the second.

> Et comme elle a l'éclat du verre,
> Elle en a la fragilité.

That is what I call *purposive comparison.* . . . The comparison takes place between two things known, each one expressible and expressed on its own account; it brings one thing already known near to another thing already known, in order better or more strikingly to express the former, by superimposing the latter on it. Poetry, of course, may use such a way of expression. But of itself this purposive comparison is a rhetorical mode pertaining to the *discursus* of reason; not a creative mode pertaining to the intuitive ways of poetry.

"On the other hand, there is the intuitive way of poetry, the way of the preconscious, nonconceptual activity of the intellect"—where the images are "keeping their own wild life, beneath the threshold of the abstractive process of formation of ideas. Thus an image is seized upon as the vehicle of some intelligible meaning, radiating from poetic intuition, and in being expressed in a word, it conveys this intelligible meaning and makes a certain thing intelligibly, though not conceptually, grasped. As when Yeats said:

> The winds that awakened the stars
> Are blowing through my blood.

Here we may observe that the image is rationally, or astronomically, rather questionable, for in nature no star has ever been awakened by any wind. But this is precisely, I think, a confirmation of my point. Yeats did not write, and could not have written, according to the classical pattern: "Just as the winds awakened the stars" (one term in a purposive comparison), "so, etc." (the other term in a purposive comparison). In reality his image was not taken from the facts of astronomy and the externals of the imagination, it came from the *preconceptual imagination,* and was used only, irrespective of any truth already known about the winds and the stars, to make known and expressed something which is not even named, say, the poet's passionate exaltation.

"That is what I call the *immediately illuminating image,* without the intermediary of any concept. . . . Two things are not compared, but rather one thing is made known through the image of another. One thing already known is not brought near to another thing already known. One thing which was unknown—only contained in the obscurity of emotive intuition—is discovered, and expressed, by means of another already known, and by the same stroke their similarity is discovered: all that, as Reverdy put it, as a result of the creativity of the spirit." He ended by quoting Marianne Moore's line: "the lion's ferocious chrysanthemum head," in which presumably the ineffable intuition, never made known before, concerned the unique decorative beauty of the lion. It seemed to the writer later that although this distinction of Maritain's was like a sword, cutting rhetoric from poetry proper in the matter of metaphor, it would have been possible to improve it in view of the lines from Yeats. The thing already known in that case was not one thing but three: winds, stars, and kindling lights, and all three were brought near the ineffable thing, the thing not yet made known, the exaltation of the poet.

The sheets mimeographed for the evening contained a further, or fourth, heading—"Perennial Poetry"—but of this great subject, since the time was up long since, the auditors were to hear nothing but the name from Maritain on this occasion. It would be Fergusson's pleasure later to prod the philosopher into writing a further essay, on Dante, in which he might satisfy the director's passion for seeing due honor paid to the Dantesque. But what Maritain had now accomplished, if it did not fully qualify as the "*organon* that would mediate between philosophy and poetry," came closer to fulfilling that ultimate end of the seminars than anyone had succeeded in doing before. His natural opponents, whenever they proved capable of articulating their reservations—as they did not do on the spot—would object that the *organon* supplied by Maritain mediated between philosophy and poetry only if one accepted Maritain's belief that philosophy was Aristotelian, Thomist, comprehensive, one, and perennial, and that he spoke for it. For their part they would recognize the existence of Maritain's philosophy and other philosophies, distinct in vocabulary and import—Cassirer's, for instance. Though he must dutifully record it, this kind of objection would not strike the writer as very grave.

But if "mediation" were achieved, as the writer thought it more or less was, that, too, left desirable things to be done. A new work of art would stand no less in need of appreciation and judgment; the rest was not silence, but was, precisely, literary criticism.

Chapter Eight

SUBJECTIVITY IS ABSOLUTE ਏ▲ ERICH KAHLER, DAVID SACHS, E. B. O. BORGERHOFF, JOSEPH KERMAN, EDMUND KING, AND FRANCIS FERGUSSON ON MANN'S *DOCTOR FAUSTUS*

L ITERARY CRITICISM would be, at least, the task of keeping things straight when it came to particular books and poems—a task made easier if it were backed by general thought as profound and clear as Maritain's, but, still, another kind of task, homelier and more social. In the spring series of seminars the Princeton people took on the specific burden of criticism with respect to *Doctor Faustus,* by Thomas Mann, six men in turn on six successive Thursdays reporting on this novel to the end that its poetic and intelligible meaning be explored and its value appraised. As usual, the question of how these proceedings availed the university and the commonweal could be answered only with argument, not with demonstration, but the argument in this case would have a little more force than usual. The author of the book was a man of letters of the heaviest calibre. At least two of his previous works, *Death in Venice* (1912) and *The Magic Mountain* (1924), were enrolled among the classics of modern literature, known to every honors candidate in the humanities. Before the war he had beguiled the readers of the United States with a prose epic of continental duration, *Joseph and His Brothers* (1933–1943). In *Doctor Faustus,* it was said, the aging master had made a valedictory fable of the artist's life and Germany's together; if the fable really applied, really struck home, then this literary work might demand a place in the liberal education; or if it did not, and in the measure it did not, then it was important that its deficiencies be noted. Would Leverkühn join von Aschenbach and Castorp in the undergraduate imagination, where intellect got its bent and portentous views were formed? The seminars at Princeton might easily determine whether he would or not.

The writer bought the book and gave it a close reading, convincing himself, at any rate, that it was going to be a difficult case. He had his bias in the matter, for he had responded with derision when young to the elaborate infatuations of von Aschenbach and Castorp, and rereading had not greatly chastened him. He felt that these famous works were mainly written from the outside as abstract problems rather than along any line of inspiration or "pulsions"—that they were engineered rather than composed. He felt a unique sympathy with Mme. Chauchat in *The Magic Mountain* if only because so far as the mountain went, and with it all Mann's people and paraphernalia, she could take it or leave it and rather tended to leave it. Bluntly stated, this was the writer's point of view—one that seemed, as a matter of taste and temperament, almost to disqualify him from rendering critical judgment. When he read the early works of Thomas Mann he blessed the wit of Jane Austen and the existential seriousness of James Joyce. But then, to complicate everything, the *Joseph* series had arrived and appealed to him mightily as an original feat of speculative comedy in a style, often enough, of great charm and elevation. He wondered if Mrs. Lowe-Porter were getting better at her job. However that might be, it gave him to think again; and now he thought he could understand the two attitudes toward *Faustus* that were already formed at Princeton before the symposium began: Fergusson's wicked irreverence and Blackmur's shrewdly fascinated respect. In this irrepressible conflict there was much amusement and a glimpse of despair, as when one evening at dinner Blackmur, a man slow indeed to impatience, was provoked to exclaim, "I won't let you say that, Francis," as if to save the director of the seminars from himself.

And in fact there now settled upon the seminars, even though the subject was prodigious, a rather relaxed and family air. Only the first of the six seminar leaders was a visitor, but even he was a Princetonian—Erich Kahler—with whom most of the company were on friendly terms. Neither Wellek nor Maritain came to any of the evenings. Warm weather was arriving, and Thursday night had become a routine. Consider the little scene putting itself together as eight o'clock comes round: the door tried by the first comer, who will step around the corner and sit on the stairs; then a couple more, sauntering down the long hall past the offices of Far Eastern studies; then the director arrives and opens up, flips the little switches, and the room displays itself alight and orderly, with four rows of collapsible chairs, seven or eight in a row, facing the big table. It is five minutes of eight. Friends greet arriving friends, coats are plumped in a corner, conversations begin, smoke rises, people fetch the atrocious ash trays of the Poetry Room and balance them on their knees or put them on the floor. The man with the briefcase or typescript arrays himself behind the table. At five minutes past the hour the last dinner party comes in from La Hière's and distributes itself in the front row. The director says a few gentle and hopeful words and the talk begins.

IT WAS appropriate enough that the first seminar should be given by Erich Kahler, an old friend of Thomas Mann's who had left Germany, as Mann did, in the thirties, and who now taught at Cornell. If Kahler's knowledge of the book's *provenance* were communicated to the company, their deliberations would be that much better informed. In talking of the origin and growth of the Faustian "motif," Kahler picked up certain mythical or archetypal rumors in a very Mannian way, noticing for example that the figure of Prometheus seemed to hold *both* protagonists of the later Faustus story—"the mortal, transgressing his God-imposed limits, and the god (or demigod) forfeiting his status through an act of revolt. In each case the punishment is perpetual torture and Inferno." He was able to say that although contact with the supernatural, and cosmic dualism, were both pre-Christian, the division of magic into white and black, propitious and evil, came about in the first Christian centuries. Then, also, the rival pagan deities were degraded to devils and left their traces in the devil's appearance: for example the goat-foot and horns of Pan, the limp of Hephaestus, the trident of Poseidon. The original Faustus was none other than Simon Magus, supposedly the founder of Gnosticism, a magician who gave a flying performance before Nero; he perished, *modo Icario,* when St. Peter called on the devils to drop him over Rome. So ran the tales or *Recognitiones* collected in writing as early as the fourth century. He not only took the name Faustus, but his consort was a woman called Helena, later confounded with Helen of Troy. Devil's partners in medieval times included Gilles de Raiz, companion in arms of Joan of Arc, an ogre and bluebeard who was burned as a repentant sinner.

"We may now consider," said Kahler, "Johannes or Georg Sabellicus Helmstedter, who, inspired by a new edition of the Simonian 'Recognitions,' represented himself as Faust junior or Faust II. The time was the beginning of the sixteenth century, the period when the Church broke asunder, when humanism, secular thinking, science, and natural philosophy were flourishing. In all this spiritual and intellectual turmoil, the borderlines between science and the magic arts were still fluid. Great thinkers like Kepler, Tycho de Brahe, and Paracelsus concerned themselves with semi-magical procedures; mysticism and demonology were rampant, witches' trials were the order of the day, and the popular imagination battened on the theme of magic and supranatural powers. All of this at least partly accounts for the tremendous and disproportionate popularity of that quack and braggart, the original Doctor Faustus. . . . The legacy of his popularity was the pseudobiographical compilation of anecdotes and stories dealing with this Doctor Faustus which was published by Spies in 1587. This book, which drew upon the motifs of all earlier Faustus stories eked out with details from current magical practices and experiences, has become the basis of all subsequent Faustus literature. Even Thomas Mann follows it closely in describing certain crucial stages of Adrian Leverkühn's career."

It would have been interesting to see just how closely Mann had followed the old book, beyond diverting his precocious and arrogant hero from theology to magic (in this case music) and putting him in league with the devil. But Kahler quoted nothing from the antique text. He noted general similarities: " . . . the recurrent feature of extensive travels, not only all over the globe but transcendent travels upward and downward, into the heights and the depths, with visits to Paradise and Hell. . . . And here, too, comes the revival of the Helena motif: Mephostophiles furnishes Faustus with a whole harem of mortal women among whom is the spirit whom he believed to be Helen of Troy. . . . Only one last element from the popular Faust Book, which found its way into Christopher Marlowe's and into Thomas Mann's Doctor Faustus requires stressing. It is the last supper—an inversion of Christ's Last Supper—to which Faust invites his dearest friends the night before he is due to be summoned by the devil." Marlowe and Mann, he thought, had at least one thing in common in their treatment of the later episodes of the tragical history. In the drama, we feel passing over the traditionally grisly action the flurry of "a very personal shudder, an anxiety springing from a deeper spiritual source, from a longing for faith, perhaps, and from a new loneliness, forsakenness, which this atheistic libertine, Marlowe, may have felt within a still thoroughly Christian world. This shudder is entirely lacking in Goethe's tragedy, but it reappears, in very different circumstances, in Thomas Mann's novel."

179

Goethe's Faust, he said, was not a specific individual but a mythical figure standing for modern man, and his tragedy was a compendium of the intellectual content of Goethe's age. "It is Goethe's final attempt to comprehend the whole of his world. . . . Hence it is one of the earliest, perhaps . . . *the* earliest great literary work to assume that cryptically abstract character which inevitably marks all important works of art in our day." (This *obiter dictum* could have been more carefully phrased, and no doubt it would have been if Kahler had heard Maritain.) "This was still the time of humanistic, classicistic *Bildung*, of the emergence of the sciences from romantic spirituality with its universalistic outlook. The borderline between the arts and sciences was still fluid; it was the time of Hegel and Schelling, when spirit, rational and poetic, was held in highest esteem. Goethe was the last to hold this intellectual universe together. The cultural climate of our present world, one hundred and fifty years later, is very different. The Christian Heaven is deserted; it is replaced by astrophysical infinities. . . . There is no haven, no resting place, no boundary in sight. The humanistic universe has broken asunder, the sciences have immensely expanded and grown apart from each other. They have become specialized and functionalized; they have parted ways with the arts—and where is philosophy? Its remains are the various kinds of logic (symbolic, linguistic, analytical)." (Here again one wished that Kahler were in a position at least to refer to Maritain.) "While rationalism triumphs in the many corners of science and technology, human reason as a controlling force is fading away. Intellect, thinking, spirit, have been utterly discredited . . . by the . . . crises . . . of our century. Between the artist, the man of Mind and his society, a terrible rift has developed. . . . As a result, art and mind have become problematic to themselves."

Maritain had also contemplated, but in his own terms, this unhappy state of affairs; but Kahler's understanding was evidently nearer to that in which Mann had moved toward the Faustus "motif." "He starts out from discipline and respectability—also artistic respectability—and ends up in a book which is an almost unveiled, almost exhibitionistic confessional. The paradoxical quality of this book is a combination of a high-strung, indeed rather overwrought, structural artistry in which not a single trait is left to playful divagation, but everything is strictly calculated in its correlation with everything else and with the whole—a combination, I say, of such an almost mathematical artistry with an outburst of what he had carefully screened and disguised throughout his life. This is what makes this book so profoundly moving."

The mathematical artistry was indeed there for all to see, though one might be of two opinions as to its value, but one apparently had to take Kahler's word for the "confessional" quality. If allusions of this sort must be made, the writer thought, should they not be explained? What was it that Mann was supposed to have carefully screened and disguised throughout his life—a visit to a brothel, for heaven's sake? A pact with the devil? Homosexuality? Kahler simply said no more on this point, leaving at least one auditor mystified as to how the steadily industrious German man of letters, father of six, resembled the diseased and fitful genius Adrian Leverkühn. Kahler had not, of course, meant to say that appreciation of the novel depended on knowledge of Mann's life, but he had clearly implied that only a knowledge of Mann's life could make the book "profoundly moving," and the writer found this irritating, especially since Kahler kept the knowledge in question to himself. A little later he was again speaking of a "fundamental, personal problem" at the root of Mann's early work and then produced a series of generalities: culture and intellect represented as decadence, love associated with decline, the artist seen as "a pariah from the start, iridescent with suspect hues, shading into the daemon, the invalid, the social outcast, the adventurer, the criminal." It was surely a loose definition of a fundamental personal problem that left one to choose among these conditions the one that might in fact fit the author. From Mann's early stories the writer had derived a suspicion that Mann's shameful secret did indeed concern his knowledge of himself as an artist, but that it was nothing very glamorous or iridescent— only his awareness of being a sensationalist who got his effects by intelligence and an iron nerve and was essentially, in Maritain's sense, no poet at all.

But now Kahler tackled the progression of import in Mann's big novels. "*The Magic Mountain* is the great divide in Thomas Mann's work. Here, we come upon an alteration in the fundamental motif. The normality of the normal is no longer secure. Before this, Mann's work had been dedicated to the problem of life's boundaries: by means of his various outcasts he had delimited an area of healthy, normal, insouciant life. Now he discovers signs of decay on both sides of the boundary—in the world of action as well as up there on the magic mountain. Dying is part of living as living is part of dying. The ambivalence, the parodox of all living things, is at last revealed. . . . The *Joseph* novels open up the remotest layers of our mythical, totemistic past. . . . Joseph rises out of these regions in a long, precarious process of sublimation, and there rises with him, within him, the sublimated, spiritualized God-image—he being the prefiguration of Jesus. He too bears a stigma from the beginning, the stigma of Grace. Grace again is full of abysses and wiles, and great discipline is required of its possessor. But for one supreme moment, the norm seems to have shifted to spiritual man. For one moment only. Joseph's counterpart was to appear, the Antichrist, the man stigmatized by the *curse* of spirit: Faustus."

As to the difference between this work and Goethe's, he made a distinction that recalled what Maritain had said of the descent of Beauty into the human heaven. "Even in Goethe's Faust there is a full recognition of the parodox of earthly life: the ever-striving, self-expanding, self-transcending spirit is by that very token unable to fulfull its destiny. But for Goethe the norm still stands . . . not down below, conventionalized in a world of middle-class normality, but high above, in the sphere of a Christian Heaven. . . . For Adrian Leverkühn no such above and beyond, no such measure and haven and authorization, is any longer available. His tragedy is seen from below, and in relation to a below. His problem is the relation of mind to its common basis, to the human community from which it is divorced. Sin is no longer the breach of an absolute norm, rather it is the Adamitic break with the community of creatures. . . . What there is of Heaven is just as internalized as what there is of Hell—on the one hand there is the ecstasy of artistic creation, on the other hand the disease as punishment of a biologized sin. Mind, in its isolation and desolation, builds its own Heaven, and has to pay for it with its own Hell. Indeed, in the career of a mind relegated to its own infinity, there is hardly any clear distinction between Heaven and Hell, between Good and Evil, for both are tainted by each other—the good being a *Fleur du Mal* and vice versa."

KAHLER'S paper noticeably lacked any extra-German framework of literary reference; there was one passing reference to Valéry but that was all—nothing to relate Mann's effort to those of his great contemporaries. The writer must note that the "dialogue" of the seminars had failed again; Kahler had not heard Maritain and Maritain was not present for Kahler. But surely the rest of the company could put things together in their heads? One of the things mysteriously revealed by the Princeton evenings was that the dark backward and abysm of time could swallow in a week or two the most brilliant discourse, or at least so obscure it that almost nobody seemed able to make play with it afresh. Fergusson obviously found this difficult to take in; he would be moved to break the ice for the indicated intercourse, recalling that Mr. So-and-so had said this and that, most pertinently; but usually that would about end it. So now, oddly enough, the company not only got nowhere in talk about the peculiar agony of

Mann's Faust but no one even mentioned the bald fact which Kahler's phrase *Fleur du Mal* must have called up: Baudelaire, of whom so much had been said in the seminars, had been, like Mann's hero, a victim of syphilis.

Modest points were briskly made on the following Thursday by David Sachs, whose subject was "Character and Value in *Doctor Faustus.*" He complimented Mann's artfulness and deliberation in characterizing his narrator, Serenus Zeitblom, whom with some acidity Sachs called a bore, and he said: "Serenus's fixity, his fixation upon Adrian, is a *sine qua non* for Faustus. If he were to have any reality as a father or husband, if he had been given the power of his humanistic convictions, he would have compromised the portrayal of Leverkühn . . . the monomania of Serenus, and of the work as a whole, would have been dissipated. . . . To refuse to accept Serenus as he is, and for what he is, is to quarrel from the outset. Yet no alternative seems possible." As to the characterization of Leverkühn, Faustus himself, Sachs considered the relationships and sentiments of the hero: with the whore, prefigured in the butterfly *Hetaera esmeralda;* with the violinist Rudi Schwerdtfeger; and with the child Echo. The first of course was the deliberate embrace of disease, the pact with the devil, "the expedient," in Zeitblom's words, "of a great gift threatened with sterility"; the second Sachs interpreted as an "experiment in happiness" against the interests of the great gift, which could only be replenished by Rudi's death, as it would again be replenished by the screaming death of the child.

Just how plausible this frightful version of inspiration might be, Sachs refused to judge, leaving that question to Fergusson who had undertaken to meditate on it for the final evening. One could anticipate a little, the writer thought. Certain things would be sure to come to mind in any such meditation. No great imagination could fail to find interest in the fiendish, and one who knew verse would think of Yeats's memorable Robert Artisson, of Tate's brooding on angels and archfiends and the next room crowded with wolves. But that imagination under any human circumstances should be fructified exclusively by the devil—this was hard to take, and to the writer it rang as false as a line that Blackmur had tried in a recent short poem of his, a line roughly epitomizing Leverkühn's case: "The fiend fouls me and I create." As to the speculation that accompanied the Faustian daring, the description of it that Mann had put in Leverkühn's mouth seemed all too plausible. Sachs quoted his summing up:

> My sin is greater than that it can be forgiven me, and I have raised it to its height, for my head speculated that the contrite unbelief in the possibility of Grace and pardon might be the most intriguing of all for the Everlasting Goodness, where yet I see that such impudent calculation makes compassion impossible. Yet basing upon that I went further in speculation and reckoned that this last depravity must be the uttermost spur for Goodness to display its everlastingness. And so then, that I carried on an atrocious competition with the Goodness above, which were more inexhaustible, it or my speculation.

This did not, incidentally, seem to bear out Kahler's statement that the "above and beyond" were not available to Mann's Faust. Evidently Mann meant to show that it became available at the end, or that the hero thought so. But in Sachs's judgment this revelation of the damned spirit was too late to save Mann's portrait of Leverkühn:

"Unlike the other excesses, the reiteration of Adrian's attributes points to the central weakness in *Faustus:* the unrealized image of greatness, the irrational exaltation of its hero. . . . Adrian's greatness is, as it were, a postulate of the system which governs *Faustus*. That his magnificence should be postulated rather than evinced is the imaginative failure of the book. Mann falters badly in his attempt to persuade one of Leverkühn's superlative intellectuality; in serious conversation Adrian is pretentious, obscurantistic, and at times ridiculous—a portrait no *Übermensch* should have to endure. True, Mann's verbal presentation of Adrian's musical genius is remarkable; but in no other regard does Leverkühn seem powerful or extraordinary. It is said, and repeatedly, that he is so, yet he affects only the lives, never the characters, of others. This, coupled with the tawdriness of his proclaimed intellectual gifts, leaves unrealized the charisma, the super-ego glow, which Mann intended."

This judgment seemed especially warranted when one thought of Mann's Joseph, by contrast so agreeable, and so fully realized, too, precisely in his quality of greatness or "charisma." But Sachs had done Leverkühn less than justice if the leader of the discussion on the third evening were right.

Now that Warren had disappeared into an Army base, Borgerhoff took his place on the program, and he prepared his study by reading all Mann's fiction from beginning to end. His paper on *Doctor Faustus* had the virtue of treating it as a work of fiction among other works of fiction—seeing it, so to speak, on the bookshelf, while interpreting its infernal or apocalyptic color in terms of *genre*. "From Nature to the Supernatural" was his title; "*Doctor Faustus* as an Expressionist Novel." If the present discussions had not yet been related to the previous year's seminars on fiction, Borgerhoff at once and firmly established a connection.

"Mann began his career at the end of the last century and therefore in a period dominated by naturalist theory . . . it was for naturalism to attack the whole logical and rational structure of the novel and the drama and to wish to substitute for this what Zola called the 'logic of nature' or 'life itself.' This was not to be accomplished simply by treating new subject matter; it had to be done by treating the subject matter differently, and in accord with a new view of it. Impressionist painting offers a useful analogy. Naturalism therefore prepared the way for the development of all sorts of modern

means for suggesting, for causing to be felt though not understood, not only the illogical and the irrational but also the
uncanny and the ultra-natural. . . . The romantics most often
chose this subject matter as something other than the dull
reality of nature, human or other, which their realistic contemporaries were trying to imitate. Whereas since 1880 or so
it has seemed more and more possible to suggest the operation
of mysterious forces in a context of nature and of society and
to set them forth in an allusive style where the logic, if there
is any at all, lies behind the events, to be sensed only in an
understanding of the whole or in a surrender to an atmosphere
or a mood. Thus the work which the illogical or the irrational
have been made to do is new. Or so it seems to me. If this
is labelled neoromanticism, and Mann has been put in that
category, I have no objection."

On this well-stated premise Borgerhoff could do all possible justice to Mann's intent as an artist and to his work as
a whole. He found it all-of-a-piece in a systematic dualism
or ambivalence, first suggested in *Buddenbrooks* (1900), in
which the personal and the autobiographical—the realistic
and naturalistic—were to become more and more clearly the
scene of action of mysterious and supernatural forces, often
sinister, conveyed not openly through events but through
increasing ambiguity of style. It was enough, for example,
in *Death in Venice,* that the operation of the supernatural was
made a possibility; in *The Magic Mountain,* besides the plain
eeriness of the setting, and the style "laid over with a perverse
glee," there were explicit suggestions of irrational and evil
forces. "Here, then, in this new magic world," the critic said,
"Mann is free to rearrange expressively the disintegrated elements of bourgeois culture . . . the work thus in some respects resembles an allegory . . . and *Doctor Faustus* by its
very title tells us that it is a morality." But by "expressively"
Borgerhoff meant—and added—that throughout this rear-
rangement there was in fact a deepening subjectivity, as the
novelist relied more and more seriously on the inexplicable

and the questionable—a subjectivity that reached its extreme, it seemed, in *Faustus*.

Here, in the first chapters, the reality or credibility of the supernatural was established in the natural—in the fantastic ambiguity of nature and the deep trickery underlying natural beauty. In keeping with Mann's usual "symphonic" structure, the fate of Leverkühn was foreshadowed; but the reader was prepared, too, to believe in it, and in Evil, and in the devil, as operating forces in the world. The critic now spoke at length on a closely related matter: the way in which the narrative handled, or "rearranged," time itself—a serious undertaking that Mann had tried before. In this case the novelist, through Zeitblom, repeated his favorite distinction between the time of the succession of events narrated, the time taken to record them, and the time taken to read the narrative; besides this, in *Faustus,* the action progressed from the primitive and archaic through atmospheres of the Middle Ages and the Reformation to modern times—and then sank back again. "In Adrian, in Adrian's music as in the destiny of the German nation, all this past is present. 'Everything must be in the air.' "

Borgerhoff's reflections on the "modern" section, in Munich, added something to what Sachs had had to say about Mann's failure to create characters. Here, for the first time in the novel, Mann presented a society—a true novelistic endeavor. "In this combination of bourgeois and bohemian society there is a strange collection of half creatures, intermediate or mixed types, all described with great care for their peculiarities and for their social, national, psychological, sexual, artistic and domestic impurity. Is this a projection of Adrian's indifference to almost all of them? Or is it Zeitblom's jealousy? Is it simply Mann's mode of character portrayal? His characters retain a quality of abstraction because they represent something larger than themselves: they represent an aspect of being and generally in some exclusive or imperfect or incomplete way. Perhaps the split which Mann has always seemed to sense in himself leads him to create almost nothing but split or half characters. . . . It is what all the characters taken together add up to that interests Mann. One penalty for this sacrifice of the part to the expressiveness of the whole is that the reader is tempted to forget that a given character has any character at all. Zeitblom is taken as caricature and Leverkühn as a symbol. But Zeitblom has a life, a profession, a family, friends, memories, ideals, hopes and fears. Leverkühn, it is true, seems to have almost none of these, yet if his heart is cold his conscience is warm and this is enough of a personal conflict for anyone. He knows his coldness and he doesn't like it. He tries indeed to overcome it in ways which are of course the wrong ways. If Mann had cared to dwell on this conflict we should perhaps have had a recognizable novelistic character."

In such a passage as this the writer for one had to recognize the great critical virtue of justice—a virtue perhaps not enough mentioned in the course of the seminars, but one upon which everything really turned. It was just to perceive within this novel, in so many ways antipathetic, and even suspect, to the sound and central tradition for which Maritain had spoken, a genuine pang of spirit as well as a special strain of artistry; this was to give the great German his due. Justice would have to take account not only of the dissatisfaction that Sachs had expressed but of other and more serious matters, soon to be defined with asperity; but meanwhile Borgerhoff placed the mind of the mature artist at the level where, in all conscience, it belonged. He also placed it in the context of creative subjectivity discussed by Maritain as the specifically modern plight of poetry.

"Here in *Doctor Faustus* we are admittedly in the extraordinary. Magic and divinity are quite completely identified with nature, society, nationality, and history. I think that if Mann had not believed that 'Everything must be in the air,' or at least had not known the novelistic possibilities of such a notion, *Doctor Faustus* would not have been written. As it is, the introduction of the supernatural into the natural which Mann pretended in *Joseph in Egypt* to dare with hesitation (though the entire work is permeated with a sense of it) is now made total and deliberate. Perhaps this fact bears some relation to a recognition of the impossibility of real or exclusive objectivity and of the fact that whether or not the novelist imitates this or that aspect of being he always imitates—that is, expresses—himself, reassured by the belief that in so doing he is after all expressing total experience, any given motion of the mind being a reflection of all being."

WITH THE FOURTH evening clarity arrived in one important if not crucial department of *Faustus* criticism—the realm of musical theory. The baton now passed into the hands of Joseph Kerman, a musician and musicologist then teaching at the Westminster Choir School in Princeton, whose essays on musical subjects appeared from time to time in the *Hudson Review*. Kerman lost no time in stating the case in the light in which it appeared to him:

"Thomas Mann's musical ideas run as follows: music is basically subjective and sensual; to achieve greatness in music, this sensuality has to be overcome by objective technique, which effects a paradoxical return to the 'truly personal.' . . . Behind this is a conviction of the diabolic nature of music: the basic sensuality is by definition diabolic; objective technique is the devil's alchemy; and the final synthesis into greatness is the devil's gift to Leverkühn, for which he suffers the pains of the little sea maiden. . . . The unanimity on this extraordinary musical system creates a hypnotic and slightly insane effect, which I am afraid characterizes only too well the sort of intellectual atmosphere in which some artists develop.

"I do not know what is more dubious about this system, the initial terms which it imposes, or the final conclusions reached. . . . I believe that behind the notion of the sensuality

190

of music must be the widely noted fact that of all the arts music seems to be able to affect human beings most immediately and most strongly. In this very special sense, then, one might call music 'basically human' or 'basically sensuous'; but to extend this to 'basically sensual' or 'basically erotic' is not only illogical but out of contact with realities; the art of music has less force in this area than the dance, the graphic arts, and several varieties of literature. Behind the notion of the necessary objectivity of music is the generally observed fact that great art is achieved by means of highly sophisticated technique. . . . The error of Mann's extension here is the idea of the necessary *objectivity* of technique, with its fetish of strictness and mathematical construction. Common sense suggests at once that the basically human quality, as I have defined it, is exactly the element to be cherished and experimented with; that technique consists exactly in nourishing this quality, rather than in contradicting it."

The attentive amanuensis of the seminars, if there had been one at this point, might have set it down that the basically human quality in the arts had been more closely defined by Jacques Maritain, who had also insisted that this quality—creative intuition—was the one above all to be cherished. Kerman's statement nevertheless refreshed the air. Common sense had as a matter of fact been very slow, in the universities and among the critics, to suggest that technique "consists exactly in nourishing this quality" rather than in mathematical construction; indeed Mann's work as a whole reflected the error with which Kerman here charged his musical theory in *Faustus*. He went on to sketch an accusation more serious than that of error. What Kerman especially wished to demolish was the master premise of all the musical theory in the novel—the antithesis between harmony and polyphony which was made to correspond to antitheses between subjectivity and objectivity, sensuality and strictness. The critic's analysis now became learned as well as sharp.

"To our ears the earliest polyphony maintains to a great degree the linear aspects of monody in each of its constituent lines; but even from the very first it was thought necessary to adjust the lines in order to form pleasing or correct vertical sonority or *harmony*, at least at the main punctuation points of the individual lines. Concern for harmony was born with the first thought of polyphony; there is no polyphony without harmony, and scarcely any harmony without at least simple polyphony; the study of writing polyphonically, *counterpoint*, consists of combining lines so that they produce satisfactory harmony at the same time that they retain some linear independence. And so harmony and polyphony are not irreconcilable opposites. Precisely speaking, they are different ways of looking at the same thing; more loosely, one can speak of 'polyphonic music' when the linear aspect seems foremost, and of 'harmonic music' when the vertical sonorities seem most important. These terms are of course imprecise and relative, and are regularly used rather differently in dealing with music of different periods. Mann's usage, however, is something still else: the desideratum is not polyphony, nor music which is primarily linear in interest, but polyphonic music which is so intent on the linear element that the harmonic is either undeveloped, slighted, ignored, or deliberately coarsened. Talk in this book of 'polyphonic' or 'contrapuntal' music is taken in this sense; all other music, including that of Bach and Palestrina, is considered 'harmonic.' Along these lines, judgments are made upon the subjectivity or objectivity of musical styles and individual compositions. In Leverkühn's *Apocalypsis cum figuris,* the music of the devils is completely harmonic, whereas the angels perform in bitterly dissonant harmony."

Kerman's close-knit argument could not be paraphrased without loss, but demanded quotation. He went on: "It stands to reason, then, that the Middle Ages is to form an important anchor to the theory as a whole. Here, at a comfortable distance from known factors, and out of earshot of known music, we seem to find the cool strict approach to musical composition, in the era of diabolism and its strict control by the Church, the era of art in the service of 'cult' rather than 'culture.' Progress, indeed, is a reaction [regression, he meant] to this distant and alchemistic age, which exerts the same sort of spell over Mann as over the romantic writers a hundred years before his time. He shares their approximate information about this period, which for him is more closely associated with Luther and Albrecht Dürer than with Charlemagne, Chartres or St. Thomas. In music, the Middle Ages is the time of the Netherlandish Schools—though only Ockeghem and Obrecht in the last quarter of the fifteenth century will really fit; neither Dufay before them nor Josquen after them can deny the charge of especial fondness for pure harmony. Within this narrow section of so-called medieval music, it can certainly be said that the linear aspect of polyphony was emphasized, and that composers had a liking for certain mathematical devices in their music, such as canons, inversions, and arbitrary *cantus firmi*. The point can be made more securely, as a matter of fact, with music of an earlier century. But these mathematical devices are much exaggerated in the old-fashioned accounts of the Netherlandish Schools, which Mann and his advisors know. They appear mainly in their largest compositions, the cyclic Mass ordinaries, and are there employed not to subdue the devil, deny the sensuality of the naked human voice, or obey dictates of the Church, but rather as a naïve and often competitive effort to answer the purely technical problem of musical organization. The close restriction exerted on these composers by the Church is likewise overstated; they were also writers of highly developed secular *chansons*. Of course no medieval composer was as emotional as Gustav Mahler, but Mann's objective frigidity is a poor description for the mysticism of an Ockeghem, the melancholy of a Binchois, or the sensitive manliness of a Landino.

"I think, in fact, that these antitheses of harmonic against polyphonic, subjective against objective, and trivial against great, exist on totally separate planes and cannot be made to correspond. This is borne out on more familiar territory by the treatment of the seventeenth and eighteenth centuries, the so-called baroque and classical periods of music. Mann is strangely silent about this whole time; we are presented with a theory of musical strictness and reaction which ignores Bach, and a theory of musical greatness which ignores Bach, Handel, Haydn, and Mozart. . . . One cannot escape the suspicion that Bach's humdrum piety lacks the flair necessary to inspire our devil-worshipers. . . . Hard, too, to deny that Bach's chorale-preludes are more subjective than the Brandenburg Concertos, for all that they are demonstrably more polyphonic. It is, however, with Mozart and Haydn that the inadequacy of the theory is most plain. I have no understanding of the idea of the 'truly personal' which does not rest on certain compositions of Mozart, and only the most arbitrary idea of 'strictness' which does not include the exquisite limitations under which the classical composers worked. Diabolism, linear polyphony, and mathematical constructions did not flourish during the Enlightenment, and its music has no meaning for the modern Faust.

"On the music of the late nineteenth century, our characters are not too frank. They say that the conventions of music have all been used up during this time, that they are now, that is, in 1900 and the succeeding decades, useful for parody only. This is at once a contradiction, of course, for if the conventions are useful for parody they are not used up—and parody as Mann seems to use the term has a broader meaning than we ordinarily expect, involving I think any objective, self-conscious use of material for some ends unsuspected in its original form. In Beethoven's last period, says Kretsehmar, conventions were employed in this special way; he does not say that they were 'used up.' But what seems to me most significant about this is the inflation of the task of the artist at the beginning of our century. All artists, not only Mann and Leverkühn, have had to revise and recreate the conventions left to them by their teachers; I do not see that conventions have ever been so depleted as to be unavailable for a succeeding time. The problems of working out a new vocabulary are the constant conditions of art, in 1600, 1750, 1900, or 1950. A truly romantic combination of fantastic faith in history and fantastic distortion of it drives Mann to the conclusion that conditions around 1900 were so intolerable as to require a Faustian link with the devil. Beethoven did not need it; only Leverkühn, with the crushing weight of romanticism upon him, has to plumb the ocean beds of pain and evil to break through again to the great, the truly personal. Let me again refer with anticipation of Mr. Fergusson's discussion of the *poète damné*, and let me quote a still voice after the Faustian hurricane, Mr. Roger Sessions: 'For those problems, though certainly difficult in the extreme, are inherently of exactly the same nature as those faced by former periods; and if we can retain our spirits before them, such pessimism will appear not only thoroughly destructive, but essentially unjustified. The problems require our best efforts, that is all.' "

IN VIEW of everything that had now been said about *Doctor Faustus,* the title of the fifth evening's paper seemed a trifle ambitious: "Where Does Mann Really Stand?" The inquirer, Edmund King of the Romance Languages department, pointed out that *Faustus* was the first of Mann's works in which he adopted the device of a narrator. "In doing this Mann is saying: I imagine an action of such magnitude that I cannot conceive it and its meaning as a whole, as I could in my earlier works; I believe that the mind of the artist engaged in such an act is inseparable from the meaning of his conception; any representation of myself engaged in this act would presuppose a kind of artistic arrogance and would be, according to my assumptions, inadequate; I will create a character less wise than myself, naïve enough to undertake what I in my sophistication cannot undertake directly, yet troubled like myself over whether he can really get at the heart of the matter; the other way, my own limitations would limit my conception; but this way my character's limitations will be a part of the conception." In this whole scheme of the book, in the technique of reporting the action through Zeitblom, King thought there was "profound irresponsibility"—not limited, therefore, to the irresponsibility that Kerman had found in the Faustian musical theory. There was another way of putting it: the whole novel could be considered a letter from Mann on the analogy of the crucial letter in which Leverkühn relates to Zeitblom his "anecdote" of the brothel. Just as Zeitblom had to supply part of the meaning of that anecdote, so "from the point of view of the reader of the book, both the inherently meaningful action and the commentary on that action become the anecdote. The process of the subjectivization of meaning reaches out of the book and embraces the audience. Subjectivism is absolute."

That haze of irony by which in fact the reader of the novel felt himself enveloped was to receive no better apologia than this. King had put his finger on it. Having done so, however, he apparently found no *point d'appui* for judging the merits of the irony, and contented himself with noting various ambiguities in the role and character of Zeitblom, including the one already crisply stated by Sachs—that there was no character there. But he came in the end to another point that had been often alluded to but never given its due in the preceding seminars: the fact that *Doctor Faustus* was about Germany personified. King first quoted Leverkühn's effort to describe the fourth movement of the Beethoven quartet, opus 132: ". . . there are things for which one cannot scare up, out of the whole rich realm of language, do what you like, any properly characterizing epithet or combination of epithets. . . . You finally land at the name: *Allegro appassionato*. That is the best after all."

"The greater the real content of a thing," said King, "the more impossible it is for it to be expressed by anything save itself; and the name of it does not obscure it with partial or doubtful interpretations; rather it stands as the sign of the thing's objective reality. Caught in the web of Mann's radical relativism are at least a few such absolute signs. I mention only one—nationality. Allowing always for the bracket of skepticism that embraces the entire work, no one will maintain, I'm sure, that the notion of Germany is equivocal for Mann even in this novel whose soul is equivocation. Germany is the name and the anecdote, the reality. Because Leverkühn *could* not say simply, nakedly, 'Pray for me,' the anecdote had to be stylistically detached from him. Pretending to be old Lutheran Kumpfy, he could write down the word that 'pressed to be written down: "Pray for me." ' Because Mann *cannot* pray for Germany, he must detach the anecdote from himself stylistically. Pretending to be old Zeitblom, he can get his prayer said, too: 'God be merciful to thy poor soul, my friend, my Fatherland!' I don't suppose that it is only Mann's sophistication that forces him into this posture. I think the vicarious style may come from the vicarious experience. When the catastrophe fell in the German tragedy, Mann was not there."

AFTER five men had done their best with this novel, the scales stood about even: on the one hand Kahler, Borgerhoff, and King had explained it with one degree or another of sympathy; on the other hand Sachs and Kerman had given reasons for regarding it as a failure in certain respects and in certain others as very nearly a fraud. But if the aim of the seminars was to arrive at a clear critical judgment of *Doctor Faustus* as a whole—the kind of judgment that would take account of explanations and fault-finding alike and usher the work to its place among the fixed stars, then some decisive summary was badly needed. This the director of the seminars undertook to supply on the last evening, and his presentation was a model of sane pungency.

Fergusson had chosen "The Devil's Recipe for Great Music" as the subject of his reflections, making it clear at once that he thought Kahler, Borgerhoff and King had discharged all the obligations to critical sympathy demanded by the occasion. Mann's irony, so well described by King, had left him unbemused—perhaps because he was familiar with it in less grandiose examples. "Dr. Mann, as Mr. King puts it, by offering alternative and mutually contradictory interpretations of every element in the book, forces the reader to make his own interpretations and adopt his own attitudes: 'subjectivity is absolute.' We, as readers, as not used to this treatment; we keep asking what the book objectively in itself is supposed to *be*. And yet, Dr. Mann's method here is that of romantic irony, and he has used it often before. The romantic ironist simultaneously affirms and denies everything; his irony is unresolved, and that is the very essence of its fun. Like the flirt who will never be serious, he invites and refuses at the same time, so leading us back to the author, who then smiles with a somewhat portentous coyness, but still eludes our grasp. That, I think, is why our discussions here have so often led to Dr. Mann—his biography, his temperament, or his philosophy. But I should like to escape this gambit."

There were, he said, three questions he should like to ask, and answer. "Why does Adrian recognize the devil's power and authority in the first place? What does the devil do for Adrian, once the pact is made, to get great music out of him? What are we to think of the whole deal?" As for the first, Fergusson said, Leverkühn has heard in music something already inclined to the diabolic: he has heard "the seductive voice of a tradition fatally headed for the void. So that, when the devil finally appears to him, he is more than ready; the devil has only to speak to him with his own ideas and emotions. . . . And, of course, this raises the question whether the devil is objectively there, or only a projection of Adrian's own *drang nach todt*. I may report that the interview strikes me as more like Coleridge's 'fancy'—a set of ingenious effects—than like his more organic 'imagination.' . . . I also do not attempt to consider the cognate question of the *real* nature of the devil. I think it probable that we are here being offered an all-purpose machine, and being invited to use it to make whatever kind of demon would best fit our own morose appetites. So instead I wish to disengage the assumptions which Adrian and the devil share, for I believe their pact depends upon certain views about art, history, and human nature which they—but not I—assume as certain."

The first of these assumptions was that music was everything. "I do not need to remind you of the illustrious line of German artists and philosophers who have felt, in music, our most direct route to the soul of the universe. But let me quote you this passage which Nietzsche wrote when still shaken by Wagner's *Tristan und Isolde:* 'I ask the question of genuine musicians: whether they can imagine a man capable of hearing the third act of *Tristan* without expiring by a spasmodic distension of all the wings of the soul? A man who has thus, so to speak, put his ear to the heart-chamber of the cosmic will . . . would he not collapse at once? Could he endure, in the wretched fragile tenement of the human individual, to hear the re-echo of countless cries of joy and sorrow from the "vast void of cosmic night" without flying irresistibly to his primitive home?' This, I think, is the *sort* of thing Adrian assumes that the devil can give him. But Adrian and the devil, three-quarters of a century later, have no thought of imitating Wagner. They wish, I think, to push music farther in the same direction; but how to do *that?*"

Here he came to the second assumption: "that music in their day is dead; that they know enough to be sure it is dead. . . . Mr. Kerman has explained this philosophy and history of music very illuminatingly. All I need to do at this point is to remark that the sense of the *fatality* of the development of music and of modern art in general, the feeling that the artist is caught by History itself, in an absolute and plainly visible impasse, is one of the most important assumptions shared by Adrian and the devil. Hence Adrian's dry desperation, his sterility and emptiness; and hence the unbreakable grip which the devil can clamp upon him. This sense of the exhaustion of art is of course not new either, nor is the effort to defy this exhaustion by destroying art as we have known it traditionally. 'The work of art? It is a fraud,' says Adrian, 'it is contrary to truth, contrary to *serious* art. . . . Art would like to stop being pretense and play, it would like to become knowledge.' Professor Maritain had a great deal of light to shed upon this desperate struggle of the modern artist.

"The fatalism of their view of the plight of art is part of a general fatalism or historic determinism. Germany is regarded as the victim of her historic fate and her incurable temperament, and so is every character in the book. If Adrian is a diabolist and a musician, that is inevitable, there is no cure, no hope of learning better. In the same way Zeitblom is what might be called a cradle humanist. The humanism of Aristotle and Plato and Dante and Racine is a most difficult attainment, a precarious equilibrium, to be maintained only by constant vigilance and moral effort. But Serenus Zeitblom I am sure was just as humane sucking his thumb in his crib as he ever became through forty patient years of *classische kulturwissenschaft*. This fatalism of the temperament is an extremely important part of the implicit creed of Adrian and the devil. It is another aspect of their German-Idealist conception of 'Freedom,' upon which everyone in the book agrees. 'Freedom is of course another word for subjectivity,' says Adrian. We are free when we obey nothing, when we are a law unto ourselves. This is the kind of freedom Adrian demands and wishes to express in his music, 'pure subjectivity' as he puts it. Some of the anomalies are brought out: the fact that this radical anarchy so soon turns into tyranny, as Nazism; the fact that music as subjectivity so inevitably generates demonically consistent forms, as Baudelaire noted in the case of Wagner—the man of passion with the despotic ideal of form. But its ultimate anomaly, one not noted by Mann, is that a man whose freedom is only that of his own unregenerate impulses is actually a slave of his temperament. That is why Adrian cannot change in any essential manner; and it is why the fatality of temperament is an essential source of the devil's power over him."

So far, no ambiguity. But now Fergusson, in his turn, had to notice one. "When the devil describes hell to Adrian as nothingness, the void, he seems to agree with the orthodox authorities. But I do not think that Dr. Mann wants us to settle for anything so simple. As Dr. Kahler has pointed out, there is an essential connection between the Faust legend itself and the Manichean heresy, according to which evil is a powerful force in its own right. The devil is *there*, in this view—another god; and the human creature may enroll under either the king of heaven or the king of hell. Adrian seems to take his devil this way. . . . Dr. Mann here seems to be trying to have his orthodoxy and his Manicheanism at one and the same time, just as Adrian, in due time, will demand the thrill of going to hell and the comfort of being saved. It is this radical inconsistency which makes this scene, like so much else in the book, bottomless—or, in other words, insubstantial. We may admire its ingenuity, but the moral imagination is balked. We cannot really imagine a man travelling two opposite directions at the same time."

As to the second question—the devil's recipe—Fergusson observed that Adrian got his assistance not in the realm of craft, *technê,* but in that of inspiration, or *mousikê.* How was it provided? "Not out of the past: the assumed creed of historic fatalism prevents that. Adrian parodies the past—picking from Shakespeare his most mannered work, from Dante his most indigestible formula, from the Middle Ages their most

superstitious and demonic stories. But he learns nothing from
the past, and his effort is to get beyond parody to the naked
human voice, something as primitive as superman and as
technically sophisticated as the whistling dive bomber. Nor
does the devil offer him any *contemporary* help or inspiration.
He has nothing much to do with his German colleagues. Italy
is represented only by the farm family he spends some time
with; England by Schildknapp's moth-eaten snobbery. As
for Paris, where Joyce, Picasso, Bergson, Maritain, Pound,
Cocteau, Stravinsky for example were then working—Paris
means to Adrian only a leering and venal press-agent.

"To sum up: the devil, as one might expect from his
ambiguous identification with Adrian's death-wish, gets great
music out of him by exaggerating his native temperament.
He prescribes, for this purpose, a mixture of agony with
bourgeois comfort, wherein Adrian's exacerbated freedom or
subjectivity may sprout what monstrous forms it will. . . .
Monstrous, I note parenthetically, is one of Dr. Zeitblom's
favorite words; he applies it to his own vast verbal output,
as he eyes it with infantile pride. Perhaps he feels that in this
free productivity he is akin to his hero. . . . Adrian's arrested
syphilis is the basic agent for exaggerating his manic-
depressive temperament. Because of it alone he lives in a
frantic alternation of freezing and burning, of exaltation and
collapse. Because of it his cerebration is speeded up, while
his erotic life is totally disordered. . . . But this is only the
basis of the devil's treatment. It is not so easy, starting with
Adrian's sterility and his blasé omniscience, to produce the
super-music, the transcendental breakthrough, which the devil
has in mind. . . . He will take off *beyond* Wagner, producing
one more *frisson* which, all of a sudden, will be, not decadent
and hysterical, but pure and primeval. Obviously, to develop
in the rather limp Adrian a head of steam sufficient for a
scream of this quality is not so easy; great ingenuity will be
required.

"The devil therefore cannot leave Adrian in peace, with
his syphilis and his scholarly quiet. In that condition he is

truly introverted, but not agonized enough. Some way must be found, without destroying his solipsism, to make it yell in ever greater agony. This is accomplished, as you will remember, by offering poor Adrian two loves, both of them narcissistic enough to leave his essential solitude intact, yet sufficiently objective to lay him open to torture. I am sure the devil had read Freud: his methods with Adrian prove it. The tenderized libido is lured out of its dark shell by an image which it mistakes for itself, and then, like some defenseless snail, it is horribly castigated. The first bait offered Adrian's moroseness is, as you remember, the flirtatious Rudi. Herr Zeitblom delicately half conceals the details of this affair; but the end is clear enough. Rudi gets murdered as the result of some uncandid, cruel and fake-naïf moves by Adrian. Adrian is left with a mixture of remorse, migraine and torpor; but then the treatment is a brilliant success: 'his mind rose up,' says Herr Zeitblom, 'a giant refreshed—indeed, his trouble might now be to keep his poise in the storm of ideas rushing upon him. This [1927] was the year of the high and miraculous harvest of chamber music.'

"The second love offered by the devil is of course little Echo, Adrian's angelic baby nephew. In investigating this episode, one must try not to be too dismayed by Herr Zeitblom's doting upon the lisping child. It is the very childishness of the child which infatuates Adrian; and though this may seem a bit monstrous it is of interest as another example of Mephisto's Freudianism. After the Rudi affair, Adrian's moral degeneration had apparently gone a step further; it now takes a child to set in motion the mechanism of amorous identification—the all-too-deceptive mirror image, or as Mann with his musical habit puts it, the Echo of Adrian's glum inner being. Little Echo is the last stop for Adrian on the way back to the womb. He can still love and envy Echo his untroubled *Freiheit,* his childish subjectivity; and the devil, who had estimated his condition correctly, having loosed him forth, pounces on him in a frenzy of murder and shame. Little Echo dies in a series of vomitings, screams and collapses, which also faithfully and of course figuratively echo Adrian's rhythm of life. Herr Zeitblom, plodding along in his heavy prose, spares us none of the symptoms. Zeitblom's literal-minded verbosity is here so unpleasing that one may feel, on first reading, that the whole little Echo affair is a piece of gratuitous and artificial *schrecklichkeit*. But, as I have indicated, it is to be explained as the ingenious work of the devil, who thus takes his place in the intrigue as an authentic Manichean *deus ex machina*. Little Echo is Mephisto's curiously old-fashioned masterpiece, a calendar painting of a cherubic child; but it works to perfection. He wrings from Adrian his *true* masterpiece, 'the most frightful lament ever set up on this earth,' yet ending not with a firewhistle, but with the pleading note on the G-string, not with a bang but a whimper.

" 'A light diet of milk, eggs, toast, vegetable soup, a good red beefsteak with spinach at midday, and afterwards a medium-sized omelet with applesauce,' says Frau Schweigestill, Mother Hushabye; and she tiptoes away to spread a rug for Adrian's feet, and adjust the light for his eyes. I remind you of this maternal creation, because she is an essential part of the devil's treatment. If Adrian is to explore the full implications of freedom as pure subjectivity, he must be freed from the cares and the uncertainties and the troublesome responsibilities which afflict the larger part of the human race. Without his damp, warm cocoon of creature-comfort, he would never have been able both to exploit the excitements of psychic degeneration and express them in his music.

"The general principles followed by the devil are clear. He is going to get great music out of Adrian by *force majeure*. The emotion, the human feeling, which Adrian lacked to begin with, are to be derived from physical and moral breakdown, from a regression of feeling back through childishness to the prehuman paradise of the womb. This is subjectivity with a vengeance. All inspiration is of course in some sense subjective; on this all the authorities agree with Adrian and Mephisto. The poet or musician lends ear to an inner awareness which is not quite our usual daylight consciousness: the subconscious or the preconscious, as Maritain called it. But the authorities also agree that the preconscious has several dimensions, that it is aware of elements both above and below. Freud thinks of it as the realm both of our unformed libido, the product of our glandular and nervous mechanisms, and of the superego, which embodies our awareness of values derived from without and not attained in our actual lives. In the process of spiritual growth, or even just growing up, we become somewhat familiar with these solicitations, and able, to some degree, to distinguish between them. I wish to remind you that all of this and much more was set forth by Maritain in his analysis of the modes of inspiration of modern French poetry. I am remembering as much as I can of that when I point out that the devil's inspiration is from below only; that it thus interprets the artist's subjectivity in one perverse way only. Hence the identification of art with disease, and the correlative gloomy dogma that, in our time at least, the triumph of art is the degeneration of the human spirit.

"What are we to make of this picture of diabolic inspiration? Must we simply accept it in the spirit in which it is offered, as *the* dope on modern art and the modern world? Or, if not, how seriously must we attempt to take it?

"Baudelaire tells us that, in his day, the Parisian journalists could not take Wagner, and that, when they heard *The Flying Dutchman,* they answered with *gaminerie professionelle.* I suppose this phrase may be translated as the kind of wisecrack with which Broadway reviewers greet Shakespeare, Chekhov, Ibsen and the numerous other dramatists whom they do not understand. I find, to my dismay, that in reading *Faustus* I am tempted to adopt the very same philistine and disbelieving attitude. On the other hand, I am even more uncomfortable with the attitude Dr. Mann seems to suggest as the proper one: Zeitblom's religious solemnity, the hysterical adoration of Nackedy, Schuell, and Mother Hushabye.

It is very difficult, I think, to find a happy medium, and that has to do with the very conception and form of the work. . . . Mann has surrounded his work with a moral wilderness or void, in which nothing that could be called taste or judgment is possible. If I have seemed to be too impudent in my remarks, my excuse must be that, against a background of nihilism, the incredulous urchin is no more inappropriate than the pious music-lover, with his bowed head and lowered eyes, who munches his rolls and Wiener schnitzel between the acts of *Götterdämmerung*.

"But there may also be another reason for my attitude, or feeling, namely, that I was brought up with other prophets of doom, who caught me young, and hit me where I really lived. I am thinking primarily of Eliot, of course. An early reading of Eliot, like an injection of ragweed, has produced in me a partial immunity. About the time when Adrian, after the first war, was venturing among the Munich highbrows and toying with the pleasing, murderous and suicidal notion of being seduced by Rudi, Eliot was writing the following lines, which I first read not long thereafter:

> I that was near your heart was removed therefrom
> To lose beauty in terror, terror in inquisition.
> I have lost my passion: why should I need to keep it
> Since what is kept must be adulterated?

After thirty years I still hear more music, and more of the authentic unheard *mousikê,* in these lines, than I do in all the screaming *Weheklage.* I feel a deeper knowledge of the dryness and isolation of soul which made Adrian a victim of his devil. I see also the clearly envisioned possibility, even after a hundred years of damned poets of every description, of trying, once again, for diabolism, titanism, and all the well-known machinery of the "free" and unregenerate genius. But this looked to Eliot like exciting the membrane when the sense has cooled—multiplying variety in a wilderness of mirrors, both of which Mann and Adrian do at such length in *Doctor Faustus.*

And Eliot, as we know, proceeded to seek his inspiration in another direction—learning from the past, trying to nourish the human spirit, and to accept its responsibilities, rather than merely asserting it in its hysterical weakness.

"Thus in reading *Faustus* I half-believe that Mann himself knew too much to write the book: that its ingenuity was no substitute for the imaginative coherence of art, its sensationalism no adequate ersatz for the human spirit, at least *trying* to be human. I am sure Mann knows, as Joyce did, that the quality of a work of art depends upon the depth of the human spirit from which it springs."

So much, in Fergusson's summary, for the quality of *Doctor Faustus* as a "morality." But before he finished he turned to that other aspect of it, and its meaning, of which King had spoken as one of the few absolutes in the book: the symbolic identification of Adrian Leverkühn with modern Germany. "In order to feel the nightmarish aspect of this identification," Fergusson said, "—a thrill like that one gets from newspaper headlines on a bad day—it is not necessary to believe with Zeitblom that Adrian's subjectivity lays hold upon the cosmos. If it, or a spirit like it, proves capable of laying hold of the dim imagination and insatiate passion of the modern crowd, as Wagner's spirit did through the Nazis, that will be enough to give it its melancholy importance for us and everyone else. I see by the *Times* that National Socialism is gaining ground once more. Perhaps, after the migraines and torpors of the defeat, the bewildered hordes are beginning to feel titanic again. We may yet see them rise, 'a giant refreshed,' having learned neither from the past nor the present, a renewed monster bearing the same relation to Hitler's punctured leviathan as the yelling *Weheklage* bears to Tristan, pleading note on the G-string and all. The irrationality and moral impotence of this being—the mob in oneself and the mob in the world—subjectivity as freedom—does not mean physical impotence. Some of these gloomy thoughts must have been in Zeitblom's mind when he hoped that pride

would turn out to be contrition after all—against all reason
and probability."

IF ANY ONE question about *Doctor Faustus* remained irksome
it was the general one, scarcely touched in the discussions,
as to the value and place of sheer will in the making of art.
Maritain had perceived and stated that if the poet were to
escape the perils inherent in his modern predicament—that
is, the predicament of conscious subjectivity—he must re-
nounce all will to power, must remain the disinterested auditor of the inner *mousikê*. Mann's work seemed the most
conspicuous, not to say flagrant, violation of this rule in
modern literature; and its cunning lay precisely in the fact
that when Mann forced and counterfeited creative intuition
he knew what it was, knew what he was doing, and knew
the suspect nature of the job. Yet what grand thing was ever
made without the tenacious will to make it? Not the *Divine
Comedy,* certainly; and it would have served discrimination
if Fergusson, or someone, could have meditated and spoken
on Dante's will; on how the disinterested artist might avoid
the Faustian risk without being guilty of that evasion of greatness, that *colpa e vergogna delle umane voglie* (sin and shame of
human wills) mentioned by Dante in the *Paradiso*.

CONCLUSION ❧

Note has been taken, perhaps too frequently, of the difficulties that beset the Princeton Seminars in keeping up the running discussion that they were meant to be. Yet in retrospect the exertions of 1950–1951 did constitute a loose sort of discussion, at a level that might be described as Olympic, if surely not Olympian, since the chief participants had shown some athletic flexibility and staying power. The *concours,* moreover, came more distinctly to a conclusion than the first year's seminars had done. There was still no formal occasion in the spring for casting up the year's gains, so to speak, or for pulling together the various minds and their various operations in an attempt at synthesis. But one thing bore more relation to another this year than before, and there had been a kind of envoi by the director.

The central event, with the star performer, seemed beyond question the Maritain seminars. But the writer's own evenings were a preparation for Maritain's and indeed it could almost be said that the basic text for eleven weeks in the heart of the winter had been Aristotle's *De Anima,* an oxygen tank of ancient clarity upon which the writer had drawn and from which the superior clarities of Maritain's discourse were partly derived. These weeks were not so far out of relation with Wellek's preceding submissions as might at first appear. The writer in his way and Maritain in his were concerned to refresh old and universal precisions in the context of that modern literature to which the German romantic movement and its thinkers were the first to contribute. As for the importance in the whole scale of thought and culture of Maritain's effort, Wellek himself had suggested it when he wrote, in his and Warren's *Theory of Literature:* "Of the creative process itself, not much has been said at the degree of generalization profitable to literary theory." When Maritain finished, a great deal had been said.

In this case, the seminars bore fruit that became publicly available almost at once. In the autumn, at the National Gallery in Washington, Maritain delivered his seminar papers with some enlargements and revisions, and two new papers on painting, as the Andrew Mellon Lectures in Fine Arts, and on the invitation of the Humanities division he repeated them in public lectures at Princeton. His undergraduate and graduate audiences on these occasions were astonishingly large, attentive, and appreciative. In 1952 the lectures were published in a handsome Bollingen Book entitled *Creative Intuition in Art and Poetry,* and in 1954 this book, already a classic, came out in a paperback edition that would reach many thousands of readers in the United States and abroad. For Maritain's addition to the literature of the arts, Fergusson's original invitation to do some work for the Princeton Seminars had given the original stimulus, and Maritain acknowledged it in his foreword.

So far as the direct "utilization" of the seminar discussions in criticism was concerned, the symposium on *Doctor Faustus* provided—for the first time—an occasion and an illustration of the problem. No doubt it should be accepted as one of the premises of any such joint effort that if one man is enabled to scale a rock his achievement belongs as well to those who hold the rope below; in this case Fergusson had been, by far, the most successful in bringing to bear on Mann's novel the Maritainist illumination—but that meant, at the last opportunity, success. By holding hard to essential and severe criteria, exacting the inner and authentic *virtu* of art, Fergusson had deflated a serious and expert artifact by one of the most eminent of writers. It was a pity that his informal observations were never published. At the end of the year he and Blackmur had it in mind, in fact, to edit the Mann symposium and to make a book out of it for the Princeton Press; this might have been still better, because it would have shown what excellent studies, in particular Borgerhoff's, Fergusson had in mind, and what sharp analyses, in particular Kerman's, helped him to resolve the critical problem. But this project fell through.

The effects of the *Faustus* symposium, like the effects of Maritain's contribution, were felt a long way beyond Princeton. As the director noted in his little report at the end of the year, Donald Stauffer proposed to work the Princetonian views of Faustus into lectures at Oxford the following year, during his term as Eastman Professor. Moreover Dr. Gunnar Tidestrom of the University of Upsala, who attended the seminars on a Rockefeller fellowship, planned to emulate the Princetonians by organizing a *Faustus* symposium in Sweden. How these events turned out the writer never knew, but it could be assumed that both retained some of the saline Princeton flavor. This was to reinforce in the world at large an intellectual service first performed in the Poetry Room.

NOTES 🍃

Prologue

p. 4 Wordsworth's mistress: The discovery was reported in Harper's *William Wordsworth: His Life, Works and Influence* (New York: Charles Scribner's Sons, 1916). A complete account followed in his *Wordsworth's French Daughter: The Story of Her Birth, with the Certificate of Her Baptism and Marriage* (Princeton, N.J.: Princeton University Press, 1921).

p. 4 The converted Tommy Eliot: More's visit to Eliot in 1928 occasioned rigorous debate between the two men of letters on questions of theology, particularly the matter of papal infallibility.

p. 4 Blackmur/Fergusson: The author of numerous essays on the craft of literature, R. P. Blackmur had, by 1949, also published several collections of original poetry, among them *From Jordan's Delight* (New York: Arrow Editions, 1937) and *The Second World* (Cummington, Mass.: Cummington Press, 1942). As director of the campus theater at Bennington College in Vermont (1936–1947), Francis Fergusson had published a translation of Sophocles' *Electra* (New York: W. R. Scott, 1938) and had been working on his *Idea of a Theatre,* which was later published by the Princeton University Press.

p. 5 H. T. Lowe-Porter/Elias A. Lowe: Helen Tracy Lowe-Porter was responsible for the first English translations of many of Mann's works, including *Buddenbrooks* (1924), *The Magic Mountain* (1927), and *Doctor Faustus* (1948). Her husband, Elias Avery Lowe, was a professor of paleography at the Institute for Advanced Study from 1936 to 1969.

p. 5 Mann at Princeton: From 1938 to 1940, Mann had been a visiting lecturer in the Humanities.

Notes

p.6   *Hound and Horn:* Published first in Cambridge (1927–1930) and later in New York City (1930–1934), the *Hound and Horn,* under the editorship of Lincoln Kirstein (who had founded the quarterly while a sophomore at Harvard), Varian Fry, Allen Tate, Yvor Winters, and R. P. Blackmur, featured original pieces by young writers, including Pound, T. S. Eliot, Katherine Anne Porter, Granville Hicks, Irving Babbitt, and Edmund Wilson.

p.6   A number of literary studies: See "Masks of Ezra Pound," in *Hound and Horn* VII, no. 2 (1934): 177–212 (reprinted in *The Double Agent: Essays in Craft and Elucidation* [New York: Arrow Editions, 1935], pp. 30–67, and in *Language as Gesture: Essays in Poetry* [New York: Harcourt, Brace, 1952], pp. 124–154); "Notes on E. E. Cummings' Language," *Hound and Horn* IV, no. 2 (1931): 163–192 (reprinted in *The Double Agent,* pp. 1–29, and in *Language as Gesture,* pp. 317–340); "Examples of Wallace Stevens," *Hound and Horn* V, no. 2 (1932): 223–255 (reprinted in *The Double Agent,* pp. 68–102, and in *Language as Gesture,* pp. 231–249).

p.6   Fergusson on dramatic art: Francis Fergusson, *The Idea of a Theatre: A Study of Ten Plays: The Art of Drama in Changing Perspective* (Princeton, N.J.: Princeton University Press, 1949).

p.7   Princeton's new library: The Harvey S. Firestone Memorial Library had been opened in June 1947, during Princeton's bicentennial pageant.

p.8   Berryman at Princeton: John Berryman joined the Princeton faculty in 1943 as fellow and lecturer in creative writing, and held the position intermittently until 1949. In 1950, *Stephen Crane* was published, as part of the American Men of Letters Series, by William Sloane Associates of New York.

p.9   The best things come: See Henry James, *Hawthorne* (New York: Harper and Brothers, 1901), p. 30.

p.9   Serious men, serious writers: R. P. Blackmur, "A Feather-bed for Critics: Notes on the Profession of Writing," in *The Expense of Greatness* (New York: Arrow Editions, 1940), pp. 288, 286 (reprinted in *Language as Gesture,* pp. 408, 406).

Chapter One

p.14   *Mimesis:* Erich Auerbach, *Mimesis: Dargestellte Wirklichkeit in der Abendländischen Literatur* (Bern: A. Francke Ltd., 1946); *Mimesis:*

214

The Representation of Reality in Western Literature, trans. Willard R. Trask (Princeton, N.J.: Princeton University Press, 1953).

p. 14   Auerbach on Pascal: Erich Auerbach, "The Triumph of Evil in Pascal," *Hudson Review* IV, no. 1 (1951): 58–79. This article represents an expanded version of the notes delivered by Auerbach in his seminar paper.

p. 14   *Pensée 298:* See *Oeuvres de Blaise Pascal: Pensées,* ed. Léon Brunschvicq (Paris: Librairie Hachette, 1904), pp. 224–225:

Justice, force.—Il est juste que ce qui est juste soit suivi, il est nécessaire que ce qui est le plus fort soit suivi. La justice sans la force est impuissante; la force sans la justice est tyrannique. La justice sans force est contredite, parce qu'il y a toujours des méchants; la force sans la justice est accusée. Il faut donc mettre ensemble la justice et la force; et pour cela faire que ce qui est juste soit fort, ou que ce qui est fort soit juste.

La justice est sujette à dispute; la force est très reconnaissable et sans dispute. Ainsi on n'a pu donner la force à la justice, parce que la force a contredit la justice et a dit qu'elle était injuste, et a dit que c'était elle qui était juste. Et ainsi ne pouvant faire que ce qui est juste fût fort, on a fait que ce qui est fort fût juste.

Justice, might.—It is just that what is just be observed; it is necessary that what is strongest be observed. Justice without might is impotent; might without justice is tyrannical. Justice without might is a contradiction, because there will always be evildoers; might without justice is open to accusation. It is therefore necessary to combine justice and might; and in so doing to make what is just mighty, or what is mighty just.

Justice is open to dispute; might is readily recognizable and indisputable. Thus we have not been able to accord might to justice, because might has worked against justice and has claimed that she was unjust. And so, not being able to make what is just powerful, we have made what is powerful just. (trans. Dana Rowan)

p. 14   Affair of Port-Royal: In 1655 Pascal had entered the religious community of Port-Royal whose members, under the direction of the Abbé de S.-Cyran, strictly adhered to Jansenist principles. The *Pensées* may be seen as a reflection of the theology of Port-Royal, whereby the notion of free will and good works had been repudiated, in favor of that of divine grace, as the only key to individual salvation.

Notes

p. 15   Auerbach in Istanbul: Before entering the United States in 1948, Auerbach had spent eleven years (1936–1947) at the Turkish State University in Istanbul, where he had completed much of his work on *Mimesis*.

p. 15   Physicist Klein: Oskar Benjamin Klein, of Stockholm, was an atomic physicist in residence at the Institute for Advanced Study.

p. 15   The thinking of Niels Bohr: Niels Henrik David Bohr (1885–1962) had proposed the notion of "complementarity" to reconcile the apparently conflicting theories of quantum mechanics and classical physics. Complementarity, Bohr believed, could be said to exist when two complementary phenomena belong to aspects of experience that, though seemingly incompatible, are in fact indispensable for a full account of that experience.

p. 16   Pascal on human affection: See Auerbach, "The Triumph of Evil in Pascal," p. 65, where Auerbach notes that toward the end of his life Pascal was reputed to have adopted an attitude of "coolness" toward his relatives and friends, "nor did he tolerate the marks of their affection for him, because such affections would mean a larceny from God . . . God alone deserved love."

p. 16   Pascal to friend in Clermont: See Blaise Pascal, *Les Lettres de Blaise Pascal: Accompagnées de lettres de ses correspondants* (Paris: G. Crès, 1922), pp. 305–309.

p. 17   Pascal and natural law: In discussing Pascal's understanding of the doctrine of "natural law" espoused by, among others, Thomas Aquinas (1225–1274), Auerbach notes that "Pascal has nothing in common with this theory . . . since he does not accept the idea of a law given by nature to mankind—except, perhaps, in the form developed by Hobbes where it means the right of the stronger. Pascal did all he could, at least in politics, to extinguish the *lumen naturale*" ("The Triumph of Evil in Pascal," pp. 75–77).

p. 18   Professor Russi: Antonio Russi, of the University of Pisa, was visiting lecturer in Modern Languages and Literatures, 1950–1951.

p. 19   Baudelaire text: All of the Baudelaire poems considered by Auerbach will be identified (unless otherwise stated) according to their position in the 1857 edition of *Les Fleurs du Mal*.

p. 19   The Sublime and the Low: Auerbach's seminars formed the basis for his later article, "The Esthetic Dignity of the *Fleurs du Mal*," *Hopkins Review* IV, no. 1 (1950): 29–45.

216

p. 19   *Spleen* IV:

Quand le ciel bas et lourd pèse comme un couvercle
Sur l'esprit gémissant en proie aux longs ennuis,
Et que de l'horizon embrassant tout le cercle
Il nous verse un jour noir plus triste que les nuits;

Quand la terre est changée en un cachot humide,
Où l'Espérance, comme une chauve-souris,
S'en va battant les murs de son aile timide
Et se cognant la tête à des plafonds pourris;

Quand la pluie étalant ses immenses traînées
D'une vaste prison imite les barreaux,
Et qu'un peuple muet d'infâmes araignées
Vient tendre ses filets au fond de nos cerveaux,

Des cloches tout à coup sautent avec furie
Et lancent vers le ciel un affreux hurlement,
Ainsi que des esprits errants et sans patrie
Qui se mettent à geindre opiniâtrement.

—Et de longs corbillards, sans tambours ni musique,
Défilent lentement dans mon âme; l'Espoir,
Vaincu, pleure, et l'Angoisse atroce, despotique,
Sur mon crâne incliné plante son drapeau noir.

When the sky low and heavy weighs down like a cover
On the mind that groans from prolonged ennui,
And when, from the horizon enclosing the whole circle,
A black day pours in upon us, bleaker than the night;

When the earth is transformed into a moist dark cell,
In which Hope, like a bat,
Flies about, beating the walls with its nervous wings
And striking its head on the rotting ceilings;

When the rain, in the cast of its vast trails,
Mimics the bars of an enormous prison,
And when a host of appalling spiders
Advances deep in our minds, tightening its threads,

Bells suddenly explode in fury
And hurl their ghastly noise against the sky,
While spirits who have been wandering stateless
Begin to whimper, quietly.

217

—And long hearses, with neither drums nor music,
Pass slowly by inside my soul; Hope,
Defeated, weeps, and a terrible Depression, despotic,
Drapes its black flag over my bowed head. (trans. Dana Rowan)

–Charles Baudelaire, *Les Fleurs du Mal*, No. LXII.

p.20 *Le Mauvais Moine:* Baudelaire, *Les Fleurs du Mal,* No. IX.

p.20 Je te donne ces vers: Ibid., No. XXXV.

p.21 Mme. Sabatier: Apollonie Sabatier, née Aglaé-Joséphine Sabatier (1822–1889), was one of the foremost figures in French literary society of the mid-nineteenth century. Her salon on rue Frochot was a frequent meeting place for the writers Flaubert, Musset, Gautier, Barbey d'Aurévilly, and Feydeau. Baudelaire was himself a devotee of Mme. Sabatier, and after 1852 turned to her for spiritual inspiration, composing in her honor some of his most beautiful and spiritual love poems, including "A celle qui est trop gaie," "Confession," and "Harmonie du soir."

p.21 A celle qui est trop gaie: Baudelaire, *Les Fleurs du Mal*, No. XXXIX. Sent anonymously to Mme. Sabatier, on December 9, 1852, together with a note bearing the words "A une femme trop gaie," this poem expresses Baudelaire's disaffection with the worldliness of his Muse.

p.21 Petrarca's *Zefiro torna:* Francesco Petrarca, "Zefiro torna, e' l bel tempo rimena" (Sonetto).

p.21 E' n belle donne . . . selvagge: And in beautiful ladies, virtuous sweet gestures/are a wasteland, and cruel and savage beasts (trans. Dana Rowan).

p.22 Vaisseau favorisé . . . aquilon: Baudelaire, "Je te donne ces vers afin que si mon nom," line 4.

p.23 Thoreau in Cambridge: A member of the Harvard class of 1837, Henry David Thoreau had lived in Hollis Hall during his freshman and sophomore years.

p.23 Isherwood: Baudelaire, *Charles Baudelaire (1821–1867): Intimate Journals,* trans. Christopher Isherwood (New York: Random House, 1930).

p.24 Sa chair . . . des anges: Baudelaire, *Les Fleurs du Mal,* "Que diras-tu ce soir, pauvre âme solitaire" (No. XXXVII), line 7.

218

p.24   Le destin . . . un chien: Baudelaire, *Les Fleurs du Mal*, "Hymne à la Beauté" (No. XXI, 1861 edition), line 10.

p.24   The Court of 1857: The Sixth Chambre de Tribunal Correctionel de la Seine (see notes for Chapter Two, p. 222, Sénard's Defense.

p.24   Sartre's essay on Baudelaire: Jean-Paul Sartre's introduction to Baudelaire's *Écrits Intimes* (Paris: Les Editions du Point du Jour, 1946), pp. i-clxv (reprinted in Jean-Paul Sartre, *Baudelaire: Les Essais* XXIV [Paris: Gallimard, 1947]), affords a lengthy philosophical perspective on Baudelaire's poetic motifs.

p.25   Mon coeur mis à nu: In Baudelaire, *Écrits Intimes*, pp. 41–79. Written in Brussels in the years immediately preceding the poet's death, "Mon Coeur mis à nu" is a collection of literary notes and introspective observations, and as such is one of the few sources to document the development of Baudelaire's poetic impulse in his later years.

p.25   Du Bos: See Charles Du Bos, "Méditation sur la vie de Baudelaire," in *Approximations, Prémière Série* (Paris: Editions de Plon-Nourrit, 1922); abridged and translated by A. Hyatt Mayor for *Hound and Horn* IV, no. 4 (1931): 461–497.

p.25   *La Mort des Artistes:*

> Combien faut-il de fois secouer mes grelots
> Et baiser ton front bas, morne caricature?
> Pour piquer dans le but, de mystique nature,
> Combien, ô mon carquois, perdre de javelots?
>
> Nous userons notre âme en de subtils complots,
> Et nous démolirons mainte lourde armature,
> Avant de contempler la grande Créature
> Dont l'infernal désir nous remplit de sanglots!
>
> Il en est qui jamais n'ont connu leur Idole,
> Et ces sculpteurs damnés et marqués d'un affront,
> Qui vont se martelant la poitrine et le front,
>
> N'ont qu'un espoir, étrange et sombre Capitole!
> C'est que la Mort, planant comme un soleil nouveau,
> Fera s'épanouir les fleurs de leur cerveau!

> How many times must I rattle my bells
> And kiss your low brow, grim caricature?

To pierce the object, in all its mystique,
How many arrows, my quiver, are there to lose?

We waste our souls in clever strategies,
And we crack away many a heavy casing,
Before beholding the great Creature
Whose hellish desire fills us with sobs!

There are those who have never known their Idol,
And those sculptors, condemned and branded with shame,
Who go forth, beating their breast and their brow,

Have only one hope, strange and sombre Capitol!
Which is that Death, hovering like a new sun,
Will bring to bloom the flowers in their soul.
(trans. Dana Rowan)

   —Charles Baudelaire, *Les Fleurs du Mal*, No. C.

p.26   *La Reniement de Saint Pierre:* Baudelaire, *Les Fleurs du Mal*, No. XC.

p.27   *L'Examen de Minuit:* Ibid., No. LXXXIX (1868 edition).

p.27   Other examples: In fact Christ appears in three more poems: "Châtiment de l'Orgueil" (No. XVI), "Le Couvercle" (No. LXXXVII, 1868 edition), and "Le Rebelle" (No. XCV, 1868 edition).

p.27   Christianity/sensuality in the *Inferno:* Dante Alighieri, *Divina Commedia: Inferno,* Canto V.

p.27   "Pietra" canzone: Canzone I, *The Vita Nuova and Canzoniere of Dante Alighieri* (London: J. M. Dent & Sons, 1939), p. 178.

p.28   *La Géante:* Baudelaire, *Les Fleurs du Mal*, No. XIX.

p.28   *La Mort des Amants/La Mort des Pauvres:* Ibid., Nos. XCVIII and XCIX.

p.28   *Aucassin et Nicolette:* Thirteenth-century tale ("canterfable") that chronicles the love between Aucassin, son of Count Garin de Beaucaire, and Nicolette, a young woman taken captive by the count during a battle with the Saracens. Early in the tale, when faced with life without Nicolette, Aucassin announces his preference for eternal damnation, despite all its horrors.

p.30   Baudelaire on les cuistres: For a discussion of Baudelaire's abhorrence of the philistine, see *Écrits Intimes*, p. 102.

p.30 La femme Sand: Baudelaire's hatred for George Sand is amply demonstrated in sections xxvi–xxviii of "Mon Coeur mis à nu," where he describes Sand as "Le Prudhomme de l'immoralité. . . . Elle a, dans les idées morales, la même profondeur de jugement et la même délicatesse de sentiment que les concièrges et les filles entretenues." ("The Wise Man of immorality. . . . She has, in her moral ideas, the same depth of judgment and the same refinement of feeling as concierges and kept women." [trans. Dana Rowan]) *Écrits Intimes,* pp. 53–55.

Chapter Two

p.32 Auerbach on Stendhal, Balzac, and Flaubert: Erich Auerbach, "In the Hôtel de la Mole," trans. Willard R. Trask, *Partisan Review* xviii, no. 3 (1951): 265–303 (reprinted as Chapter 18 of *Mimesis*).

p.32 Auerbach on Dante: Erich Auerbach, "Farinata and Cavalcante," trans. Willard R. Trask, *Kenyon Review* xiv, no. 2 (1952): 207–242 (reprinted as Chapter 8 of *Mimesis*).

p.34 Text for Auerbach's Flaubert seminar: Gustave Flaubert, *Madame Bovary: Moeurs de Province* (Paris: Louis Conard, 1921), p. 91:

> Mais c'était surtout aux heures des repas qu'elle n'en pouvait plus, dans cette petite salle au rez-du-chaussée, avec le poêle qui fumait, la porte qui criait, les murs qui suintaient, les pavés humides; toute l'amertume de l'existence lui semblait servie sur son assiette, et, à la fumée du bouilli, il montait du fond de son âme comme d'autres bouffées d'affadissement.

> But it was particularly at mealtimes that she felt completely worn out, in that little ground-floor room, with the smoking stove, the creaking door, the seeping walls, the damp flagstones; all the bitterness of existence seemed to have been served up on her plate, and, in the smoke from the beef broth, it rose up from the depths of her soul like the other fragrances of dullness. (trans. Dana Rowan)

p.34 Sentence from Chapter 12, Part ii: "jamais Charles ne lui paraissait aussi désagréable, avoir les doigts aussi carrés, l'esprit aussi lourd, les façons si communes. . . ." ("never had Charles seemed so offensive to her, nor his fingers so blunted, his mind so ponderous, his manners so vulgar. . . ."[trans. Dana Rowan])—*Madame Bovary,* p. 260.

Notes

p.35   Vauvenargues on errors clearly expressed: Luc de Clapis, Marquis de Vauvenargues, *Oeuvres Complètes de Vauvenargues,* 2 vols. (Paris: J. L. J. Brière, 1827), vol. II, p. 2

p.36   Auerbach on everyday life: In fact the discussion of Flaubert in *Mimesis,* Chapter 18, was based on an earlier piece that Auerbach had written in Istanbul in 1937, the title of which was "Serious Imitations of Everyday Life."

p.42   Auerbach's essay, as later published: Auerbach, "In the Hôtel de la Mole."

p.43   Mme. Pradier: The scandals associated with the lifestyle of Louise Pradier, née d'Arcet (1814–1885), her debts, extravagances, and her several liaisons, are reputed to have been a major source of inspiration for Flaubert in the writing of *Madame Bovary.*

p.43   Sénard's Defense: At the celebrated "Madame Bovary Trial" of January 1857, the elderly lawyer Marie A. J. Sénard, former Minister of the Interior, defended his client's work against charges of impropriety and religious and moral outrage. Sénard's lengthy *plaidoirie,* a testament to the lawyer's eloquence and conviction, eventually secured Flaubert's acquittal.

p.44   Blackmur on *Madame Bovary:* R. P. Blackmur, "Madame Bovary: Beauty Out of Place," *Kenyon Review* XIII, no. 3 (1951): 475–503.

Chapter Three

p.45   Eliot as International Hero: Delmore Schwartz, "T. S. Eliot as the International Hero," *Partisan Review* XII, no. 2 (1945): 199–206.

p.45   Eliot's Literary Dictatorship: Delmore Schwartz, "The Literary Dictatorship of T. S. Eliot," *Partisan Review* XVI, no. 2 (1946): 119–137.

p.46   Institute Director Frank Aydelotte: The progressive educator had resigned from his nineteen-year presidency of Swarthmore College in Pennsylvania to assume his duties at the Institute.

p.47   Curtius's renown in Europe: See, for example, Ernst Robert Curtius, *James Joyce und sein Ulysses* (Zurich: Verlag da Neuen Schweizer-Rundschau, 1929); *Marcel Proust* (Berlin: Suhr Kamp, 1952), *Frankreich,* vol. I, *Die Franzosische Kultur: Eine Einführung* (Berlin: Deutsche Verlag-Anstalt, 1930) (with Arnold Bergsträsser); *Europäische Literatur und Lateinisches Mittelalter* (Berne: A. Francke, 1948).

p. 47   Du Bos on Curtius: Charles Du Bos, "Ernst Robert Curtius," in *Approximations, Cinquième Série* (Paris: Editions R.-A. Correa, 1932), pp. 110–139.

p. 50   Kennan on foreign policy: George F. Kennan, *American Diplomacy: 1900–1950* (Chicago: University of Chicago Press, 1951).

p. 52   Critical theory of Kenneth Burke: See Kenneth Burke, *The Philosophy of Literary Form: Studies in Symbolic Action* (Baton Rouge, La.: Louisiana State University Press, 1941); *A Grammar of Motives* (New York: Prentice-Hall, 1945).

p. 52   Buchanan's *Poetry and Mathematics:* Scott Buchanan, *Poetry and Mathematics* (New York: John Day Company, 1929).

p. 52   Fergusson's histrionic sensibility: "A basic, primary, or primitive virtue of the human mind . . . which perceives and discriminates actions . . . in order to effect a mimetic version of them" (defined in the appendix to *The Idea of a Theatre*).

p. 52   Burke's three phases of tragic rhythm: See Burke, *A Grammar of Motives,* for a discussion of the concepts of *poeima* (purpose), *pathema* (passion or suffering), and *mathema* (perception), and their relationship to the drama.

p. 53   Eliot on Dante as a model for poets: T. S. Eliot, *Dante* (London: Faber & Faber, 1929).

p. 54   Richards summarizing Coleridge: I. A. Richards, *Coleridge on Imagination* (New York: Harcourt, Brace, 1935), p. 121.

p. 54   Fergusson on Dante's *Purgatorio:* The material in Fergusson's seminars anticipates his treatment of the *Purgatorio* in *Dante's Drama of the Mind: A Modern Reading of the Purgatorio* (Princeton, N.J.: Princeton University Press, 1953).

p. 54   Ne l'ora . . . è divina:

> At the hour close to morn
>> When the swallow begins her unhappy songs,
>> Perhaps recalling ancient woes,
>
> And when our mind, more a pilgrim
>> From the body, and less held by thoughts,
>> Is, in its visions, almost divine. . . . (trans. Dana Rowan)
>
> –Dante Alighieri, *La Divina Commedia: Purgatorio*, Canto IX, lines 13–18.

p.57   Dante on the soul free and bound: Dante, *Purgatorio*, Canto IV, lines 1–12.

p.57   Of the *anima semplicetta:* Ibid., Canto XVI, line 88.

p.62   E io a lui . . . vo significando:

> And I to him: I am one who, when
> Love breathes in me, take note of it, and in the manner
> Which he dictates within, go setting it forth.
> (trans. Dana Rowan)

> –Dante, *Purgatorio,* Canto XXIV, lines 52–54.

p.62   Dante's letter to Can Grande: For a complete version of the original letter (1319) from Dante to his patron, Can Grande della Scala, see *Dantis Alagherii Epistolae (The Letters of Dante)*, ed. Paget Toynbee (Oxford: Clarendon Press, 1920), p. 175.

p.62   Curtius on Dante's sources: See Ernst Robert Curtius, *Europäische Literatur und Lateinisches Mittelalter.*

p.62   Line 76:

> La luna, quasi a mezza notte tarda,
> facea le stelle a noi parer più rade,
> fatta com'un secchion che tutto arda;

> The moon, delayed almost to midnight,
> shaped like a bucket all aglow,
> made the stars appear sparser to us; (trans. Dana Rowan)

> –Dante, *Purgatorio,* Canto XVIII, lines 76–78.

p.65   Singleton on the *Vita Nuova:* Charles S. Singleton, *An Essay on the Vita Nuova* (Cambridge, Mass.: Harvard University Press, 1949).

p.67   A day . . . they didn't know: Ezra Pound, Canto XIII.

p.67   Eliot's dialogue on dramatic poetry: T. S. Eliot, "Dialogue on Dramatic Poetry" in *Selected Essays: 1917–1932* (New York: Harcourt, Brace & Co., 1932).

p.67   Schwartz's first book: Delmore Schwartz, *In Dreams Begin Responsibilities* (Norfolk, Ct.: New Directions, 1938).

p.67   Matthiessen on Eliot: F. O. Matthiessen, *The Achievement of T. S. Eliot: An Essay on the Nature of Poetry* (New York: Oxford University Press, 1935).

Chapter Four

p.69   Schorer on Blake: Mark Schorer, *William Blake: The Politics of Vision* (New York: Holt, 1946).

p.69   Fiction and the Matrix: Mark Schorer, "Fiction and the Matrix of Analogy," *Kenyon Review* XI, no. 4 (1949): 539–560 (reprinted in *The World We Imagine: Selected Essays* [New York: Farrar, Straus and Giroux, 1968], pp. 24–45).

p.69   The evening session on Thursday: For further formulation of the ideas expressed in the lectures, see Mark Schorer, "Technique as Discovery," *Hudson Review* I, no. 1 (1948): 67–87 (reprinted in *The World We Imagine*, pp. 3–23); Introduction to the Modern Library edition of Daniel Defoe, *The Fortunes and Misfortunes of the Famous Moll Flanders* (New York: Random House, 1950) (reprinted in *The World We Imagine*, pp. 49–60); "The Humiliation of Emma Wood-house," *Library Review* II, no. 14 (1959) (reprinted in *The World We Imagine*, pp. 60–79). See also Schorer's *Society and Self in the Novel: English Institute Essays* (New York: Columbia University Press, 1956), Introduction, pp. vii–xvi.

p.69   Lawrence on Galsworthy: D. H. Lawrence, "John Galsworthy," in *Scrutinies,* comp. Edgell Rickwood (London: Wishart & Co., 1928), p. 55.

p.75   Emma on Mr. Weston: Jane Austen, *Emma*, Part III, Chapter II.

p.75   The words of Knightly: Ibid., Part II, Chapter XVIII.

p.77   Eliot's famous remark on James: "James's critical genius comes out most tellingly in his mastery over, his baffling escape from, Ideas; a mastery and an escape which are perhaps the last test of a superior intelligence. . . . In England ideas run wild and pasture on the emotions; instead of thinking with our feelings . . . we corrupt our feelings with ideas." T. S. Eliot, "On Henry James," *Egoist* I (January 1918): 1–2 (reprinted in *Little Review* IV [August 1918]: 44–47).

p.79   James's review in the *Galaxy*: Leon Edel, *Henry James*, 5 vols. (New York: J. B. Lippincott, 1953), vol. 1, p. 261.

p.82   Five thousand a year: William Makepeace Thackeray, *Vanity Fair,* Chapter 41.

p.86   Lawrence on the intention of *Women in Love*: D. H. Lawrence, letter to Edward Garnett, June 5, 1914. See *The Letters of D. H.*

Lawrence, ed. Aldous Huxley (New York: Viking Press, 1932), pp. 199–200.

p.90 Leavis's high estimate of Lawrence: F. R. Leavis, "D. H. Lawrence," in *For Continuity* (Cambridge: Minority Press, 1933), pp. 111–148; "Comment: D. H. Lawrence Placed," in *Scrutiny* XVI (1949): 44–47.

p.90 Lawrence's last fable: D. H. Lawrence, *The Man Who Died* (New York: Alfred A. Knopf, 1931).

Interchapter

p.96 Maritain's *Art and Scholasticism:* Jacques Maritain, *Art et Scolastique* (Paris: Louis Rouart et fils, 1935); *Art and Scholasticism, with other Essays,* trans. J. F. Scanlon (New York: Charles Scribner's Sons, 1946).

Chapter Five

p.98 Wellek and Warren collaboration: René Wellek and Austin Warren, *Theory of Literature* (New York: Harcourt, Brace, 1942).

p.99 Empson–Tuve exchange: Rosemond Tuve, "On Herbert's 'Sacrifice,' " *Kenyon Review* XII, no. 1 (1950): 51–75; William Empson, "George Herbert and Miss Tuve," *Kenyon Review* XII, no. 4 (1950): 735–738.

p.99 Saintsbury's history of European criticism: George Edward Bateman Saintsbury, *A History of Criticism and Literary Taste in Europe from the Earliest Texts to the Present Day,* 3 vols. (Edinburgh: Wm. Blackwood, 1902–1904), hereinafter referred to as Saintsbury.

p.99 Wellek's history of English criticism: René Wellek, *The Rise of English Literary History* (Chapel Hill, N.C.: University of North Carolina Press, 1941).

p.99 *Mimesis* mentioned in *Theory of Literature:* Wellek and Warren, *Theory of Literature,* p. 317n.

p.100 Wellek, severe in his way: Much of the material presented in Wellek's lectures later appeared in expanded form in his *History of Modern Criticism (1750–1950),* 4 vols. (New Haven, Ct.: Yale University Press, 1955–1965).

p.100 Johnson on *Henry VIII:* Samuel Johnson, *General Observations on the Plays of Shakespeare,* in *The Works of Samuel Johnson, LL.D.,* 9 vols. (Oxford edition, London: Talboys & Wheeler & W. Pickering, 1825) (hereinafter referred to as *Works*), vol. 5, p. 168.

p. 101 Actions really performed: Samuel Johnson, "Pope," in *The Lives of the English Poets,* ed. George Birbeck Hill, 3 vols. (Oxford: Oxford University Press, 1905) (hereinafter referred to as *Lives of the Poets*), vol. 3, p. 255.

p. 101 Johnson on Milton's *Lycidas:* Johnson, "Milton," in *Lives of the Poets,* vol. 1, p. 163.

p. 101 Johnson on *King Lear:* Johnson, *General Observations on the Plays of Shakespeare,* in *Works,* vol. 5, p. 175.

p. 101 Johnson on Rousseau: James Boswell, *Life of Johnson,* ed. G. Birbeck Hill and L. F. Powell, 6 vols. (Oxford: Oxford University Press, 1934–1950), vol. 2, pp. 11–12.

p. 102 Johnson defending tragicomedy: Johnson, *Preface to Shakespeare,* in *Works,* vol. 5, pp. 103–154.

p. 102 Johnson on Shakespeare's language: Ibid., pp. 117, 118.

p. 102 On Gray's cat: Johnson, "Gray," in *Lives of the Poets,* vol. 3, p. 434.

p. 102 On Denham's Thames: Johnson, "Denham," in *Lives of the Poets,* vol. 1, p. 80.

p. 102 Johnson on genius: Johnson, "Cowley," in *Lives of the Poets,* vol. 1, p. 2.

p. 102 Johnson on *The Rape of the Lock:* Johnson, "Pope," in *Lives of the Poets,* vol. 3, pp. 233–234.

p. 103 Lessing on the limits of the arts: Gotthold Ephraim Lessing, *Laokoon oder über die Grenzen der Malerei und Poesie* (Berlin: Haude und Spenersche Buchhandlung, 1882).

p. 103 Saintsbury on Lessing: Saintsbury, vol. 3, pp. 33–34.

p. 103 Lessing on Shakespeare: Lessing, *Briefe die neueuste Literatur betreffend,* in *Lessings Sämmtliche Werke* (Berlin: G. Grote'fche Verlagsbuchhandlung, 1882) (hereinafter referred to as *Werke*), vol. 4, p. 361.

p. 104 Lessing on *Ugolino:* Lessing, letter to Friedrich Nicolai, February 25, 1768, in *Werke,* vol. 8, pp. 250–252.

p. 104 Yeats on Wilfred Owen: William Butler Yeats, letters to Dorothy Wellesley, December 21 and 23, 1936, in *Letters on Poetry from W.*

B. Yeats to Dorothy Wellesley (New York: Oxford University Press, 140), pp. 124–126.

p. 104 Lessing's celebrated dictum: Lessing, *Laokoon*, pp. 103–104. Winckelmann's aesthetic theories are expounded in his *Gedanken über die Nachahmung der Grieschischen Werke in der Malerei und Bildhauerkunst* (1755).

p. 104 Lessing's condemnation of descriptive poetry: Ibid., pp. 118–127.

p. 104 Ariosto's description of Alcina: Ludovico Ariosto, *Orlando Furioso*, Canto VII, lines 11–15.

p. 106 Lessing on poetic language: Lessing, *Laokoon*, Appendix 2, in *Lessing's Werke*, ed. Franz Bornmüller, 5 vols. (Leipzig: Bibliographisches Institut, 1884), vol. 3, p. 215.

p. 107 Butcher on Aristotle: S. H. Butcher, *Aristotle's Theory of Poetry and Fine Art, with a Critical Text and Translation of the Poetics* (London: Macmillan, 1895), p. 265.

p. 107 Saintsbury's dismissal of Herder: Saintsbury, vol. 3, p. 355.

p. 107 Herder's conception of criticism: See Johann Gottfried Herder, *Ueber die neuere Deutsche Litteratur . . . von Fragmenten*, in *Sämtliche Werke*, ed. B. Suphan, 33 vols. (Berlin: Weidmannsche Buchhandlung, 1877–1913) (hereinafter referred to as Suphan), vol. 1, p. 247.

p. 108 Herder on criticism and genius: Herder, *Briefe zu Beförderung der Humanität*, in Suphan, vol. 18, p. 131.

p. 108 Herder's *Kritische Wälder:* Herder, *Kritische Wälder oder Betrachtungen, die Wissenschaft und Kunst des Schönen betreffend, nach Maasgabe neuerer Schriften*, in Suphan, vol. 3, pp. 1–480.

p. 108 Herder on the genius of language: Herder, *Ueber die Neuere Deutsche Litteratur*, in Suphan, vol. 1, p. 148.

p. 109 Herder on knowledge from analogy: Herder, *Vom Erfennen und Empsindem der Menschlichen Seele. Bemerfungen und Träume*, in Suphan, vol. 8, pp. 170–171.

p. 109 The creating, naming Godhead: Herder, *Vom Geist der Ebräischen Poesie. Eine Unleitung für die Liebhaber derselben, un der ältesten . . .* , in Suphan, vol. 12, p. 7.

p. 109 Modern civilization was stifling and killing: Herder, *Ueber die neuere Deutsche Litteratur*, in Suphan, vol. 1, p. 335.

p.109 Herder on what is not folk: Herder, *Volkslieder,* in Suphan, vol. 25, p. 323.

p.109 Herder on what is folk: Ibid., p. 331.

p.110 Herder's catholic view of literature: Saintsbury, vol. 3, p. 355.

p.112 Saintsbury on German literature: Ibid., p. 352.

p.113 Saintsbury on Schiller: Ibid., pp. 347–384.

p.114 Babbitt on Schiller: Irving Babbitt, "Schiller as Aesthetic Theorist," in *On Being Creative* (Boston: Houghton Mifflin, 1932), pp. 134–186.

p.114 Schiller on art's civilizing role: Friedrich von Schiller, *Über die ästhetische Erziehung des Menschen in einer Keihe von Briefen,* in *Sämtliche Werke,* ed. Otto Guntter and Georg Witkowski, 20 vols. (Leipzig: Hesse & Becker Verlag, 1909–1911) (hereinafter referred to as *Werke*), vol. 18, pp. 5–116.

p.114 Schiller on the philosophy of art: Schiller, letter to Wilhelm von Humboldt, June 27, 1798, in *Schillers Briefe,* ed. Fritz Jonas, 7 vols. (Leipzig: Deutsche Verlags-Anstalt, 1892–1896) (hereinafter referred to as Jonas), vol. 5, p. 393.

p.114 For a single trick of the craft: Schiller, in Jonas, vol. 5, p. 394.

p.115 Schiller on missing the *organon:* Schiller, letter to Wolfgang von Goethe, January 20, 1802, in Jonas, vol. 6, pp. 332–333.

p.115 Schiller's most important work: Schiller, *Über naive und sentimentalische Dichtung,* in *Werke,* vol. 17, pp. 479–573.

p.115 Schiller's satirical tragedy: Schiller, *Die Räuber: Ein Schauspiel,* in *Werke,* vol. 4, pp. 49–182.

p.116 Schiller on Voltaire: Schiller, *Über naive und sentimentalische Dichtung,* in *Werke,* vol. 17, pp. 518–519.

p.116 Schiller on high comedy: Ibid., pp. 514–515.

p.117 Sublime order of a benevolent will: Schiller, *Über die tragische Kunst,* in *Werke,* vol. 17, p. 238.

p.117 Schiller on the highest aim of art: Schiller, *Über das Pathetische. Vom Erhabenen (Zur Weiteren Ausführung einiger Kantischen Ideen),* in *Werke,* vol. 17, p. 398.

p.117 Schiller on *katharsis:* Schiller, *Über das Erhabene,* in *Werke,* vol. 17, p. 630.

Notes

p. 117   Schiller on poetry: Schiller, letter to Wolfgang von Goethe, March 27, 1801, in Jonas, vol. 6, p. 262.

p. 119   Stauffer's edition of Coleridge: Samuel Taylor Coleridge, *Selected Poetry and Prose of Coleridge,* ed. Donald Stauffer (New York: Modern Library, 1951).

p. 119   Wellek's doctoral dissertation: René Wellek, *Immanuel Kant in England, 1793–1838* (Princeton, N.J.: Princeton University Press, 1931).

Chapter Six

p. 120   Blackmur's paper to the English Club: "The Lion and the Honeycomb" was later published in Blackmur's *Lion and the Honeycomb: Essays in Solicitude and Critique* (New York: Harcourt, Brace, 1955), pp. 176–197.

p. 120   Ransom's book of 1941: John Crowe Ransom, *The New Criticism* (Norfolk, Ct.: New Directions, 1941).

p. 121   Oates on St. Augustine: St. Augustine, *Basic Writings of St. Augustine,* 2 vols., ed. Whitney J. Oates (New York: Random House, 1948).

p. 124   The hearing and the sound as one: Aristotle, *Poetics,* iii, ii.

p. 125   Aristotle on objects of knowledge: Aristotle, *De Anima,* ii, v.

p. 125   Fitzgerald's text: Ibid., iii, iv, v.

p. 126   Fitzgerald's propositions: Here are some numbered propositions, in brief:

1. Between the being known to any one of us and created being as a whole there is a difference of scale.
2. Between real being and what we may call intellectual being— the abstract being of thought—there is a difference expressible as difference of scale.
3. Between actual real being and nonactual, that is, potential or possible real being, there is a difference likewise expressible as difference of scale.
4. The differences of scale mentioned are incalculable and entail for the individual being or thinking an incalculable humility.
5. Intellectual being—the being of thought—is derivative from real being and refers to it; we have some knowledge of real being.

For a more extensive discussion of these propositions, see Robert Fitzgerald, "The Place of Forms," in *The Rarer Action: Essays in*

230

Honor of Francis Fergusson (Rutgers, N.J.: Rutgers University Press, 1970), pp. 288–290.

p.128 Wellek and Warren on the critic: Wellek and Warren, *Theory of Literature*, p. 3.

p.131 On Homer's teaching poets to lie: Aristotle, *Poetics*, xxiv.

p.133 Ross on dialectical reasoning: William David Ross, *Aristotle* (London: Methuen, 1923).

p.133 Aristotle's own explicit statement: Aristotle, *Nichomachean Ethics*, I, i.

p.134 The student should be content: Ibid.

p.134 Doing and getting along well: Ibid., I, ii.

p.134 Participation in The Good: Ibid., I, iv.

p.134 Solon on not being happy alive: The authority for the warning Solon is said to have addressed to Croesus is Herodotus, *History*, I, xxxii.

p.135 From Hemingway's "Today Is Friday":
1st Soldier—I thought he was pretty good in there today.

. . .

3d Soldier—The part I don't like is the nailing them on. You know, that must get to you pretty bad.
2d Soldier—It isn't that that's so bad, as when they first lift 'em up. [*He makes a lifting gesture with his two palms together.*] When the weight starts to pull on 'em. That's when it gets 'em.
3d Roman Soldier—It takes some of them pretty bad.
1st Soldier—Ain't I seen 'em? I seen plenty of them. I tell you, he was pretty good in there today.

–Ernest Hemingway, "Today Is Friday," in *Men Without Women* (New York: Charles Scribner's Sons, 1928), pp. 209–210.

p.137 Things fall apart: William Butler Yeats, "The Second Coming," in *The Collected Poems of W. B. Yeats* (New York: Macmillan, 1933), p. 215.

p.137 What Time takes away: Edwin Arlington Robinson, "Hillcrest," in *Oxford Book of American Verse*, p. 492.

p.138 Witnesses of the invisible: Aristotle, *Ethics*, II, ii.

p.139 Athenian débâcle in Sicily: Thucydides, *The History of the Peloponnesian War*, VII, xxiii.

231

Notes

p. 139   Longinus quoting Thucydides: Longinus, *On the Sublime*, xxxviii.

p. 143   Habimah Theatre: The 1946–1947 production of *Oedipus Rex* at the National Theatre of Israel, directed by Tyrone Guthrie.

p. 144   Aristotle on chance: Aristotle, *The Physics*, ii, vi.

Chapter Seven

p. 148   Maritain on the perennial subject: Much of the material in Maritain's lectures would be reproduced, in expanded form, in *Creative Intuition in Art and Poetry* (New York: Pantheon, 1953).

p. 148   Dicendum est . . . quod facit:

> It should be said that art is nothing other than right reason [applied to] making certain works. The excellence of these does not consist in human striving being directed in a certain way but in the work that is made being good in itself. For the craftsman's intent in making the work does not stand to his credit, but only the quality of the work he makes. (trans. Robert Fitzgerald)

–Thomas Aquinas, *Summa Theologica*, i, ii, q. 57, a. 3.

p. 149   Wilde on being a poisoner: Oscar Wilde, "Pen, Pencil and Poison: A Study in Green," in *Intentions* (New York: Brentano, 1905), pp. 59–92.

p. 149   To engender in beauty: See Plato, *Symposium* (206), in *Plato: Phaedrus, Ion, Gorgias and Symposium with Passages from The Republic and Laws,* trans. Lane Cooper (New York: Oxford University Press, 1938) (hereinafter referred to as Cooper), pp. 256–257.

p. 152   Maritain's quote from the *Ion:* Plato, *Ion* (534–536), in Cooper, pp. 83–86.

p. 152   Maritain's quote from the *Phaedrus:* Plato, *Phaedrus* (245), in Cooper, pp. 27–28.

p. 156   Baudelaire and Eliot on emotion in art: Baudelaire, Fusées i, in *Écrits Intimes,* p. 8. See also the views expressed by T. S. Eliot in "The Perfect Critic," in *The Sacred Wood: Essays on Poetry and Criticism* (London: Methuen, 1920), pp. 1–16.

p. 157   St. John of the Cross: St. John of the Cross, "Canciones entre el alma y el Esposo," in *The Poems of St. John of the Cross,* trans. Roy Campbell (New York: Pantheon, 1951), pp. 16, 26.

p.157 Schiller on the first dark total idea: Schiller, letter to Wolfgang von Goethe, March 27, 1801, in Jonas, vol. 6, p. 262.

p.158 Aquinas's definition of beauty: Thomas Aquinas, *Summa Theologica*, I, q. 39, a. 8.

p.158 Baudelaire's *Hymne à la Beauté:* Baudelaire, *Les Fleurs du Mal,* No. XXI (1861 edition).

p.158 Rimbaud's prescription: Arthur Rimbaud, letter to Paul Demeny, May 15, 1871. First published by Paterne Berrichon in *La Nouvelle Revue Française,* October 1912.

p.160 Baudelaire on beauty:

> You tramp on corpses, Beauty, with contempt;
> And Horror is not the least bewitching of your jewels,
> And Murder, one of your dearest trinkets,
> Dances infatuated on your insolent belly. (trans. Dana Rowan)
> —Charles Baudelaire, *Hymne à la Beauté,* strophe 4.

p.161 Assault on the absolute: Jacques Rivière, "La Crise du concept de littérature," in *Nouvelle Revue Française,* February 1, 1924. Reprinted in Jacques Rivière, *Nouvelles Études* (Paris: Gallimard, 1947), p. 313.

p.161 Rousseau's "astonishing sentence": Jean-Jacques Rousseau, *Confessions, Livre Premier.*

p.162 Baudelaire on disinterestedness of poetic creation: "L'inspiration vient toujours quand l'homme le *veut,* mais elle ne s'en va pas toujours, quand il le veut" ("Inspiration always comes when a man *wants* it, but it does not always go away when he wants it to") (trans. Dana Rowan)–Charles Baudelaire, Fusées XVII, in *Écrits Intimes,* p. 19.

p.164 To be a modern poet: Max Jacob, "L'Art chrétien," in *Art Póetique* (Paris: Emile-Paul, 1922), p. 63.

p.170 Landor on Rose Aylmer's death: See Walter Savage Landor, "Rose Aylmer," in *The Complete Works of Walter Savage Landor,* 16 vols., ed. Stephen Wheeler (London: Chapman & Hall, 1927–1936), vol. XV, p. 339.

p.171 Sous le pont Mirabeau: Guillaume Apollinaire, "Le Pont Mirabeau," in *Alcools: Poèmes 1898–1913* (Paris: Gallimard, 1920), pp. 16–17.

p.171   I am gall, I am heartburn: Gerard Manley Hopkins, "I Wake and Feel," in *Poems* (New York: Oxford University Press, 1918), p. 66.

p.172   Et comme elle . . . la fragilité: "And just as she has the brilliance of glass,/So also does she have its fragility" (trans. Dana Rowan)– Pierre Corneille, *Polyeucte: Tragédie,* iv, ii.

p.173   The winds that awakened: William Butler Yeats, "Maid Quiet," in *The Collected Poems,* pp. 79–80.

p.173   As a result of creativity of spirit:

> L'image est une création pure de l'esprit. Elle ne peut naître d'une comparaison, mais du rapprochement de deux realités plus ou moins eloignées. . . . On crée . . . une forte image, neuve pour l'esprit, en rapprochant sans comparaison deux realités distantes dont *l'esprit seul* a saisi les rapports.

> The image is a pure creation of the mind. It cannot be born of a comparison, but from the drawing together of two more or less disparate realities. . . . A strong image is created . . . that is new to the mind, by bringing together, without comparison, two separate realities, whose relationship has been grasped by *the mind alone.* (trans. Dana Rowan)

> –Pierre Reverdy, "Image," in *Nord-Sud, Self-Defence et Autres Écrits sur l'Art et la Poésie (1917–1926)* (Paris: Flammarion, 1975), pp. 73–75.

p.173   The lion's ferocious chrysanthemum head: Marianne Moore, "The Monkey Puzzle," in *Collected Poems* (New York: Macmillan, 1951), p. 88.

Chapter Eight

p.175   Mann's *Doctor Faustus:* Thomas Mann, *Doktor Faustus: Das Leben der deutscher Tonsetzers Adrian Leverkühn, erzahlt von einem Freunde* (Stockholm: Bermann-Fischer Verlag, 1947); first U.S. edition: *Doctor Faustus: The Life of the German Composer, Adrian Leverkühn, as told by a Friend,* trans. H. T. Lowe-Porter (New York: Alfred A. Knopf, 1948); hereinafter cited as *Doctor Faustus.*

p.177   Erich Kahler on Mann: Kahler gives further expression to the ideas presented in his seminar in *The Orbit of Thomas Mann* (Princeton, N.J.: Princeton University Press, 1969). See, in particular, "Sec-

234

ularization of the Devil: Thomas Mann's *Doctor Faustus*," pp. 20–43; "Doctor Faustus from Adam to Sartre," pp. 86–116.

p.179 Marlowe on Faust: Christopher Marlowe, *The Tragical History of the Life and Death of Doctor Faustus*.

p.184 Yeats's Robert Artisson: See William Butler Yeats, "Nineteen Hundred and Nineteen," in *The Collected Poems*, pp. 239–243.

p.184 Tate's brooding on angels: See Allen Tate, "The Wolves," in *Poems 1928–1931* (New York: Charles Scribner's Sons, 1932), p. 17.

p.185 A short poem of his: R. P. Blackmur, "All's the Foul Fiends," in *Poems of R. P. Blackmur* (Princeton, N. J.: Princeton University Press, 1977), p. 150.

p.185 My sin is greater than . . . my speculation: *Doctor Faustus*, p. 502.

p.197 "Pray for me": Ibid., p. 142.

p.197 "My friend, my Fatherland": Ibid., Epilogue, p. 510.

p.203 The year of chamber music: Ibid., p. 455.

p.204 A frightful lament: Ibid., p. 485.

p.204 Mother Hushabye's light diet: Ibid., p. 256.

p.206 I that was near your heart: T. S. Eliot, "Gerontion," in *Selected Poems* (New York: Harcourt, Brace & World, 1934), pp. 31–33.

p.208 Dante on sin and shame: Dante Alighieri, *La Divina Commedia: Paradiso*, Canto 1, line 30.

Conclusion

p.210 Of the creative process itself: Wellek and Warren, *Theory of Literature*, p. 82.

BIOGRAPHICAL DIRECTORY ❧

AUERBACH, ERICH (1892–1957) German philologist, scholar, and critic. 1929–1935, professor of Romance Philology at the University of Marburg; 1936–1947, professor of Romance Languages at the State University of Turkey, Istanbul; 1948–1949, visiting professor at the Pennsylvania State College; 1949–1950, member of the Institute for Advanced Study at Princeton; 1950–1957, Sterling Professor of Romance Philology at Yale University. Principal works: *Mimesis: The Representation of Reality in Western Literature* (1953); *Scenes from the Drama of European Literature* (1959); *Dante: Poet of the Secular World* (1961).

BERRYMAN, JOHN (1914–1972) Poet, fiction writer, and critic. Author of *The Dispossessed* (1948); *Stephen Crane* (1950); *Homage to Mistress Bradstreet* (1956); *77 Dream Songs* (1964, Pulitzer Prize winner). 1955–1972, taught in the English department of the University of Minnesota.

BLACKMUR, RICHARD PALMER (R. P.) (1904–1965) Scholar and critic, and early proponent of the critical movement known as the New Criticism. 1940–1965, member of the faculty of Princeton University, and professor of English (1951–1965); 1943–1946, member of the Institute for Advanced Study; 1957–1965, director of the Gauss Seminars; 1961–1962, Pitt Professor of American History and Institutions at Cambridge University. Principal works: *The Double Agent: Essays in Craft and Elucidation* (1935); *Language as Gesture: Essays in Poetry* (1952); *The Lion and the Honeycomb: Essays in Solicitude and Critique* (1955).

BORGERHOFF, ELBERT BENTON OP'T EYNDE (E. B. O.) (1908–1968) Scholar and critic. 1939–1942 and 1946–1948, assistant professor of French at Princeton; 1948–1956, associate professor of

French, Princeton; 1952–1958, 1965–1966, director of the Princeton/ Gauss Seminars in Literary Criticism; 1956–1968, held Class of 1900 Chair in Modern Languages, Princeton. Principal work: *The Freedom of French Classicism* (1950).

CASTRO, AMERICO (1885–1972) Spanish/Brazilian scholar and critic. 1915–1923, professor of Spanish Language History at the University of Madrid; 1923–1924, 1936–1937, visiting professor at the University of Buenos Aires; 1924, visiting professor at Columbia University; 1931–1932, Spanish ambassador to Berlin; 1937, left Spain with the rise to power of Franco; 1937–1939, University of Wisconsin; 1939–1940, University of Texas; 1940–1972, professor of Spanish at Princeton. Principal works: *Vida de Lope de Vega* (1919); *The Thought of Cervantes* (1925); *Spain in Her History* (1948).

CHERNISS, HAROLD FREDRIK (b. 1904) Classicist and critic. 1946–1948, professor of Greek at the University of California, Berkeley; 1948–   , professor at the Institute for Advanced Study. Principal works: *Aristotle's Criticism of Presocratic Philosophy* (1935); *Aristotle's Criticism of Plato and the Academy* (1944).

CURTIUS, ERNST ROBERT (1886–1956) German scholar, critic, and philologist. 1913–1919, professor of French at the University of Bonn; 1920–1924, professor of French at the University of Marburg; 1924–1929, professor of French at the University of Heidelberg; 1929–1951, chairman of the department of Romance Literatures and Languages at the University of Bonn; 1949, fellow of the Institute for Advanced Study. Principal works: *James Joyce* (1929); *The Civilization of France* (1932); *European Literature and the Latin Middle Ages* (1953).

FERGUSSON, FRANCIS (b. 1904) Literary and dramatic critic. 1927–1930, associate director of the American Laboratory Theatre, New York; 1930–1932, drama critic for the *Bookman*; 1932–1934, lecturer at New School for Social Research, New York; 1934–1947, professor of Humanities and Drama, Bennington College, Vt.; 1948–1949, member of the Institute for Advanced Study; 1949–1952, director of the Princeton Seminars (later the Gauss Seminars) in Literary Criticism; 1952–1953, visiting professor at Indiana University; 1953–1958, University Professor of Comparative Literature at Rutgers University; 1973–1981, professor of Comparative Literature at Princeton. Principal works: *The Idea of a Theatre: A Study of Ten Plays: The Art of Drama in Changing Perspective* (1950); *Dante's Drama of the Mind: A*

238

Modern Reading of the Purgatorio (1953); *Aristotle's Poetics: A Critical Introduction* (1961).

GAUSS, CHRISTIAN (1878–1951)   Educator and teacher of modern languages. 1903–1905, assistant professor of Modern Languages, Lehigh University; 1905–1907, assistant professor of Romance Languages, 1907–1936, professor of Modern Languages, and, 1913–1936, chairman of the department, Princeton; 1925–1945, dean of Princeton College, and first chairman of the Creative Arts Program. Author of *Life in College* (1930).

HOWE, IRVING (b. 1920)   Writer, historian, and critic. 1953–1961, associate professor and professor of English at Brandeis University; 1961–1963, professor of English at Stanford University; 1963– , Distinguished Professor of English at Hunter College of the City University of New York. Principal works: *Sherwood Anderson: A Critical Biography* (1951); *William Faulkner: A Critical Study* (1962); *Decline of the New* (1970); *World of Our Fathers* (1976); *A Margin of Hope* (1982).

KAHLER, ERICH GABRIEL (1885–1970)   Czech author, lecturer, and scholar. 1941–1942, lecturer, New School for Social Research, New York; 1947–1955, professor of German Literature at Cornell University; 1949, member of the Institute for Advanced Study; 1955–1956, visiting professor at the University of Manchester; 1959, Mershon Visiting Professor at Ohio State University; 1960–1963, visiting professor of German Literature at Princeton; 1963–1964, visiting professor at the Technisches Hochschule, Munich. Principal works: *Der deutsche Charakter in der Geschichte Europaer* (1936); *The Arabs in Palestine* (1944); *The Tower and the Abyss: Inquiry into the Transformation of Man* (1957); *The Jews Among the Nations* (1967); *The Orbit of Thomas Mann* (1969).

KERMAN, JOSEPH WILFRED (b. 1924)   Musicologist and critic. 1949–1951, Westminster Choir College, Princeton; 1951–1963, taught in the Music department of the University of California, Berkeley and, 1960–1963, chairman of the department; 1971, Heath Professor of Music at Oxford; 1974– , professor of Music at Berkeley. Principal work: *Opera as Drama* (1956).

KING, EDMUND LUDWIG (b. 1914)   Scholar and authority on Spanish literature. 1936–1941, assistant professor of Spanish, Missouri State College; 1946– , professor of Romance Languages and Literatures at Princeton and, 1966–1972, chairman of the department; currently professor of Romance Languages and Literatures Emeritus. Principal work: *Becquer: From Painter to Poet*.

MARITAIN, JACQUES (1882–1973) French philosopher and man of letters. 1913–1940, professor of Philosophy at the Institut Catholique de Paris; 1940–1944, visiting professor of Philosophy at Columbia University; 1945–1948, French ambassador to the Vatican; 1948–1953, professor of Philosophy at Princeton; 1953–1973, Professor Emeritus. Principal works: *Saint Thomas and the Problem of Evil* (1942); *The Philosophy of Nature* (1951); *Creative Intuition in Art and Poetry* (1953).

MEREDITH, WILLIAM (b. 1919) Poet and translator. 1946, 1947–1948, 1949–1950, Resident Fellow in Creative Writing at Princeton; 1950–1951, assistant professor of English at the University of Hawaii; 1955–1983, taught in the English department at Connecticut College, and 1965–1983, professor of English. Author of *Love Letters from an Impossible Land* (1944); *Alcools* (translation from the French of Guillaume Apollinaire) (1964); *The Wreck of the Thresher* (1964).

OATES, WHITNEY J. (1904–1973) Classicist and humanist. 1931–1970, taught in the Classics department at Princeton, professor of Classics (1945–1970), chairman of the department (1945–1961); 1953–1970, chairman of Special Program in the Humanities. Principal works: *Basic Writings of St. Augustine* (1948); *Aristotle and the Problem of Value* (1963).

OPPENHEIMER, JULIUS ROBERT (1904–1967) Physicist. 1929–1947, member of the faculties of the University of California and the California Institute of Technology, professor of Physics (1936–1947); 1943–1945, director of Los Alamos Laboratories, New Mexico; 1947–1966, director of and professor of Physics at the Institute for Advanced Study.

PANOFSKY, ERWIN (1892–1968) German art historian. 1921–1933, professor of the History of Art at the University of Hamburg; 1931–1935, visiting professor of Fine Arts at New York University; 1934–1935, visiting lecturer in Art at Princeton; 1935–1968, professor of Art at the Institute for Advanced Study. Principal work: *Idea: A Concept in Art Theory*.

240

SACHS, DAVID (b. 1921) Philosopher and scholar. 1947–1951, junior fellow and teaching assistant in the department of Philosophy at Princeton; 1952–1953, research fellow at the Institute for Philosophical Research; 1953–1955, instructor of Philosophy at the State University of Iowa; 1955–1960, instructor and assistant professor of Philosophy at Cornell University; 1962–1963 associate professor of Philosophy at Brandeis University and visiting lecturer at Harvard; 1963–1969, associate professor and professor of Philosophy at Cornell; 1969– , professor of Philosophy at Johns Hopkins University.

SCHORER, MARK (1908–1977) Educator and critic. 1937–1945, taught on the English faculty at Harvard; 1945–1965, associate professor, professor, and chairman of the department of English at the University of California, Berkeley. Principal works: *A House Too Old* (1935); *William Blake: The Politics of Vision* (1946); *Sinclair Lewis: An American Life* (1963).

SCHWARTZ, DELMORE (1913–1966) Poet, critic, and fiction writer. 1943–1955, editor of the *Partisan Review*. Author of *In Dreams Begin Responsibilities* (1938); *The World Is a Wedding* (1948); *Vaudeville for a Princess and Other Poems* (1950); *Summer Knowledge: New and Selected Poems* (1938–1958).

SINGLETON, CHARLES SOUTHWARD (b. 1909) Educator and linguist. 1937–1948, taught in and was later appointed chairman of the department of Romance Languages at Johns Hopkins University; 1948–1957, professor of Romance Languages and chairman of Italian Studies at Harvard; 1957–1983, professor of Humanistic Studies at Johns Hopkins; 1983– , professor of Hispanic and Italian Studies at Johns Hopkins. Principal works: *An Essay on the Vita Nuova* (1949); *Decameron* (translation from the Italian of Boccaccio) (1954); *Dante's Divine Comedy* (6 vols.) (editor) (1970–1975).

STAUFFER, DONALD ALFRED (1902–1952). Educator and critic. 1927–1945, member of the English department at Princeton and, 1946–1952, chairman of the department. Principal works: *English Biography before 1700* (1930); *The Art of Biography in Eighteenth Century England* (1941); *The Nature of Poetry* (1946).

TATE, ALLEN JOHN ORLEY (1899–1979) Critic, poet, novelist, and teacher. 1922–1926, founding editor, with John Crowe Ransom, of the *Fugitive*, Nashville; 1934–1936, lecturer in English, South-western College; 1938–1939, professor of English, Women's College, University of North Carolina; 1939–1942, poet in residence at Princeton; 1944–1946, editor, the *Sewanee Review*; 1946–1948, lecturer in the Humanities and professor of English, New York University; 1947–1968, member of the English department at the University of Minnesota, Professor Emeritus (1968); 1968–1969, Senior Fellow at Indiana School of Letters. Author of *Poems: 1928–1931* (1932); *The Fathers* (1938); *On the Limits of Poetry: Selected Essays 1928–1948* (1948).

WADE, IRA (1896–1983) Scholar, educator, and linguist. 1919–1921, head of the department of Romance Languages, Marietta College; 1927– , professor of French at Princeton, chairman of the department of Modern Languages and Literatures (1946–1958). Principal works: *The Clandestine Organization and Diffusion of Philosophical Ideas in France from 1700 to 1750* (1947); *The Search for a New Voltaire* (1958).

WARREN, ALBA HOUGHTON (b. 1915) Scholar and critic. 1950–1954, assistant professor of English at Princeton; 1955–1957, associate professor of English at Washington College, Md. Principal work: *English Poetic Theory, 1825–1865* (1966).

WELLEK, RENÉ (b. 1903) Critic and literary historian. 1935–1939, lecturer in Czech Language and Literature at the School of Slavonic Studies at the University of London; 1939–1946, member of the English department at the University of Iowa, professor of English (1944); 1946–1952, professor of Slavic and Comparative Literature, and chairman of the Slavic department, 1947–1959, chairman of the department of Comparative Literature, 1952–1972, Sterling Professor of Comparative Literature, Yale University; 1972– , Sterling Professor Emeritus. Principal works: *Immanuel Kant in England, 1793–1838* (1931); *Theory of Literature* (with Austin Warren) (1942); *A History of Modern Criticism* (4 vols.) (1955–1965); *Concepts of Criticism* (1963).

INDEX ❧

Index

Isherwood, Christopher, 23

Jacob, Max, 154, 164
James, Henry, 43, 77, 84–86, 91, 127, 139
  review of *Middlemarch* by, 79–80
  visualization of characters of, 105
Johnson, Samuel, Wellek on, 100–103
Joseph and His Brothers (Mann), 175, 182
Joseph in Egypt (Mann), 190
Joyce, James, 33, 127, 158, 176
Jude the Obscure (Hardy), 72, 73
Justice and force, in Pascal's *Penseé* 298, 14–16, 58–59

Kahler, Erich, seminar on *Doctor Faustus* by, 177–183, 185
Kant, Immanuel, Schiller and, 113, 117
Kennan, George, 50
Kenyon Review, 69
Kerman, Joseph
  on harmony in poetry, 192
  on polyphony, 192, 193, 194
  seminar on *Doctor Faustus* by, 190–195
King, Edmund, seminar on *Doctor Faustus* by, 195–197
Klein, Oskar Benjamin, on Pascal, 15–16, 18–19
Knowledge, nature of, 125–126
Korean War, effect on Princeton Seminars by, 146–147
Kritische Wälder (Herder), 108

Laboratory Theatre in New York, 51
Lady Chatterley's Lover (Lawrence), 89–90
Landor, Walter Savage, 170, 171
Language of poetry, Lessing on, 105–106
Laokoon (Lessing), 103, 104, 105–106
Lawrence, D. H., 69–70, 71, 86–90, 91
Leavis, F. R., 81, 90
Lectures on Aesthetics (Hegel), 118
Leibniz, Gottfried Wilhelm von, 113
Lessing, Gotthold Ephraim
  on descriptive poetry, 104–105
  interpretation of *Poetics* by, 106–107
  language of poetry and, 105–106
  Wellek on, 103–107

Letters on the Aesthetic Education of Man (Schiller), 114
L'Examen de Minuit (Baudelaire), 27
"Lines" (Shelley), 171
"Lion and the Honeycomb, The" (Blackmur), 120, 121, 145
Literary criticism, 136
  seminar on transition in, 97–119
  See also Critic, literary; New Criticism
Lowe-Porter, Helen Tracy, 5, 176
Luther, Martin, 193
Lycidas (Milton), 101

MacLeish, Archibald, 106
Madame Bovary (Flaubert)
  realism in, 34–37
  seminar on, 32–44
Magic Mountain, The (Mann), 175, 176, 182, 187
Mahler, Gustav, 193
Mallarmé, Stéphane, 18, 161, 167
Mann, Thomas, 5, 161, 187
  failure to create characters by, 188
  seminar on *Doctor Faustus,* 175–208
Man Who Died, The (Lawrence), 89–90
Maritain, Jacques, 8, 66, 191, 208, 209, 210
  on Baudelaire, 22
  on beauty, 158–162
  on classical poetry, 170, 171
  on metaphor, 172–174
  seminar on poetry and reason by, 146–174
Marlowe, Christopher, 179
Matthiessen, F. O., 67
Mauvais Moine, La, (Baudelaire), 19, 20
Melville, Herman, 154
Meredith, George, 76–77
Meredith, William, 8, 18
Metaphor
  in style of Austen, 75
  Maritain on, 172–174
Metaphysics, 163
Michaux, Henri, 165
Middlemarch (Eliot), 82–83, 91
  analysis by Schorer on, 77–81
  review by James of, 79–80
Miller, J. G., 109

246

Designed by Marianne Perlak

Composed in Bembo by the Eastern Typesetting Company, South Windsor, Connecticut. Printed and bound by the Murray Printing Company, Westford, Massachusetts. The paper is Glatfelter Writer's Offset, an acid-free sheet.